LIBERATED FRANCE

LIBERATED FRANCE

by

CATHERINE GAVIN

Patria
C'est l'ange de nuit.
Rois, il vous suit
Marquant d'avance
Le fatal moment
Du firmament.
Son nom est France
Ou Châtiment.
*
C'est l'ange de Dieu.
Dans le ciel bleu
Son aile immense
Couvre avec fierté
L'Humanité.
Son nom est France
Ou Liberté!

VICTOR HUGO, *Les Châtiments*

ST. MARTIN'S PRESS · NEW YORK
1955

PRINTED IN GREAT BRITAIN

CONTENTS

To my husband
JOHN ASHCRAFT

FOREWORD

LIKE many people in Britain, Canada and the United States, I regarded the defeat of France by Germany in 1940 as a tragedy of classical dimensions, and our physical, as well as political, separation from France as not the least of the calamities of World War II.

It was my good fortune to return to France at the Liberation as a British war correspondent, and thereafter for a number of years to share in the daily life of the brilliant and indestructible French people.

As an accredited foreign correspondent I was able to meet many of the personalities, listen to the debates and witness the events described in this account of the Liberation era. In preparing and documenting it I received the patient and expert help of the following persons:

At the Quai d'Orsay: MM. James Baeyens, Henri Wolinar, Jean Hallaire, Mill.

At the Présidence du Conseil, Service de Presse et d'Information, Paris: MM. Henri Pavard, Pierre de Sarcuse.

At the Commissariat Général au Plan, Paris: M. de Fleuriau.

At the French Embassy Press and Information Service, New York: M. Roger Vaurs, Madame Jeanine Lien, Mr. Donald Thomas.

To all of those, and particularly to Madame Lien and Mr. Thomas, my grateful thanks are due.

CATHERINE GAVIN

London, November 1954

9

THE GAULLIST LEGEND

ON the afternoon of June 4, 1944, a group of distinguished men, among them Mr. Winston Churchill and General Dwight D. Eisenhower, were gathered in a wood near Portsmouth, not far from the advance headquarters of the Allied Expeditionary Force. It was a typical English summer Sunday of rising wind and rain, and General Eisenhower, Supreme Commander of the greatest invasion force ever assembled, recorded it as a day of unbearable tension. The weather reports were bad, and he had ordered the postponement for at least twenty-four hours of the allied attack on German power in Western Europe; the thoughts of nearly all the men in the wood were with the 4000 invasion vessels which had already put to sea, and with the 150,000 troops crowded between their pitching decks. The ports and camps of southern England were crammed with men. Three airborne divisions were already alerted, an escort fleet of battleships, cruisers, destroyers and minesweepers waited to cover the landings, and special crews were ready to install five artificial anchorages on the French side of the Channel.

General Eisenhower and his Chief of Staff, General W. Bedell Smith, who had accompanied him to the meeting with the Prime Minister and his party, were preoccupied by the enormous responsibilities of the assault on Hitler's Fortress Europe and the subsequent campaign in which thirty-seven Allied divisions would be matched against the fifty-three German divisions commanded by Field-Marshal Karl von Rundstedt in the West. In Normandy, the chosen assault area, the Germans were known to have one Panzer and nine infantry divisions, supported by the 15th Army in the Pas-de-Calais. Against this the Allies in their initial attack would launch five assault and two follow-up divisions, supported by local elements of the French Forces of the Interior (F.F.I.), whose commander, General Pierre Koenig, had been one of Mr. Churchill's luncheon guests before they drove from his special train, halted near Droxford, to confer with the Americans.

PROLOGUE: THE GAULLIST LEGEND

Four years, to a month, had passed since the short summer campaign in which the French had been defeated by the Germans after the British Expeditionary Force had been driven off the continent with a total loss of weapons and equipment. For half of that period France had been partly occupied, for the rest of the time completely occupied, by German troops and organizations, and, in spite of endless reports by neutral travellers and by French and British secret agents, no accurate picture of civilian morale had as yet reached Supreme Headquarters. An active Resistance movement had been harassing the Germans for years, often at the risk of death and torture; the F.F.I. had been supplied with arms and equipment dropped by parachute, but how much forty million citizens could or would do to effect their own liberation was still a matter for conjecture. General Eisenhower's hope was that the French would give help to the Allied troops as and when it was needed, avoiding ill-timed uprisings and vain sacrifices; he also wished them to obey orders given by Headquarters, to avoid a repetition of the confusion and traffic jams of 1940. He intended to broadcast his instructions by radio and leaflet on D-day.

This was why, at a time of almost intolerable stress and responsibility, a group of exasperated soldiers and statesmen had to devote several of the last precious hours before the invasion started to a wrangle over the order of precedence and the wording of the D-day messages to France.

Three leading members of the British Government took part in the argument, which had already lasted throughout an unsuccessful lunch party: the Prime Minister; the Foreign Secretary, Anthony Eden; and the Minister of Labour, Ernest Bevin. The Commonwealth was unofficially represented by Field-Marshal Jan Christian Smuts, Prime Minister of the Union of South Africa, whose interest in the liberation of France was presumably academic, since he had already decided and publicly announced that 'France has gone and will be gone in our day and perhaps for many a day'. Diplomacy had its representatives in a former French Deputy, the ailing but accomplished Pierre Viénot, a probable choice as French Ambassador to Britain after France was freed, and in Alfred Duff Cooper, an equally probable choice as British Ambassador to France, who of all the argumentative group felt the most sympathy with the man providing the stumbling-block to international harmony: a French brigadier-general by the name of Charles de Gaulle.

General de Gaulle, who had been officially recognized by the British on June 28, 1940, as 'the leader of all Free Frenchmen, wherever they may be', had spent three years in London before transferring his headquarters to Algiers, where he presided over a group of men, endorsed by himself, whom the Allies called by their original title of 'French Committee of National Liberation', but whom he now called the Provisional Government of the French Republic. Mr. Duff Cooper, the British Representative to this Committee, had had some difficulty in persuading its president to leave Algiers for the conference on the eve of D-day, but he had been backed up by most of the Committee members, who threatened to resign if the general refused to fly to London in Mr. Churchill's own York aircraft, which had been sent to fetch him. De Gaulle's own feeling was that 'he was merely being sent for because it now happened to suit the convenience of the Allies to put him up to make a speech which would give the French people the false impression that he was in agreement with the British and the Americans, which was not the case'.[1]

Duff Cooper, who was convinced that the whole people of France would accept de Gaulle as their leader after the Liberation, knew how often the general's self-esteem had been wounded, during his four years' struggle towards this position, by the often peremptory orders he had received from the Allies to travel here, to remain there, to speak, or to be silent; how often, for varied reasons, he had been kept in the dark about decisions affecting French territories; while even now he was being presented with a *fait accompli* in the shape of a speech by Eisenhower of which 40,000,000 copies had already been printed for distribution. But he sympathized with the indignation felt by Mr. Churchill, then obsessed by the thought that 'the first landings might be attended by fearful casualties', when de Gaulle refused to give precedence to General Eisenhower in a broadcast by which, it was hoped, many Allied lives would be saved, and in a fit of pique and temper forbade his liaison officers to accompany the invading forces.

De Gaulle announced that he was only prepared to make this, the ultimate and most important of all his many broadcasts to the French, on condition that the Allies would come to a preliminary agreement with him on the financial and civilian administration of Liberated France: specifically, that the American-printed French notes, called liberation currency, be not circulated; that Allied Military Government be not established, and that he himself and his Committee be recognized *de facto et de jure* as the Provisional Government of the French Republic.

Since the policy of the Allies was that they would impose no government upon France from without, and that no group could call itself a government until free elections had been held, de Gaulle's demands had no chance of success, and Eisenhower, taking his stand on a Presidential directive which left him free to decide whether he should deal with de Gaulle's Committee or any other French body, flatly refused to discuss financial and civilian questions further. Eisenhower, a notable conciliator who piqued himself that his dealings with de Gaulle had 'never developed the heat that seemed to be generated frequently in his meetings with many others', was thoroughly provoked by this encounter, and his naval aide noted sympathetically that it was 'another of those last-minute things that worry the devil out of the Supreme Commander'.[2]

The British, too, were angry and distressed. Mr. Eden 'had never been so unhappy or so perplexed about anything' and Mr. Churchill barked out that he had no intention of 'giving de Gaulle the title deeds of France'. No agreement had been reached when the Americans had to return to advance headquarters and Mr. Churchill to his temporary office; and the French general, accompanied by M. Viénot and Generals Koenig, Bethouart and Billotte, returned in dudgeon to London.

It was not the numerical strength of the Fighting French forces which nerved de Gaulle to outface the Supreme Commander. On D-day the American troops in Britain numbered 1,562,000,[3] while the ground forces of the Fighting French amounted only to some 15,000. They were nearly all included in General Leclerc's 2nd Armoured Division (2ᵉ D.B.), then in camp in Yorkshire. Many of these, like Leclerc himself, had been followers of de Gaulle since 1940. A few were survivors of Force L, the heroic little band which had fought and marched from Cameroun to Chad and on to Tripoli and Tunisia. It was on Mr. Churchill's insistence that the 2ᵉ D.B. had been brought from Casablanca

14

to Swansea in a convoy of Landing Ship Tanks returning empty
from Italy, so that a French force might participate in the
liberation of France, but Eisenhower had not been able to arrange
transportation for their Shermans; and Leclerc's men were kept
cooling their heels at Dalton Hall until they disembarked in
France as part of 3rd U.S. Army on D-day plus 56. One battalion
of French marine commandos took part in the assault landings on
D-day, attached to the 3rd British Division in Operation Sword;
the cruisers *Montcalm* and *Georges Leygues*, with other French naval
units, were part of the support in the Channel, while three French
bomber squadrons and four pursuit units flew with the Royal Air
Force.

The French force of 256,000[1] ground troops then divided between Italy and North Africa was not, strictly speaking, of Gaullist
inspiration, for it dated from the Anfa agreement made with
General Henri-Honoré Giraud in January 1943, by which the
United States undertook to outfit and re-arm the French troops
in North Africa, subsequent to the Allied landings there. General
Jean de Lattre de Tassigny, commander of part of the force, had
not joined de Gaulle in London until 1943, and he held his command from General Giraud. De Lattre's Army B, attached to
6th U.S. Army, was preparing to liberate the island of Elba on
June 17 and proceed to the invasion of the south of France.
General Alphonse-Pierre Juin, who had originally put himself
under the command of General Giraud, was in command of the
French Expeditionary Corps in Italy, where his 100,000 men had
fought magnificently alongside the 8th British and 5th U.S.
Armies in the gruelling winter campaign of 1943-44. At the time
when de Gaulle was arguing in the wood, Juin had 'miraculously
cracked the German defences in the mountains before Rome',
and on the next morning, June 5, he was to lead his men in a
Roman triumph through the streets of the capital.

A total force of 300,000, however courageous, might have seemed
a poor bargaining weapon compared with the mighty French
Army of 100 divisions which had faced the Germans in May 1940,
and of which two million men had been taken prisoner, but de
Gaulle, as Duff Cooper had already noted, could talk 'as if he
were Stalin and Roosevelt combined', and he had positive
assurances to add to his own conviction that he had an entire

nation behind him in his transactions with the Allies. It was true that his example of resistance, his broadcasts to France, the whole *mystique* which had been built up around him, had inspired hundreds of Frenchmen to join his forces, thousands to risk imprisonment and torture by joining the underground, and millions to regard him as the symbol of liberation. This was why the resentment felt by Mr. Churchill at the crucial moment, when as he told de Gaulle 'the United States and Britain were willing to risk the lives of scores of thousands of men to liberate France', came for all practical purposes four years too late. It was Winston Churchill himself who by his impulsive acceptance of de Gaulle in 1940 had laid the foundation stone of the Gaullist legend.

★

In 1940 the French had been beaten by an enemy superior in numbers, air power, armour, mobility and morale, attacking on a terrain encumbered by civilians in flight. What had happened to them was just what might be expected to happen when a diminishing population, bled white in two wars — in 1871 by a 5000 million franc indemnity, in 1914-18 by the lives of one and a half million men — was attacked for the third time in seventy years by a people twice as numerous and all swayed by the same fanaticism. As a defeat it was a straightforward military proposition, but so complete had been the belief in the invincible French Army and the impregnable Maginot Line that the watching world insisted on regarding it as a moral collapse, attributable to some fatal flaw of character in the victims. This theory received some support from Marshal Philippe Pétain, who, after becoming premier of France on June 16, 1940, and suing for an armistice with Germany next day, declared that his country had been defeated because of her sins, and must now endeavour to expiate them by her sufferings.

It was at this moment of despair and doubt that General Charles de Gaulle returned to London, which he had visited twice during the previous week as Under-Secretary for National Defence in the cabinet of Paul Reynaud. De Gaulle had been a junior minister for eleven days and a brigadier-general for less than one month; before that he had been Colonel de Gaulle, an officer more

famous for his accurate predictions* of what a mechanized force
could do than for his actual handling of armour. He had had bad
luck in the Battle of France and just before being summoned to
join the government had been extricated from an untenable
position near Abbeville by the 2nd Seaforth Highlanders.[5] At
Bordeaux, where the French cabinet was in session, and in London
he had made a favourable impression on Mr. Churchill, who
quickly came to regard him as 'the Constable of France', and on
Brigadier-General Edward L. Spears, British liaison officer to
the French premier. It was Spears who brought him to London
in his own aircraft on June 17 and provided the office space at
St. Stephen's House which was the first headquarters of 'Free
France', and it was Spears who obtained Mr. Churchill's approval
of the appeal which de Gaulle read on the B.B.C. at 6 p.m. next
day,[6] the one hundred and twenty-fifth anniversary of the battle
of Waterloo.

> . . . Has the last word been spoken? Must all life disappear?
> Is the defeat final? No!
> Believe me, I who address you with a knowledge of the
> facts, tell you that nothing is lost for France. The same
> means as conquered us will some day bring about the victory.
> For France is not alone. She is not alone. She is not alone.
> She has a vast Empire behind her. She can unite with the
> British Empire, which holds the seas and continues the
> struggle. Like Britain she can draw endlessly on the immense
> industrial resources of the United States.
> . . . I, General de Gaulle, now in London, invite the French
> officers and soldiers now in Britain, or who come to Britain,
> with their arms or without — I invite the engineers and
> technicians of the armaments industry who are in Britain or
> who come to Britain to get in touch with me.
> Whatever happens, the flame of French resistance must not
> and will not go out.

These words, which were sane, patriotic, brave and simple,
established de Gaulle in British opinion as an honourable soldier

---

* The conclusions in his book, 'The Army of the Future' (*Vers l'Armée de Métier*, 1934),
had been rejected by the French General Staff, and applied by General Guderian,
the German tank expert.

who wished to rally his countrymen in a fight which for Britain was only beginning, and they shone by contrast with the declarations of the Pétain government. By Article 8 of the armistice the French Fleet was intended to pass under the supervision of Germany and her new ally Italy. To prevent this the British seized all French vessels in their own ports, came to terms with the French squadron at Alexandria but were forced to open fire on the squadron stationed at Mers el Kebir near Oran, which caused the government, now installed at Vichy, to break off diplomatic relations with Britain on July 5. On July 11, in the Vichy Casino, the members of the Chambre des Députés voted plenary powers to Philippe Pétain by 569 votes to 80, with 17 abstentions, upon which the eighty-four-year old marshal assumed the title of Chief of State. The legality of these proceedings was to be a cause of debate in France for years to come, while in transactions with the Vichy Government Adolf Hitler showed himself to be Bismarck's superior as a stirrer-up of strife. The Iron Chancellor had made an attempt to embroil the defeated French of 1871 with their British colonial rivals, but Hitler had made the breach complete, and at the same time set the French at loggerheads with one another. He was well aware of their weakness for divided counsels.

The establishment of a collaborating government meant that General de Gaulle was now a *général en dissidence*, condemned to death *in absentia* for desertion, while all those who joined him were equally liable to be condemned as traitors to the French State. To the British de Gaulle was now the personification of their favourite image, the forlorn hope, and the government had no hesitation in confirming its recognition of him by an agreement dated August 7 and beginning:

> General de Gaulle is engaged in raising a French force, composed of volunteers. This force, which includes naval, land and air units and scientific and technical personnel, will be organized and employed against the common enemies.
>
> This force will never be required to take up arms against France.

The memorandum went on to say that de Gaulle, supreme commander of the French force, had agreed to accept the general direction of the British High Command. The pay and pensions of his volunteers (on the British Army scale) and other personnel would be paid, retrospectively as from July 1, by the British Government, the repayment to be a matter for subsequent arrangement.[7] There was nothing in the agreement to imply that the British regarded de Gaulle as a political leader, or as a man who four years later would be calling himself President of the Provisional Government of France, for they assumed from the tone of his continued broadcasts that in him they had acquired a belligerent ally, whose one object was to fight the Axis Powers.

The Free French movement being thus established, the government provided de Gaulle with more spacious headquarters at 4 Carlton Gardens for the reception of the volunteers who were slowly rallying to his cause. He had a considerable pool of French service personnel on which to draw, for at the time of the armistice there were 13,600 navy men at Aintree, 5530 ground troops, survivors of the Norwegian campaign, at the Trentham Park depot and 260 at the Glasgow base, with a number of hospital cases in different centres. Their response was not favourable. In defeat, with lack of reliable news from France making their situation more bitter, they wished only to be reunited with their families, salvage their property and above all get out of the foreign country and home to France, like the half-crazed refugee who

> *Leur cria Nous tant pis on rentre*
> *Mieux vaut cent fois chez soi crever*
> *D'une ou deux balles dans la tête*
>
> *Mieux vaut cent fois chez soi crever*
> *Que d'aller en terre étrangère*
> *Mieux vaut la mort où vous vivez*

By the end of July most of them had been repatriated, and Mr. Churchill ordered only 2000[8] weapons when he indented for rifles for the 'Free French Volunteers'. But replacements were already on their way, and by devious routes: volunteers whom no personal considerations halted on their way to fight for France. The Comte de Hautecloque, a captain in the 4th Infantry Division, left his château, his wife and six children to win fame under his war-name of Philippe Leclerc, making a vow that he would never cease the fight until the *tricolore* flew again over Metz and Strasbourg. Gilbert Renault, exempt from army duty as a *père de famille nombreuse*, left his children to go to England, and when he returned to them it was under the name of Rémy, first and bravest of all the secret agents of Free France. With such men as these came many hundreds less famous, *les braves p'tits gars* who did the fighting, manned the vessels seized by the British which formed the nucleus of the *Forces Navales Françaises Libres** (F.N.F.L.), flew with the air squadrons of the *Groupe Lorraine* and covered their flag with glory at Koufra and Bir-Hakeim. But of a mass movement out of France, or in France, to support the general there was no sign.

De Gaulle had another pool of recruits to draw upon in England, although most were over military age. On July 1 he was presented by Pierre de Malglaive, an executive of the Compagnie Générale Transatlantique (who later spoke twenty-seven times on the B.B.C. in his favour) to the French colony in London, assembled in the central Y.M.C.A. — a gathering of sad and anxious men who had not been reassured by de Gaulle's radio announcement of June 28 that he had taken them all under his authority. The younger members of the French colony in Britain — business men, teachers, hotel employees, hairdressers — had been mobilized in 1939, and the veterans of World War I who remained feared that they would either be conscripted into the Free French forces or interned by the British as enemy aliens. They tried to please both sides by forming, on July 9, an association called *Les Français de Grande Bretagne*, which at its peak claimed 5000 members and 7500[9] adherents, and which by money-raising drives, auxiliary movements and publications added considerably to the Gaullist propaganda. Meantime fears of conscription were allayed by the passing of the Allied Forces Act in August, which preserved British jurisdiction in the civil affairs of the various 'Free' units organized in Britain, and forbade the foreign authorities controlling them to conscript their own resident nationals, exempt under the Military Service Act.

This Act of Parliament had a special bearing on de Gaulle's movement (the only 'Free' force not under the authority of a

---

* Raymond Aglion, their chronicler, gives the enlistment in the F.N.F.L. as 2500, in the Royal Navy 1000.

legally constituted government-in-exile) because there had been disagreeable rumours about de Gaulle's recruiting methods. It was established during the Commons debate on August 21 that he had already interned regular military personnel who had deserted rather than be press-ganged into joining his movement, and refused to hand them over to the British authorities. This had happened in the north of England, while in Glasgow one of his men, a blackavised Lieutenant Lahana, had been threatening a group of merchant captains, awaiting repatriation with their wives. Such incidents made the government uneasy; so did the failure of any notable Frenchmen to join de Gaulle. No other member of the Reynaud cabinet made his appearance in London. Ambassador Charles Corbin asked for his passports; Roger Cambon, the chargé d'affaires, remained in London but kept aloof from Carlton Gardens. General Catroux, Governor-General of Indo-China, was the ranking officer to join de Gaulle, but he came alone from Saigon; so did General Legentilhomme from Djibouti, so did Colonel de Larminat from Syria. Admiral Muselier, the only naval officer of flag rank to join, had been dug out of the reserve list in 1939 to supervise arms factories in Bordeaux. It was some time before it dawned on Mr. Churchill that French respect for the chain of command was strong enough to keep most officers and administrators faithful to Vichy, and that this was one reason why the great territorial possessions of the French Empire — Indo-China, Madagascar, French West Africa, North Africa, Martinique — held fast to Marshal Pétain.*

Mr. Churchill was sufficiently dissatisfied with his impulsive bargain to suggest to General Catroux, when the latter reached London in September, that he might care to take over the Free French movement;[10] and in November to receive an envoy from Pétain, Louis Rougier, and send him off to North Africa to see if General Weygand would consider returning to the fight as a leader of Frenchmen.[11] Between these two proposals there had been the disaster at Dakar, the one feat of arms led by de Gaulle in person with British naval and air support. On September 23 he appeared before the key port of French West Africa, which, he had assured the British, would declare for him. But Governor Boisson

---

* Declared for de Gaulle, 1940: French Equatorial Africa, Cameroun, French Establishments in India, New Caledonia, French Oceania, New Hebrides.

had had time to get reinforcements from Vichy, thanks to the imprudence of Gaullist officers who drank *à Dakar!* in their favourite London restaurants, and after three days of ship-to-shore bombardment the British Defence Committee ordered the expedition to withdraw.

It was after this fiasco, when his stock was very low in London, that a close observer perceived that the general was turning away from the military to develop the political side of his movement. It was his good fortune that during the three months when he had been leading his movement from above it had been steadily filling from below with the men who made it possible for him to continue in his rôle, and who were the real creators of the Gaullist legend.

These men included Gaston Palewski, who had been Reynaud's *chef de cabinet* and took the same place with de Gaulle; André DeWavrin, *dit* Passy, a regular officer who had been teaching fortification at St. Cyr, and who became G-2, or head of the 2ᵉ Bureau, when the Free French forces could be counted by the score; Jacques Soustelle, a young anthropologist; Georges Boris, a middle-aged Socialist, editor of *La Lumière* and former associate of Léon Blum; René Cassin, a Jewish law professor who gave La France Libre its juridical basis, and a group of London-accredited or refugee journalists. The Agence Havas provided Maurice Schumann, François Quilici, Pierre Bourdan, *dit* Maillaud; *Le Journal*, Jean Oberlé and Yves Morvan, *dit* Jean Marin; the defunct French Ministry of Information, Pierre Comert and Georges Gombault. From the Sorbonne came the scientist André Labarthe and the philosopher Raymond Aron, and the arts were represented by Maurice van Moppès, a cartoonist; Michel St. Denis, *dit* Jacques Duchesne, a theatrical director, and Pierre Lefèvre, a youth who had appeared at the Old Vic. as one of the three witches in *Macbeth*. Some of these adherents were looked at askance by *Les Français de Grande Bretagne*, who clung with all their souls to two articles of faith: one, that Pétain, whom most of them secretly admired, was playing a *double jeu* with Hitler, having a secret understanding with de Gaulle (this was a line of wishful thinking which stretched from Surrey to Singapore) and two, that de Gaulle was a fine man whose only handicap was the aides he had chosen. *'Son entourage est lamentable!'* they liked to whisper; but in this they were less than fair to the Carlton Gardens team, who although without experience of advertising or sales techniques were rapidly building up the general as a political leader.

With the British propaganda machine at their service, they were able to distribute an imposing number of publications. There was a newsprint allocation* for Labarthe's intellectual monthly, *La France Libre*, and for Comert's daily, *France*, and later for *La Marseillaise*, the organ of de Gaulle's personal opinion. Edited by François Quilici, it became violently anti-American in tone after the North African landings, in which de Gaulle was not asked to share, and the British Government revoked its licence—Quilici, one of whose sallies had been to call the Americans 'star-spangled slavers', later reappearing in North Africa as editor of the *Marseillaise d'Alger*. There was also an allocation for the broadsheet *A Tous les Français*, which appeared on the walls and hoardings of London during the first week-end in August 1940.[12]

This challenging poster, beginning

Français!
La France a perdu une bataille.
Elle n'a pas perdu la guerre!

passed in time into the Gaullist legend as the actual speech delivered by de Gaulle on June 18, for his original broadcast had been heard by few people in France. As a text it was better edited and more workmanlike than the 'flame of French resistance' speech, but the honesty and the spontaneity were gone, never quite to be recaptured in any of the twenty-nine broadcasts made by de Gaulle before the end of the year. After he had an uncensored outlet at Radio-Brazzaville he spoke less often on the B.B.C., but until 1943, when he established himself in sole control at Algiers, he appeared twice a month before the government-controlled microphones of Portland Place. Once his stage-fright was over he turned out to be a natural radio performer, and a highly individual one, with a diction modelled on Bossuet, a harsh voice and a style of punctuation all his own. It was not difficult for the British Broadcasting Corporation, a non-commercial network, to 'sell' him

* Other publications on the newsprint allocation list included *Le Journal Officiel de a France Libre*; *Entente*; *Le Glaive de l'Esprit*; *Volontaire pour la Cité Chrétienne*; *Bulletin de la Marine Française*; *La Lettre de la France Libre*; *Newsletter of the Amis des Volontaires Français*.

to the French in the biggest package deal in the history of European radio.

Every day his personal spokesman, Maurice Schumann, broadcast at 12.25 and 8.25 p.m., while the team of Oberlé, Duchesne, Jean Marin and company, which presented features like *Ici Londres* and *Les Français Parlent aux Français*, increased their radio time allowance to a peak of five hours each day.

The B.B.C. was easily the most important asset of de Gaulle's publicists. Next, because appealing to a wider readership than their own periodicals, came the books written by various witnesses of *la débâcle*, as the French called their defeat and Occupation. In Britain and America all the events of midsummer 1940, including the Vichy arrangement, went under the collective name of 'the fall of France'.

In the literature of invective the fall of France has a place all its own. It was a series of attacks on a helpless victim, for nobody living in France could then refute the accusations of defeatism, corruption, indolence and greed, made by refugee French writers, who brought to their task a venom seldom found in British journalism, as they raked over old scandals of the Third Republic and emptied their spleen on its last two premiers, Édouard Daladier and Paul Reynaud, then under trial for 'war guilt' at a Vichy court at Riom. When it was revealed that each of these middle-aged politicians had had a mistress, and that Paul Reynaud's *chère amie*, the Comtesse de Portes, had had some influence on policy-making, it was clear to the scandalized British that France had deserved to lose, and that even if two such libertines survived the Occupation they were out of public life for ever.

What Happened to France. The Truth about the Tragedy of France. Farewell France. I Saw France Fall. Guilty Frenchmen. Adieu Paris. Gravediggers of France. The Central European refugees to whom France had given asylum, but who had been arrested for security reasons at the outbreak of war, added new titles to the list— *The Devil in France. Scum of the Earth. Suicide of a Democracy.* A British historian, Philip Guedalla, was not above tacking an incomplete sketch of Pétain to a study of Bazaine and rushing it out as *The Two Marshals*, 'an unbroken picture of the French Army for one hundred years'. A novelist, Bruce Marshall, poured contempt on the Parisians of the 1930s in *Yellow Tapers for Paris*. Hollywood produced *Casablanca*, with the corruption of a Vichy official as part of the story line, and Tin Pan Alley cashed in on *The Last Time I saw Paris*. *Last, fallen, yellow, guilty, farewell* — the key words of defeat made the perfect frieze against which to set the contrasting figure of France's First Resistant, Charles de Gaulle.

With these advantages already on their side, de Gaulle's propagandists could plan their promotion of the man they were to present no longer as a tank general but as the depositary of republican legality and national honour. He started with one tremendous advantage, a perfect name, for Charles de Gaulle made a natural translation into 'Charles of France' (his enemies called him Charles de Gauleiter). He was of commanding presence, six feet four inches tall, and just as Mr. Churchill, with his strong sense of the past, had seen him first as a character from French history (the last Constable of France left office in 1627) some of his volunteers thought he looked like 'a being from another age'. His head was better suited to the encircling medieval helmet than the two-starred képi, for the features were arranged in a series of ellipses, barred above the small pouting mouth by the clipped moustache fashionable in World War I; the eyes were hooded by heavy lids, and the pouches beneath the eyes were symmetric with the rings of flesh, not yet a double chin, where the small head met the craning neck. General Spears's wife thought his appearance lifeless, 'wrapped in a palpable coldness that hid him as a damp cloth hides a sculptor's clay', and most of those who set out to describe him ended by comparing him to someone else — to St. Louis, Eamonn de Valera, George Washington.

The de Gaulles were a respectable middle-class family from the north, able to trace their direct ancestry back to one Antoine de Gaulle, living in Châlons-sur-Marne in 1713.[13] The future general was born in 1890 in the city of Lille, where his father was a teacher in the Jesuit school system; he himself was educated by the Jesuits in Paris and at the military college of St. Cyr. He was highly articulate, like all his family: his father's mother, born Joséphine Maillot, had written eighty-one books. His paternal uncle, Charles, had been crowned *Barz Bro C'hail*, the bard of Gaul, in recognition of his published studies in Breton and Welsh, while his uncle Jules had devoted the rare leisure of a bureau chief at the Préfecture de la Seine to preparing an exhaustive catalogue of the bees, wasps and ants of France.[14] The general himself was steeped in the learning of the sixteenth and seventeenth centuries, but he was also a student of Nietzsche and Clausewitz.

His cold and haughty personality, which chilled so many of the men with whom he came in contact, made a strong appeal to young people and to women. The volunteers literally stood in awe of him and were proud to wear his emblem, the Cross of Lorraine,* the sixteenth-century badge of the Holy League for the defence of the King of France and the Catholic Church. Scores of young women wrote or came to Carlton Gardens, seeking to enrol as secretaries or members of the women's auxiliary corps, and one remarkable girl, Elisabeth de Miribel, great-granddaughter of the Marshal-President MacMahon, became de Gaulle's representative in Canada at the age of twenty-five. By 1943 she was at the head of a sixteen-man bureau in Ottawa, handling posters, radio and film publicity for 250 Free French Committees across the country.

In spite of his attraction for women, de Gaulle's aides noted contentedly that although ill-wishers compared him to General Boulanger there was not likely to be a Marguerite de Bonnemains in this man's dedicated life. He spent his week-ends in suburban Berkhamsted with Madame de Gaulle and their children. His son, Philippe, joined the Free French Naval Cadets and the elder daughter, Elisabeth, attended a convent school; the younger, Anne, then ten, was a handicapped child who died some years later. On Mondays he returned to a modest suite in the Connaught Hotel in London, where the meals to which he invited his officers were extremely frugal. He drank English beer without comment, and often said that the only pleasure remaining to him was a good cigar.[15]

The profile of de Gaulle which emerges from his supporters' memoirs shows how great was their achievement in creating his legend. Coldness is his dominating quality. He is seldom cheerful, though once or twice he cracks a leaden joke, commenting on the large feet of a waitress and wondering if she is 'a British spy', or tells a hotel cook: 'You are a greater *chef* than I.' He is unemotional. When Madame de Gaulle telephones to tell him that

---

* Numerous and conflicting reasons have been given for the choice of this emblem, carried, before the days of the Holy League, by St. Joan of Arc.

she and the children are safe in England he ejaculates '*Ah! c'est toi!*' and goes on working. When his niece, Geneviève, is arrested by the Gestapo and put in a concentration camp, he forbids the mention of her name. He cheers his courageous agent, Rémy, leaving for France on a dangerous mission, with the words: 'You'll get pinched, you know! Everyone gets pinched at that game!'[16] Begged to show some human interest in his volunteers he barks at an orderly: 'How are you? Have you any news of your family?' — the man is petrified. At Algiers, in the midst of plenty, his receptions are still frugal and chillingly formal. He drinks an infusion of lime blossom while the men stand round him, the women being segregated at the far side of the room. There is no warmth, relaxation, humour; the reverse of the legend is splendidly null.

But the cool negations of de Gaulle's private life were balanced by the heat and passion of his life in public, constantly fed by his own belief that he did not only speak for France but *was* France, and therefore entitled to act like an autocrat in all his relations with the Allies. This was the cause of many errors. Having signed an agreement never to make war upon his countrymen, he joined his troops to the British in an attack on the Vichy French in Syria, ostensibly to prevent the use of strategic airfields by the Germans, and sulked because the Free French were not signatories to the treaty ending the short campaign.[17] He guaranteed liberty and independence to the French mandated territories of Syria and Lebanon in 1941; then, having fallen out with his benefactor, General Spears, now British Minister in the Levant, he made an excuse of undue British influence to postpone the promised free elections until 1943. When the results displeased him he caused his delegate-general, Jean Helleu, to imprison the Lebanese President, four cabinet ministers and one deputy.

As early as December 1941 he was urging Churchill and the Chiefs of Staff to let him organize an expedition, with British support, against the Vichy French of Madagascar — an operation from which, when it was undertaken, he was rigidly excluded. At Christmas, when Churchill and Roosevelt were conferring in Washington after the attack on Pearl Harbour, he overrode the express injunctions of them both by sending a naval detachment to capture St. Pierre and Miquelon, two French islands off the

Newfoundland coast, where he believed the radio station was of strategic importance to the enemy. In that action he gained one hundred recruits and lost the State Department's goodwill.

The United States presented a rich field for de Gaulle's publicists. A thriving movement of sympathizers took the name of 'France Forever', while influential and talented refugees who for political or racial reasons had judged it wiser to leave France for New York or Washington, enjoyed the polemics of Henri Bernstein (pro-de Gaulle) and André Maurois (pro-Vichy) and the asperities of the rival papers, Émile Buré's *France-Amérique* and Geneviève Tabouis's *Pour la Victoire*. With newsprint unlimited, de Gaulle's saga could be told everywhere, from a cover story in *Time* magazine to a children's version in *True Comics*, where the protean general was shown winning the battle of Abbeville ('almost the only French success of this war'), sailing a motor launch under the guns of Dakar and flying through a tornado above Uganda with the unlikely cry of 'This American-made plane is marvellous!'[18] Although the Free French movement was not included in Lend-Lease until November 1941, when payments were made through the British Government, a French National Committee was established in the United States by the middle of October 1940. Others were set up in Argentine, Australia, Brazil, Canada, Chile, Egypt, Mauritius, Mexico, South Africa and Uruguay, which was announced in the House of Commons with the comment that 'the British Government is rendering all the assistance in its power'.

The government's assistance seemed indeed to be unlimited. More and more housing was allocated to the Free French as headquarters spread from one to three houses in Carlton Gardens, the Secret Service moved to St. James's Square and then to Duke Street, W.1, and other branches appeared in Mayfair, Bloomsbury and Westminster. But the entourage was never satisfied. If there was a breath of criticism in the usually laudatory British press it was called 'the assertions of Goebbels'; a delay in authorizations or credits became 'unheard-of difficulties'. The British directives to the B.B.C. team were resented at Carlton Gardens and so, to a much greater extent, were the interventions of the British Intelligence Service and their right to process all new arrivals from France through the so-called 'Patriotic School' *before* they were interrogated by Passy's branch. As early as February 1941, de Gaulle ordered Passy to give no information to the British.[19]

André DeWavrin, *dit* Passy (many of the *émigrés*, and nearly all members of the French Resistance, used aliases to protect their relatives from German reprisals) was at that time nearly as high in the general's councils as Gaston Palewski, the favourite among his aides. As head of the Secret Service (through the years it had a varied set of initials: 2ᵉ Bureau, S.R., B.C.R.A.M., D.G.E.R., S.D.E.C.E., but Passy was a fixed star) Colonel Passy specialized in tale-bearing, and was as much responsible as any one man could be for President Roosevelt's criticism that de Gaulle's 'whole movement was honeycombed with police spies — he had agents spying on his own people'.* He also specialized in vendettas: notably against Maurice Schumann in London and Emmanuel d'Astier de la Vigerie and Georges Bidault in the underground networks of France. Georges Boris, another good hater, fell out with Duchesne and Bourdan, the broadcasters, because they were 'not *gaulliste* enough'[20] and the whole press section was at war with the editors of *France* and *La France Libre* for the same reason. Admiral Muselier ('naturally suspicious') quarrelled with General Catroux, whom he suspected of a desire to lead, and General de Gaulle, though irritated by tittle-tattle, was not above hating Muselier, whom he called 'an insufferable meddler'. After the movement changed its name and became *Fighting France*, one of England's liveliest wits, A. P. Herbert, summed up the Carlton Gardens situation in a few lines of verse:

FIGHTING FRENCH†

(Three Odd Thoughts)

Mon Général, it might be wise
To fight the foe, not our Allies.

· · ·

* When a volunteer named Maurice Dufour withheld information he had given to the British he was beaten and imprisoned in the cellars of Duke Street. He escaped from detention in the country through the help of a friend at Scotland Yard, and with the assistance of some disillusioned members of *Les Français de Grande Bretagne*, filed suit against de Gaulle, Passy and others. In return for money compensation and facilities to enlist in the Royal Canadian Air Force, Dufour, who was making and selling handbags for a living, was persuaded by the government to drop the suit just before D-day, on the grounds that it might produce a bad reaction in France.

† In the *Sunday Graphic*, November 21, 1943. Reproduced here by kind permission of the author.

What is this noise of strife, this martial babel
It's a committee of the Fighting French.
And if they're so alarming at the table
My hat, they must be tigers in the trench!
.   .   .
Some people have a genius for the game
Of pouring oil upon the troubled flame.

But by 1943 de Gaulle was impervious to criticism. Thanks to his agents he was known throughout the world as the Frenchman whose name meant freedom, while liaison with the separate undergrounds then being welded into the *Conseil National de la Résistance* had established his position inside France. The French Communist party had approached him in March 1942, proposing collaboration until the final victory. Before Germany attacked Russia in 1941 the Communists had made few attempts at resistance, and had dismissed de Gaulle as 'the lackey of British capitalism', but now they talked as if they were the only patriots in France, although many non-Communist undergrounds had preceded theirs. One of the earliest resistance movements in France, as it happened, had been set up by a Scotsman, the Rev. Donald Caskie. Minister of the Scots Kirk in Paris until *la débâcle*, Mr. Caskie had opened a Seamen's Mission in Marseilles at the end of June 1940, which he used as a front for processing British troops, stranded at the time of the armistice, across the Pyrenees into Spain, and this he did with the aid of French helpers who directed the men to Marseilles and helped to smuggle them out. Mr. Caskie had been arrested, and was on his way to the House of Torture at Nice, before ever the Communists were permitted by their party line to take a hand in the game.

About the same time that they approached de Gaulle, Pierre Brossollette, *dit* Pedro, arrived in London. One of the few men liked by Colonel Passy, Brossollette quickly became the man most important, to the future of France, of all the *Compagnons* — a name conferred by de Gaulle, after the example of William the Conqueror, on those who rallied to him in England. Brossollette, a product of the École Normale and *Le Populaire*, a Socialist who venerated Léon Blum, gave the Gaullist movement a sharp push towards the Left. He insisted that all broadcasts should be oriented to the idea that 'France must learn that the anti-German aspect of Gaullism cannot be separated from its political aspect',[21] for he felt that Gaullism needed 'the unreserved support of the Socialist masses'. He summed this up in a memorable letter to another Socialist recruit, André Philip:

> There is no possible salvation of France other than de Gaulle, or outside the Gaullist myth, so he must now be recognized as a political leader.[22]

This tallied with the general's own ambitions, and he began to learn the new technique of Left-wing speeches, which contrasted oddly with his earlier oratory and its many conventional allusions to saints and soldiers. In April 1942 he went so far as to say:

> It is a Revolution, the greatest in her history, which France, betrayed by her *élite* of leaders and her privileged classes, has begun to accomplish. And I may say on this point that those who imagine they will find, after the last shot has been fired, a France politically, socially and morally similar to the France they knew before commit a cardinal mistake. In the secret moments of her anguish and at this very time a new France is being created, whose leaders shall be new men.[23]

This was a definite promise which led, after a period of negotiation, to de Gaulle's concordat of May 15, 1943, with the National Resistance Council, the charter of his acceptance by 'the Socialist masses', and two weeks later, after his definitive removal to Algiers,* he regrouped his hand-picked Commissioners as the French Committee of National Liberation. In November he added, though in an advisory capacity only, a Consultative Assembly of 102 members, 49 being drawn from the metropolitan Resistance, which went to work at once on the blueprints for the France to be led by the 'new men'. With the *mise en place* of these organizations the work of the Carlton Gardens experts was almost done. If what they had accomplished was not what the British Government had intended when they agreed to pay a French Volunteer Force to fight the Germans, then so much the worse for those who had officially recognized de Gaulle as 'the leader of all

---

* The transactions at Algiers, like those of the government of Vichy, lie beyond the scope of this Prologue, but books bearing upon them are noted in the Bibliography.

31

Free Frenchmen, wherever they may be'. This pledge was an excellent basis for the claims to total recognition with which de Gaulle bombarded the Allies even before the Committee of National Liberation decided to call itself the Provisional Government of the French Republic.

The agreement entered into so impulsively, in an hour of mortal danger, had given Britain the asset of a small but courageous body of French forces, plus the advantages of strategy and communications provided by the line opened across Africa by the gallantry of Leclerc and the adherence of certain French colonies to de Gaulle. What, if any, the asset to France might be could scarcely be estimated on the eve of D-day, but one thing was certain: Britain had given de Gaulle the subsidies, the publicity and the propaganda machinery to return to France as its liberator and saviour.

British taxpayers, who long before the United States provided Lend-Lease or Anfa supplies to the Free French forces had assumed the responsibility of paying for the general, for the Duke Street Gestapo, and for the Communist Deputy, Fernand Grenier,[24] to come to London and speak on the B.B.C., had occasionally inquired through their Members of Parliament what the cost of it all might be. The Treasury answered that it would not be in the public interest to reveal the figures. But Cordell Hull made a shrewd guess at the government's total expenditure when Lord Halifax, the British Ambassador, told him on June 17, 1943, that British subsidies to de Gaulle's London headquarters were being terminated, any future payments to be made to Algiers. Mr. Hull noted that the June 1943 payment, had been £1,300,000 ($5,200,000) and calculated that the annual subsidies must have run to a minimum of $60,000,000.[25] 'Unfortunately,' he commented, 'some of the subsidies had financed de Gaulle's attacks on the United States Government.'

★

On June 6, 1944, General Eisenhower delivered the first of the D-day broadcasts to France. He said:

Prompt obedience to the orders that I shall issue is essential
... As France is liberated from her oppressors you yourselves

will choose your representatives and the government under which you wish to live.

Later in the day General de Gaulle, yielding to persuasion, went to the familiar microphone and said:

The orders given by the French Government and the French national and local leaders appointed by it and entitled to give orders in its name must be followed exactly.

And, over Radio-Vichy, Marshal Pétain countered:

Obey the orders of the government. The German Army might be compelled to take special measures in the combat areas. I beg you to obey them in the best way you can.[26]

Thus, on the long-awaited day of liberation, the French people found their obedience demanded by no fewer than three conflicting authorities, S.H.A.E.F., de Gaulle and Vichy. In spite of the anxiety felt by the high echelons, however, there was never any evidence that harm was done at population level by the Allied divergence of opinion. Under the German occupation the French had brought disobedience to a fine art, and had fully developed their constitutional unwillingness to obey any orders at all.

PART ONE

THE LIBERATION
1944, 1945

CHAPTER I

AUX ARMES, CITOYENS!

WHEN the French marine commandos waded ashore at Ouistreham on D-day they at once found themselves fighting side by side with their countrymen, for the local fishermen rushed down to the beach and seized the weapons of the fallen Germans.[1] It was an exact fulfilment of the liberators' hopes, but one which the civilian population of Normandy did not often provide in the early days when the beachheads were established and forces deeply committed on both sides. The reaction of the Normans was incalculable: sometimes they came out to greet the Allies with flowers and wine, even after their farms and hamlets had been wrecked in one or two days of the savage hedgerow fighting; sometimes they were sullen and unco-operative, sometimes they looked more hostile than they dared to be. This was not because Normandy was a province given to active collaboration with the Germans, or particularly devoted to Vichy, but because it was hotly resentful of being at last caught up in the tide of war which on other occasions had flooded Alsace and Lorraine, French Flanders, Picardy and the Marne. For some time prior to D-day the Allied saturation bombings of German installations along the coast and at railheads had been an accurate forecast of what would happen when the invasion began, and as town after town was pounded into rubble the Normans, first refugees of the Liberation, became the first members of the 'club' invented by cynical Parisians and dubbed the *Libérés Malgré Eux* — liberated in spite of themselves.

During the Occupation Normandy had been a valuable source of dairy produce and meats for the Paris black market, then regarded — at least by those who could afford to buy in it — as a patriotic activity. As the hay harvest and young wheat went down beneath the Shermans, and dead cattle sprawled in the ditches, the Norman farmers saw heavy losses in store. There was no market for the stocks they had in hand, for the most intrepid *trafiquant* could not cross the lines of two armies when by the end

37

of June every bridge across the Seine below Paris and all the principal bridges of the Loire had been destroyed. It was not surprising that General de Gaulle, when he was given facilities to visit France for twenty-four hours on June 14, walked up the main street of Bayeux in a silence which Palewski who, with General Koenig, was by his side tactfully described as 'impressive'.[2]

The general got satisfactory applause at other moments of the visit from the crowds which surged forward to touch his jeep and gathered to join him in singing the *Marseillaise*. Bayeux was an important halt on his strange journey, for it contained some hints of his future relationships. The fact that he shook hands with Monsieur Rochat, the *sous-préfet* of the district, who was accused of collaboration, raised a teapot tempest in Algiers, where the Communists protested with a vigour which showed how sure they were of their rights in the general. The miniature *coup d'état* which he carried out on a visit not intended to have any political significance showed what his diplomacy might be like if he were called to govern: it consisted in presenting two of his entourage, travelling as 'French journalists', as 'François Coulet, Commissioner of the Republic, who will represent the Provisional Government in this area' and 'Colonel de Chévigné, commanding the liberated subdivision of the 3rd Military Region'. This performance was intended to show the Americans the power and organization of the Provisional Government and prevent them from setting up military rule in France, and it was described in the Algiers press as 'a commando operation calculated to inflame a true soldier'.[3] It was not, perhaps, calculated to make de Gaulle's projected visit to President Roosevelt a harmonious one, but the general went back to London well satisfied with his trip. From there he went to Washington and on to Algiers, where he remained until he returned to France on August 23. The Bayeux visit, on D-day plus 8, was the only time that the 'Liberator of the Territory' stood on French soil until Paris had risen, and he entered the capital on D-day plus 80.

Bad weather delayed the break-out from the beachheads, and the British and Canadians settled down to what Eisenhower called 'the brutal, slugging battles for Caen and Falaise' which protected the flank of the Americans in their turning movement and capture of the Channel ports. It was soon apparent that the process of liberation would be slow. The German Army had beaten the French in one month after crossing the frontier in 1940, and it was disconcerting to find, after all the sneers at French weakness, that even the mighty Allied Expeditionary Force was unable to repeat the process in reverse. It was five and one-half months before the Germans were pushed as far as the Rhine (by the 1st French Army at Rosenau), nine before the Rhine was crossed (by the 9th U.S. Army at Remagen) and nearly twelve before the last German resistance pockets in France surrendered.

During this slow and costly start the Gaullists at Algiers were criticizing the Americans more and more freely. De Gaulle had not obtained complete satisfaction in Washington, for although President Roosevelt was prepared to give the Provisional Government *de facto* recognition he insisted that General Eisenhower must retain full military authority in France and make decisions on the civil administration. *Alger-Républicain* and Quilici's *Marseillaise d'Alger* felt free to attack the vexatious 'liberation currency' and warned the Americans that 'the French must not be made to feel that the arrival of their welcomed comrades-in-arms merely means changing the forces of occupation'! The whole situation, as seen from Algiers, was 'distressing for the French and prejudicial to the Allies in French eyes'.

Inside France the picture was much more favourable, for the French Forces of the Interior (F.F.I.) had risen in Normandy, 30,000 strong, and were particularly active in helping to clear the Brittany peninsula, where the Germans had been driven back into the four principal ports. The rising in Normandy gave the Allies leave to hope that enlistments in the F.F.I. had increased over the estimate of the paramilitary strength of the Resistance — 200,000 effectives — made early in 1943 by Colonel Passy and Pierre Brossollette and checked by a British officer. At that time the Communist *Front National* had claimed to be the best organized for military action. It had 25,000 shock troops, the *Franc-Tireurs et Partisans* (F.T.P.), carrying out an average of 250 monthly attacks on the German occupants, and these shock troops would be increased to 100,000 on D-day.[4] But recruiting grew brisk through all the networks after the invasion had taken place, and at the end of the war General Eisenhower reckoned that the F.F.I.'s overall support had been worth fifteen army divisions to Supreme Headquarters.[5]

As both sides poured reinforcements into the battle area there was a stirring through all the shackled country. At Vichy the government began to disintegrate. At Oradour-sur-Glane in the Limousin a hideous tragedy took place within a week of the invasion, when a detachment of German S.S. men, alleging that an officer had been killed near the village, carried out the mass murder of almost the whole population (650), adding the Teutonic refinement of penning the women and children inside the church to be asphyxiated and burned alive. It was not the first such massacre in Occupied France, for similar tragedies had been enacted at Nantes, Comblanchien, Nantua and elsewhere, but the peculiarly horrible circumstances kept the name of Oradour alive for years after the Liberation, as a memorial to the German way of life.

In the south of France the F.F.I. waited for the signal to rise in support of the invasion of the Riviera. In the centre and the south-west their comrades grew bolder; along the Swiss border, in Haute-Savoie, Ain, Jura, they were not only harassing the German garrisons but enforcing local sanctions. The mayor or policeman too co-operative with the enemy, the girl too notorious for 'horizontal collaboration', the farmer too willing to turn over all his produce to the Vichy food control, all began to feel the weight of patriotic disapproval. Still Paris was silent. As the flame leapt the bridgeless Loire and licked into Yonne and the Morvan, the splendid capital where the swastika banner still flew seemed to be drowsing in the summer heat. But whatever charters or ordinances might be promulgated at Vichy or Algiers only from Paris came the law: on the judgment of Paris Roosevelt and Churchill waited, and on the leadership of Paris waited France.

The hour struck in the middle of August. Leclerc's 2e D.B. had arrived in France on August 1, distinguishing itself immediately in the battle of the Falaise Gap and the liberation of Alençon. De Lattre's Army B, disembarking between Cavalaire and St. Tropez on August 16, was fighting along with the 6th U.S. Army the brilliant series of actions which liberated Toulon and Marseilles. The Caen break-through had sent the Allies racing through Normandy, on August 15 to Argentan, on August 16 to Domfront, Tinchebray, Le Mans. From north, south and west the liberators were hurrying upon Paris, and still Paris made no sign. On August 15 a favourite summer holiday, the Feast of the Assumption, was celebrated by thousands who flocked to the banks of the Seine for hours of fishing, swimming and basking in the sun.[6] The capital seemed almost paralysed; but two days later the early housewives, forming in line outside the bakeries, saw the first unobtrusive movements of troops and trucks which started the German retreat from Paris.

At the first sign of flinching Paris leaped upon the enemy. It was a spontaneous action, a spasm of deliverance from within which was absolutely necessary to the city's humiliated heart, permitting the Parisians to say for ever after that without waiting for the Allies they had won back freedom with their own hands. It was achieved in a strange week of street fighting, breaking out in one *arrondissement* and dying away in another, moving from the classic barricades flung up against the tanks of the Occupants to fusillades from the roof tops and man-hunts among the twisted Paris chimney cans, and punctuated with conversational interludes when an armistice was under discussion. It began with an attack by *Honneur de la Police*, a Resistance network stiffened by the presence of Charles Luizet, one of de Gaulle's *Commissaires de la République*, who had been flown from Algiers to the Vaucluse *maquis* in June and from there had made his way to Paris. It was directed from beginning to end by the National Resistance Council (C.N.R.) whose names and intentions were now revealed to the citizens of Paris.

> *Aux Armes, Citoyens!*
> People of Paris! —
> The long-awaited day has come!

So the C.N.R. began its exhortation, in the old language of glory, but the C.N.R. posters, appearing by the thousand on the walls of Paris, were not the only appeals to action which the citizens read.

On August 18, the day before the police uprising, posters issued in the name of de Gaulle's Provisional Government had urged patriots to form in bands of five for guerilla fighting. At the same time, in the name of the French Republic, the commander of the F.F.I. in the Paris area and the Île-de-France called upon all officers and soldiers not already in the organization to report for

41

duty immediately, adding the warning that only enlistment in the F.F.I. gave a citizen the right to membership of the Resistance.[7]

This order deferred in due form to General Pierre Koenig as commander of the F.F.I. and as de Gaulle's representative on the C.O.M.A.C., or military action branch of the National Resistance Council, but to the excited citizens scanning the posters for information about those who had been working in the dark or in exile towards their deliverance it almost seemed as if two new authorities were directing them instead of one; nor did instructions come only from the C.N.R. and the Provisional Government at Algiers. The Paris Liberation Committee, headed by a Communist named Georges Marrane, was also publishing directives, and the Communist *Union des Femmes Françaises* was issuing staccato orders:

> Women!
> You, too, can kill the Boches!
> Help to construct the barricades,
> There are arms! The enemy has arms!
> *Take them from him!*[8]

For some of the citizens this was strong meat. They re-read the order of the F.F.I. commander in the Paris area; he followed it up on August 19 with an Order of the Day defining the mission of the F.F.I. — 'to open the road to Paris to the victorious Allied armies and to welcome them' — and enforcing general mobilization, the requisition of all vehicles and the regular patrol of all Paris by the F.F.I. Then they began to ask questions about the man who signed these orders with the name of Colonel Rol.

Georges-Henri Tanguy, *dit* Rol, had taken for his clandestine name that of a fallen comrade in the International Brigade, in which he fought in Spain in 1937. A Communist, he had previously been discharged from both the Renault and Citroën automobile works for agitation, and since 1941 had been active in the Resistance. He had commanded the F.T.P. in his native Brittany and the Atlantic area before becoming the underground commander of Paris, and he was a natural soldier, with not only the leadership but the fine square face and strong features seen in many portraits of great French soldiers. In the French Revolution he might have won permanent fame and charged with Bonaparte at Arcola or Lodi Bridge: in 1944 his rôle was to requisition all the clandestine petrol in Paris and one-tenth of the official supply, and issue another poster:

> *How to Make an Incendiary Bottle.*
> Bottle ¾ Petrol,
> Add ¼ sulphuric acid,
> Shake well. Throw![9]

The thought that a man of this temper had 50,000 F.F.I. under his command in Paris alone was alarming to the *attentistes* of the capital, who would have preferred to see the Germans marching out by an eastern gate while the Allies marched in through the Bois de Boulogne, without any interlude in which dishevelled youths from the St. Antoine quarter roamed the placid streets of Passy, with F.F.I. brassards on their arms and no safety catches on their rifles. Incendiary bottles and barricades and *pétroleuses* snatching up the weapons of the fallen made a picture of revolution all too reminiscent of *la rouge commune insurrectionelle*, and although even the oldest inhabitants of Paris could hardly remember the terrible Sunday in May 1871 when the *Communards* burned the Tuileries and shot their hostages, including the Archbishop of Paris, they were well aware that history might repeat itself. It was a relief when, after six inconclusive days of fighting, messengers from the F.F.I. left Paris to tell General Leclerc that ammunition was running low in Paris and to beg for haste in his march towards the capital.

Leclerc had been fretting to start for Paris since the Allied victory at Argentan which closed the Falaise pocket, and had already made one attempt to break out of the sector. For this he had been reprimanded by General Leo S. Gerow, commanding V U.S. Corps, who translated by the word 'indiscipline' Leclerc's obsessive ambition to be first into Paris. General Omar Bradley, commanding XII U.S. Army Group, gave the order to march, but did not fail to note the delay of about twelve hours before Leclerc got the 2ᵉ D.B. out of camp at Fleure. The division moved about 6.30 a.m. on August 23, with 125 miles to go to Paris, and met with little enemy opposition on that day. On the 24th they ran into fire from German .88s on the Paris perimeter and heavy machine-gun firing at Fresnes, but even allowing for these delays their rate of progress was too slow to please the American generals, who refused to admit the need for celebrations en route as the delighted French welcomed their countrymen as liberators. Bradley was especially impatient, declaring that he 'could not wait for them to dance their way to Paris'.[10] He had been told that the deliverance of Paris by French troops would add to French prestige, but at last he growled to his chief of staff: 'To hell with prestige, tell the 4th Division to slam on in and take the liberation!'[11] With this competition, the 2ᵉ D.B. made better time, and at 9.22 p.m. on Thursday, August 24, advance elements of the division entered Paris and stood before the Hôtel de Ville.

There was little sleep in the capital that night and the dawn of August 25 broke on one of the great Paris *jours*. In the morning there was the triumphal entry of the 2ᵉ D.B. and the first delirious contact with American troops; then fighting broke out again all over the city. The Germans made the Hôtel Crillon into a strong point and defended it fiercely; there was fighting in the Place de la Concorde and the rue de Rivoli. The Quai d'Orsay was set on fire. At last the German commandant of Paris, General von Choltitz, prepared to leave his headquarters at the Hôtel Meurice to offer the surrender of the garrison to General Leclerc.

It was not at the Hôtel de Ville but at the Montparnasse railway station, where a command post had been set up, that Leclerc realized his four years' dream and accepted the German admission of defeat. The Hôtel de Ville was still occupied by the leaders of the National Resistance Council, who had followed the events of the week of liberation with mingled feelings. It was known that Hitler, in his fury, had ordered mass bombings of Paris if the revolt continued, and some of the Council were for delay until protection by Allied fighters could be assured; others, and particularly the Left-wing members, insisted that the F.F.I. attacks should continue. Their boldness was justified, for the few German bombers which reached Paris did little damage, and the city's historic beauty was still intact when General de Gaulle, having visited Leclerc at the Montparnasse station, presented himself, first to the C.N.R. in the city hall and then to the great throng assembled to cheer him in the Place de l'Hôtel de Ville.

The sound of firing was still heard across the city, for although

Colonel Rol had issued his last Order of the Day — a laconic 'mission accomplished' — the F.F.I. were still joyfully hunting stray Germans and Vichy militiamen across the roof-tops, and in the setting sun of August 25 there was fresh blood on streets where the paving stones had been torn up with crowbars to block the German tanks. It was the feast of St. Louis, the Crusader king of France; by all omens, a happier moment for de Gaulle's arrival in Paris than the Waterloo anniversary of his first radio appeal, and as liberated Paris cheered itself hoarse he seemed to be at the very pinnacle of success. Few men were likely to remind him at that moment that only four months earlier Marshal Pétain had stood in the same place, looking at another sea of enthusiastic faces, on the occasion of his only visit to Paris during the Occupation.[12]

Some days earlier the Marshal had been forcibly removed from Vichy in spite of protests to Hitler, and was being conveyed by easy stages to Sigmaringen in Germany. Before the uprising in Paris broke out he had attempted to make what dispositions he could for the future. He had written to Jules Jeanneney, the president of the former Senate, offering to give an account of his transactions during the 'mandate' which the Deputies had given him at Vichy in 1940; but Monsieur Jeanneney, to the displeasure of the Communists, was about to take office in de Gaulle's first cabinet. Pétain had also confided to Admiral Auphan the delicate mission of discussing with General de Gaulle the best 'solution to the French political problem' and 'the avoidance of civil war',[13] but General de Gaulle, in his triumph, was not disposed to negotiate with Admiral Auphan. To the partisans of the Marshal — and the enemies of the Communists — it seemed that a great opportunity was thereby missed, but it was one which de Gaulle could hardly be expected to seize. Even if all the insults which he, and most of the French broadcasters, had heaped on the man they called *Père la Défaite** had been struck from the record, the slightest move towards a *rapprochement* with Pétain, who had signed decrees sending Frenchmen to forced labour in Germany, would have turned all the fury of the Left against himself.

---

* This title was bestowed on the Marshal at the beginning of the Free French movement, long before he committed the supreme error of siding with the Germans at the time of total Occupation in 1942.

The excitement and the triumph continued through the following day, and the sense of tragedy began to fade with the charnel-house odour which hung over Paris for the better part of a week. Like all other Paris tradesmen the undertakers had pulled down their iron shutters at the outbreak of revolt, and the unclaimed dead had lain unburied until they were shovelled into hospital lawns or public gardens.[14] Now the F.F.I. chaplain, Father Bruckberger, was saying funeral masses for the members of the organization, who alone had the right to church services, and here and there at the street corners the first pitiful handwritten cards and bunches of flowers commemorated the men and girls who had died there *pour la France*.

General de Gaulle proposed to make on foot the classic journey from the Tomb of the Unknown Soldier under the Arc de Triomphe to give thanks for victory at the altar of Notre Dame, and Leclerc's tanks were early in parade order to line the route. This caused another clash with General Gerow, for the American had ordered Leclerc to get out of Paris on August 25 and join in the pursuit of the enemy. On August 26 the order was thrice repeated and thrice ignored, an act of insubordination which was no more than the pessimistic General Bradley had expected. 'Within a week', he was to comment, 'we would be rooting Leclerc's Shermans out of every back alley in Paris, even threatening his division with dissolution to get it on the road.'[15] But it was at de Gaulle's wish that the 2ᵉ D.B. was detained as protection[16] against the Vichy *miliciens*.

De Gaulle appeared at last, the radio word made flesh, under a rain of flowers and waves of cheering, walking down the Champs Élysées with an odd assortment of men around him. Some of the *Compagnons* were there, and the National Resistance Councillors, and others never heard of before or since, like the tall negro with a bandaged arm who was close enough to jostle the general's footsteps, and who was identified as Sergeant Dickson, of the 17th *arrondissement* F.F.I. The best reporting team of the *Figaro*, resuming publication in its 118th year, were grateful for the sergeant and for any other human angles; their reports revealed, by the paucity of such details about the general, how difficult it might be to make the legend come to life. De Gaulle's impressive height was duly noted, also that he 'looked about him' and had a special 'way of accepting homage — gathering it to him with open hands'. It was a gesture he had seen performed, although more gracefully, by the consort of King George VI; his countrymen soon learned that the solemn upward flap of both hands meant that de Gaulle was about to ask them to sing the *Marseillaise*.

The welcome Parisians gave that day to Charles de Gaulle seemed to prove beyond a doubt that they accepted him as their natural leader, and the newsreel cameras and radio reporters gave Britain and America instant proof that Mr. Churchill's Problem Child (as Roosevelt called him) was the centre of such adulation as no French general — not Condé, not Foch, not even Bonaparte — had ever won as battle honours. In that hour it seemed as if de Gaulle could do nothing which would not win the entire support of his countrymen. It was not until three years later that Colonel Rémy, who in four perilous years had learned to make hard appraisals of men under emotional stress, published his estimate of the number of true supporters of de Gaulle in the whole of France at that time. He put it no higher than 500,000,[17] being those who had rallied to the general's appeals *before* he landed in France, and their immediate sympathizers among the working class. Rémy realized that the photographs of de Gaulle which now appeared in every window covered space from which the picture of the Marshal had just been torn, and that the Crosses of Lorraine cut out of old linen and hastily stitched on the *tricolore* flags hanging from every balcony were too often the badges of last-minute adherents, destined to be known as *septembrisards*, or Resistants of September.

The liberation of Paris was an orgasm of triumph and vengeance, in which the frustrations of four years were compensated by the sight of bedraggled German troops, last scourings of the *Heimwehr*, kicked along by the F.F.I. with their hands clasped behind their necks in abject surrender. With them trailed a handful of wretched prostitutes, whose shaven heads were to add the epithet *Tondue!* to the recriminations of the Paris streets. The prison gates, thrown wide to release the victims of the Gestapo, now opened again for a miscellaneous throng of Germans, prostitutes, society women, persons slack in cheering Leclerc's tankmen, civil servants accused of collaboration, tenants in bad odour with their *concierges*, the innocent and the guilty pell-mell;

within a week Drancy, Fresnes, St. Denis and the Cherche-Midi held more prisoners than before.

There was a tremendous coming and going in the city. All those cooped up in their narrow rooms for years past, dreading the summons of the Gestapo, or going out with eyes made blank and ears that refused to hear the German speech, now asked nothing better than to stroll and stare and listen. There was always something to see: on August 29 it was the march of two American divisions, taken through the city on their eastward route at the request of de Gaulle,[18] who thought a show of Allied force would impress any remaining collaborators. There was the sight of the swastika banners and the German-language street-directions being torn down and thrown into the gutters; there were also the traces of the fighting, though within a week of liberation these had diminished in the centre of the city to the shattered 'fifth column' on the façade of the Hôtel Crillon and a capsized *cabinet d'aisance* opposite the United States Embassy. The crowds drifted to and fro in the tranquil September sunlight which gave the Paris air its old illusion of being filled with powdered gold; the scent of boxwood came from the unclipped hedges in the Tuileries, and the roses of Picardy, of Anjou, of Dijon had a late flowering everywhere.

Now was the time, in that short pause of grateful calm, for men of perception both French and Allied to try to heal the wounds of France; wounds which the Germans had dealt not only to her man-power and to her whole economy but to her very soul. France was a country which had been defeated from the outside, and by the same power which twice before had subjected her to cruel suffering; if she was to rise to her feet again it was imperative that she be whole and united within herself and that those who claimed the right to help her should do so with the charity of the Epistle to the Corinthians as well as with the material supplies which — and it was part of her humiliation — she so urgently required. But the new men raised up in France proved to be narrow sectarians, willing to promote dissension and revenge, and the Allies, unable to get beneath the surface of the French bravado, forgot to include loving-kindness in their Liberation gifts.

After the first few days the Parisians were less eager to stroll on the liberated Champs Élysées or up and down the boulevards, for it was not easy to get from point to point on foot. Public transportation was at a standstill. The *métro* was not running and little petrol remained from Colonel Rol's incendiary bottles to supply omnibuses or automobiles. A few cars had *gazogènes* bellying on the roofs, and ransom prices were paid for rides in two-passenger rickshaw attachments to ordinary push bicycles. Even the *fiacres* turned out again, and apocalyptically thin horses dragged the musty straw-smelling cabs along the boulevards, while from a starting-point in the Place de la Concorde a few brewers' drays, drawn by percherons, carried office workers and shop assistants towards their suburban homes.

The young girls, riding on bicycles, added a gay note to the scene. Their sun-tanned legs were bare, for it was still warm, and they wore sandals with wooden platform soles and short, very full skirts; their hair was dressed *à la pompadour* above their laughing painted faces. They were the exact opposite of the girls whom the Allies had left in Britain, rationed in cosmetics and dress goods for years, wearing uniform and dungarees and with hair cut to conform with army regulations or the safety rules of the ordnance factories. Male eyes, justifiably charmed by the Parisiennes, failed to see that the pretty bright dresses would turn into blotting-paper under a shower of rain, that the slim heels wore sticking-plaster where the springless shoes had chafed, that the perfumed hair was lustreless because of the long shortage of fats. Only beauty and gaiety were described in the first reports from liberated Paris, which also emphasized the delicious food and drink served to all the liberators who came within range of French hospitality. Those reports came out quickly via a Resistance radio, and half a dozen war correspondents were temporarily suspended by S.H.A.E.F. for the transmission of uncensored material. 'Fortunately,' commented General Eisenhower's naval aide, 'none of the messages contained anything the censor would have stricken out.'[19]

Although these messages contained no military information they had an unfortunate effect in Britain and America, as did the next batch received through the army communications system. In Britain, where austerity had become a way of life, it was gloomily supposed that the French were *at it again*, guzzling and swilling as in 1940, while in America, where so many funds had been raised to alleviate French distress, there began to be doubts that any distress existed. When it was reported early in September that the Paris fashion houses would proceed with their usual showings there was an outcry against the frivolity of the French, who could interest themselves in hats shaped like pagodas, minarets and tea-cosies at a time when the Allies had run into serious reverses in Holland. It was not understood that high fashion was a major source of export revenue and employment to Paris, while champagne, which had figured so largely in all reports of the Paris celebrations, was a major money-earner for the north-east just as wine was the most valuable export of Bordeaux. It was wonderful how the hat-perfume-and-champagne story was revived again and again as proof of French frivolity, even in the years when textiles, mining and metallurgy, the real leading industries, had passed their pre-war production levels.

War reporters going to or from the front soon became familiar with every well-lit showcase in the long corridors at the Ritz Hotel and the Scribe, which contained changing displays of *l'article de Paris* in the form of lingerie, leather goods or costume jewellery. They described these things because they had little time to go beyond the radius of fashionable streets between the rue du Faubourg St. Honoré and the Avenue de l'Opéra and see how the Paris workers were faring in Aubervilliers or the bombed districts of Boulogne-Billancourt. There the talk was not of luxuries but of food in its simplest and scantiest form.

Rémy had seen men dying of hunger in the Paris streets during one of his secret missions,[20] while aged persons rummaged feebly in the garbage cans for food. As far back as 1942 he had estimated the average weight loss in the capital to be 40 lb. per person, in spite of the system, practised by nearly everyone, of getting food parcels from the provinces. This was not a black-market operation, for prices remained more or less normal, and the farmers who were willing to outwit the Vichy produce inspectors, or German requisitioning, kept a strict mental tally of the *quid pro quo* their relatives or friends in Paris would owe them for their trouble. It was, however, so difficult to send meat and poultry that Parisian diet leant too much to the cereal or the vegetarian: 1941 was known as the Rutabaga Year.[21] Deficiency ailments made their appearance, children became prone to tuberculosis, and women were plagued by a complaint shown by a puffy softness under the skin and called *la cellulite*, for which those who could afford it would undergo spa treatment for years to come.

Since food was the object of so much planning and physical effort it had naturally become the principal topic of conversation, especially when the last cheeses, *quenelles* and Strasbourg *pâtés* had been sacrificed to the Liberation feasting and Paris was once again a famished city. The Allies, through the Civil Affairs branch which the Gaullists hated, rushed in 5000 tons of food and medical supplies in British and Canadian Army trucks, but this was only a palliative measure, and it was clear that organization of food supplies should be the first care of the Provisional Government.

De Gaulle had installed himself at the War Ministry, in the office used by Clemenceau when he assumed the direction of affairs in the grim closing stages of World War I. The only Commissioners with him were Parodi and André Le Troquer, a one-armed veteran of Clemenceau's war; the others were still in Algiers, chafing at the need to wait until S.H.A.E.F. could spare air transport to bring them to Paris. It was a very short breathing-space for the general, but one which might well have allowed him to take his measure of the city, in which — he professed to have known by instinct since he was twelve years old — he had been predestined to rule.

Since Bonaparte had surveyed the Paris of the Revolution, no leader had ever had such an opportunity of studying the capital as a world within a world, for never since 1793 had Paris been so completely cut off from the provinces. There was radio, but radio could not be used for the multiple administrative transactions usually carried out by telephone or telegraph, and most of the wires had been cut by patriots as a way to harass the enemy. Destruction of road bridges and railways made the postal system slow and unreliable. The only way to find out what was really happening in liberated Lyons or Marseilles was to send a man there, and since fewer than 3000 steam locomotives were serviceable for the entire rail network it was as hard to get a seat on a train as a priority for a S.H.A.E.F. aircraft.

At this moment, when he and the capital were isolated from the world, it would have been of advantage to Charles de Gaulle, the amateur of seventeenth-century prose, to know some of the signposts left by writers of a later date. Taine, for instance, had left some precise guidance on what might be expected of the Parisians, as true in 1944 as in 1863:

> Every day they need a supply of vivid words, biting jests, new truths and varied ideas. They weary quickly and cannot endure boredom. They exaggerate their work, their spending, their needs and their efforts.
> But how subtle they are! How free their spirit! How quick to grasp, to comprehend! In their great and cosmopolitan city any idea can come to birth. The immense field of thought opens before them with no forbidden road.
> Custom neither hinders nor guides them: government and church are there to release them from the cares of national leadership and are supported with the same patience and mockery as the beadle or the policeman. Here, in short, the world is a stage show, a matter for criticism and argument. And you can be sure that the arguments and criticisms are absolutely free.

*

Few Frenchmen, except possibly a *maquisard* in search of a refuge, had visited the sources of the Seine during the years of the German occupation. Unadmired in its little grotto, the nineteenth-century statue erected to *Sequana flumen* had continued to guard one of the several rills which bubble up ceaselessly among the cresses and rushes and wild flowers of a certain valley of the Côte d'Or. But three hundred miles nearer the sea, where the Seine holds Paris in its curves, the springing impulse of the source had been translated as steadily as in past centuries into the creations of the spirit of man.

The liberators had been officially informed for years that France was existing in a mental vacuum, in which such original work as might be done was exclusively political and representative of the patriotic spirit of the Resistance. From clandestine presses the free world sometimes obtained, and frequently overrated, such books as Vercors's *Le Silence de la Mer* or Aragon's *Le Crève-Cœur*, which were received, said one francophile critic, 'like a present from the moon on the banks of the Acheron'.[22] Even more lunar in its superb ignoring of *la débâcle* was Colette's romance called *Julie de Carneilhan*, which reached her British admirers in 1943 by way of a Montreal publishing house. It was a surprise to find, when Paris was free, that there was nothing clandestine about *Julie*, who had made her Paris début in 1941 via Arthème Fayard et Cie, publishers of the anglophobe weekly *Candide*, and that other noted writers whose patriotism, like Madame Colette's, was never in question, had continued to produce freely under the Occupation. André Gide's *Imaginary Interviews* had been appearing in the *Figaro* before it suspended publication in 1942. Paul Valéry was still working on his *Faust*. François Mauriac had written *Les Mal Aimés*, while two exciting new writers, Albert Camus and Jean-Paul Sartre, had been exceedingly prolific. A new play by Sartre, *Huis Clos*, which the liberators crowded to see as soon as the Paris theatres re-opened on September 10, had been put on under the Occupation, not long before D-day, and the playwright had also developed a new and casuistic system of philosophy called existentialism. Many of these writers had been subjected to the discipline of the Resistance, but all had used their minds in freedom, and Sartre summed up their situation when he said: 'We were never more free than during the German occupation. We had lost all our rights, including the right to talk . . . and because of all this we were free.'

Everywhere in the arts there was something new. Pablo Casals had been playing his violoncello in aid of Vichy's *Secours National*. Maurice Thiriet's new composition, *La Reine des Îles*, had been performed over Radio-Marseilles. Van Dongen's sensuous canvases had been on show at the Galerie de France. Jean-Louis Barrault, most brilliant of the younger actors, had staged *Hamlet* and *Antony and Cleopatra*, while in the cinema so much new work had been done by Marcel Carné, Christian Jaque and others that a 'Fortnight of the Cinema' was held in the Normandie theatre in December to show the best motion pictures of the Occupation years.

The cinemas reopened later than the theatres, later indeed than the race tracks and the *vernissage* of the Salon d'Automne on October 6, chiefly because of the cuts in electric current. The Germans, as a parting courtesy, had destroyed the hydro-electric plant in the Massif Central, and new restrictions were added to

53

the rationed use of electric power. Elevators stood motionless in office and apartment buildings. Clumsy pot-bellied stoves with long L-shaped pipes to carry the smoke outdoors burned wood and *mazout* in living-rooms where central heating had been used, and the tops of such stoves usually held a few simmering pots and pans transferred from the useless electric ranges. Water ran cold in all the taps, and only certain types of sufferers, like rheumatic patients, could obtain permits for the restricted use of electric water-heaters. When the nights grew longer, the black-out, already relieved in London, remained in operation in Paris, and only a few street lamps shed a ray of light at an oblique angle across the ancient streets.

But the Parisian appetite for entertainment was superior to all material difficulties. One of the great deprivations, it was said, had been the ban on British and American movies, and any re-issue that could be rushed to Paris was sure to play to packed houses. There was a revival of *Entente Cordiale*, a propaganda piece of the Munich era, and of *The Story of Vernon and Irene Castle*, which as *La Grande Farandole* soothed the twitching nerves of Marseilles, of *Wuthering Heights* and the perennial *Gold Rush*. But the topical titles brought out the biggest crowds. Chaplin in *Le Dictateur* and Bette Davis in *Victoire sur la Nuit* (Dark Victory) held audiences in their seats through *séances* rendered interminable by repeated failures of electric current.

The cinema, like the theatre, was medium-price entertainment, but for those with money to burn new bars and night clubs seemed, in spite of the restrictions on building materials, to spring up almost overnight. Black-market restaurants, operating *dans la clandestinité*, went through the farce of displaying an official list of prices at the door which bore no relation to the charges for steaks, whipped cream from liberated Normandy and citrus fruits from the Riviera. Night clubs had difficulty with their floor shows, for star performers were liable to sudden arrest for collaboration, and closing orders were issued arbitrarily. Closed for dancing, on de Gaulle's command, to honour the World War I dead on November 11; closed completely at Christmas during the Battle of the Bulge, these clubs had to face heavy competition from the endless gala evenings in aid of war charities, at which appeared such stars as Noel Coward or Maurice Chevalier, who had recently been exonerated of collaboration at a drum-head court-martial in Périgueux, conducted by an F.F.I. captain *dit* Double-Mètre.[23] The principal patrons of the night clubs were known as the B.O.F. (*beurre, œufs, fromages*) from the dairy products on which their illicit profits had been made, and they cut odd figures in the ornate and luxurious surroundings of rose satin walls and white rococo pillars — the men ordering food and drink lavishly, the women loaded with jewellery in the new style, with diamonds set in rings cut in cubes and squares of 18-carat gold, the symbols of a calculating age.

Young people learned to jitterbug at the dances given for American troops on leave, and took with enthusiasm to *le swing* and *le jazz hot*: they were all making the most of their time now, for France had re-entered the war, and new mobilization orders were not appreciated by the generation too young to fight in 1940, which had learned to make its way *dans la clandestinité*. The *zazous* who hung round the Place de l'Opéra in their zoot-suit wear of dark grey flannel *complets*, with trousers ending just below the knee and white socks turned down over suède shoes, did not appreciate being drafted to serve under de Lattre and having to give up rackets made more than ever profitable by access to U.S. Army medical supplies and petrol. But patriotism was still in fashion, and thousands of Parisians ignored the transport shortage and trekked to the Champs Élysées on foot on November 11, when Winston Churchill visited the city in which his faith had never faltered. That day the cries of *Vive Churchill! Vive de Gaulle!* echoed from top to bottom of the Champs Élysées, and only stopped when the long parade of Allied troops began, headed by a British detachment (Paris had seen too little of the British troops) which swung past the saluting base to the tune of 'The British Grenadiers'. On another day the spectacle was provided by General Eisenhower, down from the front for a press conference at the Hôtel Scribe, and pausing, taut and smiling in his battle-dress, long enough to impress the delighted crowds with his complete indifference to the reported threats of assassination. And on another there was the sensation of the ammunition train at Vitry, which exploded with hideous crashes while de Gaulle was making a speech in memory of war victims and caused wild rumours that the general had been murdered.

In short, the autumn of the Liberation was one long thrill for the inhabitants of Paris, and when Mistinguett, who by the most generous count had reached her seventies, reappeared on the stage of the Théâtre de l'Étoile attired in a khaki uniform and riding in a property jeep, it was conceded that the ultimate in patriotic fervour had found expression. But the Americans brought the Parisians back from the clouds to the realities of 'business as usual', well expressed by posters which appeared in the principal streets with the message:

Congratulations on a Job well done!
Hart Schaffner & Marx Clothes
U.S.A.

CHAPTER II

THE AFTERMATH OF THE RESISTANCE

Monsieur Hamel turned to the blackboard, took the chalk and wrote with all his force in the biggest letters possible:

VIVE LA FRANCE—

Then he stayed where he was, leaning his head against the wall, and without speaking he made a sign with his hand—
'It is finished . . . go away.'

THE famous ending of *La Dernière Classe*, which described an Alsatian schoolmaster's reaction to the French defeat of 1871, suggested that Alphonse Daudet's Monsieur Hamel had accepted disaster, and was not preparing to organize resistance. But times had changed in 1942, and when a history teacher named Georges Bidault was dismissed from his post at Lyons by the Vichy government, on the grounds that his teaching was 'too patriotic', he wasted no time in turning his face to the class-room wall. He had been a schoolmaster all his life, except for the brief period when he had gone to war, been taken prisoner in 1940, worked as a grocery counterman in Hanover and won repatriation with an over-age group, but his dismissal did not move him to the biblical *It is finished*: Georges Bidault took to the underground and left Lyons. A devout Catholic, he reappeared at the Paris home of the devoutly Protestant Misses Poincenot in the garb of a Protestant pastor.

From that time on Georges Bidault, *dit* Rousseau, had risen in the ranks of the Resistance, as it was beaten into shape by the remarkable Frenchman who was the first president of the National Resistance Council. This was Jean Moulin, *dit* Max, who had publicly withstood the German occupants as Prefect of Chartres, and who, in the underground, had assumed the herculean task of welding together the seven major groups of the Resistance,* all

---

* North: *Organisation Civile et Militaire, Ceux de la Libération, Ceux de la Résistance, Front National* (Communist). South: *Combat, Franc-Tireur, Libération.* The smaller *réseaux* and their membership may never be accurately counted.

of which were extremely articulate, had dissimilar blueprints of the France they wanted to live in after the war, and were able to express their ideas in the pages of clandestine newspapers.

There was a Gaullist and an anti-Gaullist wing in the early Resistance which Max tried hard to bring together. He himself was an ardent Gaullist, who wanted to see 'One chief alone: De Gaulle' as the slogan of a clandestine paper instead of 'One struggle only: for the Country', and he took issue with dissidents like Henri Frenay, leader of the *Combat* network, who held that 'since de Gaulle was in England and not in France he could not follow, day after day, our difficulties, our servitudes and our desires'.[1] Unlike Bidault, whom he had put in charge of his press and information section, Max was in personal touch with de Gaulle; he had reported to the general in London, and represented the Resistance on the French National Committee. This plurality of offices, inside and outside France, gave him power superior to de Gaulle's own, and the anti-Gaullists wondered pleasurably if the general realized that Max's dynamic personality and political address might carry him, and not the 'Leader of all Free Frenchmen', to the first Presidency of the Fourth Republic.

In June 1943, after a visit to London, Jean Moulin was betrayed to the Germans and died under the tortures of the Gestapo. His successor was Georges Bidault, who immediately decided to separate the functions of the C.N.R.'s leader and its representative on the French National Committee, a move which Colonel Passy, who had started a vendetta against Bidault, declared to have been inspired by the Communists.[2] Georges Bidault, as it happened, was a Christian Democrat, who had taken his first steps in politics as a member of that not very powerful group, and had written editorials for its daily paper, *L'Aube*. By religion and training he was completely opposed to Communism, but he was also determined that the National Resistance Council should be fully representative of French opposition to the common enemy, and it was broadened to include members of the political parties of the Third Republic: Communists, Socialists and Radicals on the Left and Christian Democrats, *Alliance Démocratique* and *Fédération Républicaine* on the Right. The trade union groups, *Confédération Générale du Travail* (C.G.T.) and *Confédération Française de Travailleurs Chrétiens* (C.F.T.C.) were also represented on the Council.

This was the powerful body which Georges Bidault was justified in calling, on his first meeting with Charles de Gaulle, 'the Resistance out of uniform', and with it de Gaulle, leader of the Resistance in uniform, was first of all obliged to come to terms. Monsieur Bidault, its president, seemed to be the very opposite of the general. He was a halting orator without much physical presence; modest and even demure in appearance, he allowed a half-smile to appear often on a rather kittenish countenance. Paul Reynaud had been nicknamed *Le Chat*, but there was little similarity between the feral Reynaud and the feline president of the C.N.R. Bidault's later nickname was the Dear Little Man.

General de Gaulle, slipping easily into place as head of the Provisional Government, did not make the mistake of underestimating Georges Bidault or the power of the body he led, which had its own palace guard, the C.O.M.A.C., and its household troops, the F.F.I. The National Resistance Council had placed 'the establishment of the Provisional Government of the Republic formed by General de Gaulle' at the top of the programme drawn up in the previous March, and by September 8, when the definitive list of de Gaulle's first cabinet was published, this aim had been achieved. The rest of the programme included:

Punishment and purge of traitors.
Confiscation of the property of traitors and black marketeers.
Restoration of egalitarian and democratic principles.
Reforms implying the eviction of the feudal directors of economy and finance.

With this programme de Gaulle had been in official agreement ever since his concordat with the Resistance in May 1943, and there was nothing in it which clashed with the fiery resolves drawn up by his own Consultative Assembly in Algiers. The Consultative, presided over by Félix Gouin, former Socialist Deputy for Marseilles and leader of the *Fleurs* underground network, was the only thing resembling democratic representation in the autocratic Gaullist movement, in which all the groups from the Imperial Defence Council of 1940 to the Provisional Government of 1944 were hand-picked by the general. The Assembly, which included anti-Vichy Deputies and Resistants from the underground networks went farther than the C.N.R. in the details of its programmes. Its various commissions had spent an enjoyable winter in drawing up *Ordonnances* for the future Constitution, education, and foreign policy of France — decisions which were to affect Liberated France for years to come — but their function in regard to de Gaulle was purely advisory, and after the return to Paris their advice was not very often sought.

The C.N.R. had not gone so far in working out such matters as the future status of the French Empire. What they wanted was the national insurrection so often promised them in the speeches of Charles de Gaulle, which should bring about the punishment of all those whom they, an army of shadows, had opposed during their years underground.

The language of national insurrection had not come naturally to Charles de Gaulle. He had been coached in it by men like Brossollette and Henry Hauck, his Director of Labour, who preached his cause to the British Labour party and the Trade Union Congress. By the spring of 1943 he had been in fine form, broadcasting condemnation of 'the System' which had caused the French disaster, and demanding that 'the Vichy caricature of fascism' be swept away. But in spite of many such speeches, and in spite of the places given to Communists in the C.N.R. and the Consultative Assembly of Algiers, not all the comrades inside France were persuaded that de Gaulle really meant to lead the promised 'national insurrection' as far as they meant to go. Without waiting for his appointees, the Commissioners of the Republic, to reach France from Algiers, or to obtain transportation inside the country, the Communists had set up administration by lynch law. Their paramilitary *Franc Tireurs et Partisans* joined with elements of the F.F.I. to form the *Gardes* (or *Milices*) *Patriotiques*, who claimed the right to bring collaborators before a kangaroo court and thence to summary execution. Some captains and colonels in the *Gardes Patriotiques* became famous for their severities, like Maurice Chevalier's interrogator, Capitaine Double-Mètre of Périgueux; others for the mass attacks they led on prisons, stormings of the Bastille in miniature and also in reverse, for the collaborators held inside were to be killed and not set free. On many nights that autumn the Minister of Justice, François de Menthon, and the Minister of Information, Pierre-Henri Teitgen (both Christian Democrats), had to rise in the dead of night and make the best of their way to some distant town where the populace was in an uproar round the scaffolds raised for summary execution.[3] There was nothing like a good killing for purging the shame of the Occupation, and there were many citizens ready to scream: 'They died too soon! too soon!' when they saw the young *miliciens* of Vichy drop to the well-aimed volley.

An outbreak of anarchy after a great war was no new thing in France. Waterloo had been followed by the 'White Terror' in the south, and in 1944 it was in the south again that the Red excesses were at their worst. The Allied armies were far away to the north and east, the capital was isolated, and the F.F.I., which had liberated Lyons, Brittany, Corrèze, Haute Vienne, Haute Savoie and the Limousin, was not only strong enough in those regions to carry out any number of summary executions* but continued, through the month of November, to receive supplies of weapons and ammunition from Great Britain.

The British had forwarded these supplies to equip the F.F.I. for integration with the regular army, and the order for such an integration was made by the cabinet on October 28, the day when the national insurrection was officially declared to have ended. The C.N.R. twice protested against the government decree but was compelled to fall back on platitudes about national solidarity and sacrifices for the general good. The police were ordered to confiscate illegal weapons and detain their owners. The Departmental Liberation Committees, all-powerful in the days of lynch law, saw the end of their project to turn themselves into an alternative government, or States General. The Paris Liberation Committee had to console itself by changing eighteen street names in honour of Resistance martyrs, mostly Communist. The F.F.I. in Paris had to give up the lucrative practice of extorting sums, at the rate of 50,000 francs fine for a contribution of 1000 francs, from business men and tradespeople who, for the sake of peace, had contributed to Doriot's *Parti Populaire Français* or any other Vichy group.

De Gaulle had suppressed a state of anarchy, and at the same time had shown the C.N.R. and the Departmental committees (who now had 146 representatives in the enlarged Consultative

* The exact number will never be known. The French Ministry of Information put it at 3000 or 4000; it has been put as high as 50,000.

Assembly) that the Provisional Government intended to be the sole authority in France. But he had also roused the animosity of the Left, who used his own words against him with telling effect. Thus Claude Roy in *Les Lettres Françaises* of September 30 commented: 'Charles de Gaulle himself has said that national insurrection is inseparable from national liberation' and Pascal Copeau, protesting against the sentence passed on two F.F.I. officers for summary executions at Maubeuge, wrote in *Action*:

> For four frightful years, the best of Frenchmen learned to kill, to commit sabotage, to derail trains, to steal and to defy what they were told was the law. And who taught these young Frenchmen to kill, who gave them the order to assassinate? Who but you, *mon général*? Who but you, Monsieur Maurice Schumann, Pasionaría of the microphone? Who but you, Georges Bidault, president of the National Resistance Council?

The only way to appease the avengers was to punish collaborators through the regular channels of justice, and de Gaulle, who had faced down the Resistance over the *Gardes Patriotiques*, did nothing to hinder their demands for punishment. He was, for one thing, too busy consolidating his position by a series of personal appearances throughout the country. He visited Lyons, Toulon, Marseilles and Orléans in mid-September, heard a *Te Deum* in his native Lille on October 2, and went on to the sound of the *Marseillaise* into devastated Normandy. He had shown no leniency at Algiers, in spite of protests by Roosevelt and Churchill, when he became the warder of MM. Peyrouton and Flandin, and of Governor Boisson of Dakar, who finally brought French West Africa to the Allied side. Now his views on *l'épuration*, the Purge, were summed up in the words: 'God will judge all their souls and France will bury all their bodies!'[4]

He thus lost a great opportunity of pouring oil on the wounds of his country. The purge became an ulcer in the side of France, keeping hate alive and engendering new bitterness, denying the country the services of men of talent and immuring others in prison as completely as the Bourbon kings had sent men to the Bastille under *lettres de cachet*. It ought to have ended before the first Christmas of the Liberation; it dragged on, in one form or another, for ten mortal years.

★

Not many days after Paris was set free, a new column appeared in the daily papers after the births, marriages and deaths and before the racing and theatre news. Headed 'Arrests and Purges', it named those arrested in the previous twenty-four hours, and the sentences passed on those brought to trial; soon it was a lengthy as well as a popular feature, for 100,000 persons were taken into custody in the first five months after the Liberation, and 52,000 were detained in prison. The entire prison population of France in 1939 had been 18,000.[5]

Those acquitted, or who could give satisfactory excuses, for their alleged collaboration, were said to be *blanchis* (whitewashed), and their names, too, were published, but the wheels of justice turned slowly, and as the weeks passed at Poissy or Fresnes, while the dossiers passed from one slow-reading revolutionary to another, many prisoners on remand began to feel that there was something to be said for a drum-head court-martial in the brisk style of Captain Double-Mètre.

An *Ordonnance* passed at Algiers on June 26 had set up a framework for the collaborator trials, and the only hitch in establishing it at Paris was that so many of those who administered justice were themselves accused of collaboration. There were 30 sanctions in the Council of State, 370 vacancies in the tribunals and courts of appeal, 266 suspensions in the magistrature and 215 among the justices of the peace. Competent judges and prosecutors had therefore to be chosen from a purged list of law-givers, and juries could not be empanelled without giving proof of good Resistance records.

The *épuration* worked on three levels. A High Court of Justice tried all those who had taken direct part in the government of Vichy. Courts of Justice tried crimes classifiable as action favouring the enemy, and Civic Chambers cases of the new crime, 'National indignity'. This covered all forms of dishonourable conduct and was punishable by 'national degradation', which meant loss of civil and political rights, return of medals and decorations, and exclusion from certain professions. This was by far the largest category of punishment and the one most easy to abuse.

Unluckily for the prestige of the *épuration* the big game was not immediately available. The Vichy ministers were either in

Germany with Pétain or in some neutral territory, and the best interim arrangement that could be made was the creation of a *Jury d'honneur*, consisting of the president of the C.N.R., the vice-president of the Council of State and the chancellor of the new Order of the Liberation, to hear the pleas of the 569 Deputies who had voted plenary powers to Pétain in the Vichy Casino. Two-thirds were banned from public life, and only those were exonerated who could prove that they had taken part in the Resistance.

These cases were deferred until the following spring. In the autumn of 1944 the Court of Justice had to open its hearings with the case of Georges Suarez, director of the newspaper *Aujourd'hui* (circ. 80,000) accused of intelligence with the enemy in time of war.

The proceedings, which opened in the Palais de Justice on October 23, were brief and dramatic. In technique a happy blend of the new and the old, the prosecution employed such devices as the playback of wax recordings of the accused man's opinions, while the court made no protest against the occasional shrieks of 'Kill him! Death to the traitor!' which arose from as many of the Paris mob as could carry their garlic-sausage sandwiches and revolutionary enthusiasm into the public area. Twenty-four jurors — four, for the first time in the history of French justice, were women — deliberated for only twenty minutes before bringing in a verdict of guilty, and the pallid Suarez heard the death sentence with exemplary calm. Two weeks later his execution in the yard of the Fort de Montrouge set the pattern of most of those which followed: twelve riflemen in two ranks of six, condemned man refusing to have his eyes bandaged or his wrists bound, a final cry of *'Vive la France!'* The pattern changed only a few times as what François Mauriac called in January 'the bloodstained labyrinth' grew more involved. Jean Luchaire, director of *Nouveaux Temps*, walked to the *peloton* in a disdainful silence. Pierre Laval attempted suicide in Fresnes and was shot in the courtyard, having no strength to walk to the place of execution. Joseph Darnand, leader of the hated Vichy militia, offered, if his life were spared, to lead a commando battalion in Indo-China; when this was refused he varied the classic *'Vive la France'* with a parting shout of 'Long live God!'[6]

These niceties of firing-squad deportment were still some months away, and what was chiefly proved by the early trials of the *épura-tion* was the occupational hazards of the writer's trade. The *Comité National des Écrivains* had prepared such a long list of sus-pected collaborators that it was well for the editors of the liberated press that they had an equally large choice of employees, all guaranteed Resistants, all well trained in clandestine journalism. The writers of the Occupation were indicted one by one. After Suarez, Paul Chack of *Le Matin* and Robert Brasillach of *Je Suis Partout* were executed, while Drieu la Rochelle of the *Nouvelle Revue Française* cheated the firing squad by committing suicide. Charles Maurras, the venomous old royalist of the *Action Française*, stood his trial in Lyons and got life imprisonment, Henri Béraud of *Gringoire* was sentenced to death and went to prison instead, Stephane Lauzanne of *Le Matin* received a sentence of twenty years in jail. Those not completely blinded by the sweat of the Libera-tion murmured that the politicians, officers and financiers of Vichy had slipped through the net while a group of venal journal-ists suffered in their stead.

It emerged that court proceedings were not necessary to smear a man or woman suspected of collaboration. Added to the 'Arrests and Purges' column was a tailpiece giving details of 'the Purge in the Army', or it might be 'in the University', or 'in the Finance Ministry' — for the civil service was severely purged, and the Provisional Government had hard work to replace trained men in the various public services. In the army, which for the most part had been loyal to the Marshal, 3035 officers were dis-charged at the Liberation, 14,379 dropped from the staff lists and 2635 graded as retired or resigned.

Through all this patriotic activity loomed one great moral question: where to draw the line of collaboration? What was the ethical difference between the Renault worker of Communist sympathies, earning money in a factory then adding to the German war potential, and the newspaper hack who had signed his name to some silly flattery of Otto Abetz? Who among those who had taken any part in public affairs during the Vichy régime had not, however patriotic, furthered the enemy's cause in spite of himself? This question was propounded with dramatic effect during the trial of Admiral Esteva, Vichy's Resident-General in Tunisia.

E 65

This case, the first to be heard by the High Court of Justice, came on in March 1945, before a blue-ribbon jury of twenty-four chosen by lot from a list of fifty candidates drawn from the Resistance and from among the Deputies voting against Pétain in 1940. It was heard by three judges, and Constant Victor Mornet, a man with the face of a bad-tempered bison who was Honorary Chamber President of the *Cour de Cassation*, was the Public Prosecutor. Esteva, accused of having permitted Axis troops to invade Tunisia and of exhorting the French under his command to 'fight against Bolshevism', was a pink-cheeked, lachrymose old gentleman who got his fair share of barracking and hissing from a mob delighted to see a Vichy admiral in the dock at last, but he was not the star of the performance. That was Maître Chresteil, his counsel, a bearded man with clean-cut features and a voice which seemed to beat like hail against the choleric cheeks of Monsieur Mornet, when he attacked the Public Prosecutor for having himself served Vichy! For having even emerged from retirement to serve on a commission to revise naturalizations, aimed at French citizens who were also Jews! Pale and cold, Maître Chresteil outfaced the lowering Prosecutor in his crimson robe. Monsieur Mornet's war record, he said, proved that 'even loyal Frenchmen might commit an error of judgment'. It was not quite good enough to save Esteva from the anticipated sentence of life imprisonment, but the argument — who in France dared sit in judgment on his neighbour? — awakened misgivings in many hearts. By that time 20,000 cases had been heard and 1458 persons condemned to death. Could it be that the *épuration*, in which the Communists never ceased to call for more arrests and harsher sentences, was the country's compensation for its hidden feelings of guilt and shame? Even the Provisional Government had ceased to make the purge a main issue, for by the beginning of 1945 it had moved on to a pursuit far more congenial to Charles de Gaulle: the restoration of France to her old position as a first-class military and diplomatic Power.

CHAPTER III

LA GRANDE NATION

O N August 25, the day of de Gaulle's arrival in Paris, the Allies had signed a Civil Affairs Agreement transferring administration of the interior zone of France to the Provisional Government, leaving only the military or forward zone under the jurisdiction of the Supreme Commander. The Agreement pledged Britain and the United States to back the vexatious liberation currency, which was also placed under the Provisional Government's control, and which in any case soon found its own level by the refusal of French shopkeepers to accept it.

This removed two of the main grievances of the Gaullists, and the frantic welcome given to the general in the capital and the provinces seemed convincing proof of the support he commanded all through the country. The refusal to grant full recognition to his government, *de facto et de jure*, in which President Roosevelt, his chief antagonist, obstinately persisted until October 24, created a diplomatic situation which verged on farce as Roosevelt accredited Ambassador Jefferson Caffery to a government at Paris which his own government declined to recognize, and without the protocol of ascertaining whether the envoy would be *persona grata*. De Gaulle refused to receive Mr. Caffery. The British Government dispatched Ambassador Alfred Duff Cooper, with a cross-Channel escort of forty-eight Spitfires[1] — a parade which hardly compensated the Duff Coopers for the discovery that the old Embassy on the rue du Faubourg St. Honoré was crammed with the furniture of thirty-two British refugee families of 1940. General de Gaulle refused to receive Mr. Duff Cooper.

This deliberate shunning of the Allied ambassadors alarmed some of the clearer heads in the French cabinet. Already there was a hierarchy of lucidity at the Quai d'Orsay, where Georges Bidault was installed as Foreign Minister. Henri Bonnet and René Massigli were appointed ambassadors to Washington and London respectively — posts which they were to hold without interruption for the next ten years. Massigli remonstrated with de

Gaulle on his treatment of their good friend Duff Cooper, which he called very different from the cordial reception he himself had been given by King George VI and Mr. Churchill. Why — he asked — since the Russians too had delayed recognition of the Provisional Government, did de Gaulle receive the Russian envoy, Bogomolov, and ignore Caffery and Duff Cooper? De Gaulle replied darkly that 'the Russian and British positions were entirely different, owing to the way the Prime Minister had treated him'.[2]

This highly personal approach to diplomacy cast a gloom over the formal entertainment offered to the British ambassador when the belated recognition at last took place, and it was clear that de Gaulle, active in 1940 in promoting an abortive Franco-British Union, proposed then in an attempt to prevent *la débâcle*, would not revive the Entente Cordiale in 1944. If he looked for an alliance it would not be in that direction, and yet the *politique de grandeur* which he had mapped out might demand alliances, since it was based on a nineteenth-century concept of the rôle of France in Europe. De Gaulle, who intended that France should sit among the victors as a first-class Power, with prestige undiminished by early defeat and subsequent misfortune, was attempting to copy Talleyrand, who had manœuvred in the same way at the Congress of Vienna; and had the general been a diplomat with the skill and patience of Talleyrand he might have been equally successful, especially as France in 1945, unlike the France of 1815, would be an Allied, not an ex-enemy nation at the conference table.

From a hand that held few trumps he was disposed to play the card which had already served him well as head of the Free French movement, when he had used the existence of a very small body of fighting men to extort political concessions from his backers. There was once again a French Army in the field, for on September 19 de Lattre's Army B had been integrated with U.S. 6th Army Group as the 1st French Army — reviving honourable memories of 1940, when the 1st French Army defended the British retreat from Dunkirk[3] — and on the dash and drive of de Lattre's command and the 2e D.B. de Gaulle staked part of his claim for France to become one of the occupying powers in a conquered Germany. He failed to realize that, although they were delighted to cheer the flags at the military parades he staged as often as circumstances permitted, the French people had lost interest in the army almost as soon as the whole territory, except for the German pockets in the west, had been set free. No one as yet had gauged the profound depths of their disillusionment: they were not prepared to halloo for any army, not even their own, until it had justified the claims of its own propagandists. Bedevilled for four years by the contending voices on the airwaves — Churchill, de Gaulle, Philippe Henriot, Ferdonnet, Joseph Goebbels — the French had allowed their natural scepticism to degenerate into the permanent condition of disbelief which was one of the most serious results of the Occupation.

They were still, however, susceptible to the dramatic appeal of a fighting general, although the war had diminished their faith in admirals (after Esteva was sentenced there were four more awaiting trial for the scuttling of the fleet at Toulon), and there was ready admiration for Generals Koenig, Juin, Leclerc and de Lattre.

The four generals, not one of whom was a Parisian, presented a composite picture of the French provinces from which Paris drew her strength. General Pierre Koenig, the hero of Bir-Hakeim, was a Norman from Caen, where his father had been in business as an organ-builder; the family had originally come from Alsace. General Koenig, the commander of the F.F.I., had remained in Paris with de Gaulle and was now military governor of the city. General Juin, who like Koenig had walked with the general on his famous descent of the Champs Élysées, was now, with his brilliant Italian campaign behind him, Chief of the General Staff for National Defence.

Alphonse-Pierre Juin, a burly, bullet-headed, self-made man, was born at Bône in North Africa, where his father was a *gendarme* stationed in the export centre for Algerian products. The elder Juin, employed after his retirement from the *gendarmerie* as *concierge* at the Constantine courthouse, had come from the Vendée; his wife, a dressmaker, was a native of Corsica. This crossed strain, General Juin liked to say, was responsible for his own energy and stamina. A fine school record had won him a place at St. Cyr, and in October 1911 he passed out first in a graduating class which included Charles de Gaulle 'among the top ten'.

69

Wounded in World War I (and carrying a stiff arm as a result), he served in Morocco with Marshal Lyautey and was taken prisoner at Lille in World War II. The conditions of his release were often called in question, and his loyalty to Marshal Pétain, who named him commander-in-chief in North Africa, went no further than the opposing of some token resistance to the Allied invasion of November 1942. Then he threw in his lot with the Allies — 'enough of your dirty politics! Now we're going to fight the Germans!'[4] an American vice-consul heard him say to the Vichy Resident-General — and left for the Tunisian front. Liberator of Corsica and commander of the French Expeditionary Corps in Italy, Juin's victories at Cassino, on the Garignano, before Rome, had won him not only the admiration of the Allied commanders, but — to an extent achieved by no other French officer of the period — their personal friendship. He was on excellent terms with General Alexander, commanding the 8th British Army, and General Mark Clark of the 5th U.S. Army thought so highly of him that he overcame General George Marshall's reluctance to 'give a decoration to a foreigner'.[5] Juin received the first D.S.M. awarded to a Frenchman in World War II.

At this period in his life General Juin appeared to have little interest in international politics. His military routine held no place for *mystique* or melodrama. His Alpine campaign, which drew from him a few conventional remarks on Hannibal and Napoleon, suited him no better and no worse than his years in the desert, and he was in his element in a trailer high in the snow-swept mountains with his pipe drawing well and a good operational map before him, and later on the chance to relax with his officers over a bottle of *pinard* and a few shouted choruses.

The Comte de Hautecloque, *dit* Leclerc, liberator and idol of Paris — a city he neither cared for nor understood — had roots which went deep into the history of France. A noble family of Picardy, the de Hautecloques wore the cockleshells of Crusaders on the shields displayed at their château of Belloy-Saint-Léonard. A twelfth-century de Hautecloque, Guy, had fought in the Fifth Crusade in Egypt; his grandsons Wauthier and Pierre had been among the *Compagnons* of the royal Saint Louis in his Tunisian campaigns against the infidel.[6] The Captain Philippe de Hautecloque of 1940, in spite of his peace-time soldiering, his country

70

house and large young family, was a complete throwback to his Crusading ancestors. He was the genuine fanatic, dedicated to his troops and the cause for which they fought. A woman's bicycle may be a less splendid mount than a caracoling charger, but when de Hautecloque, soon to be Leclerc, pedalled his way across France[7] to stand in his dusty knickerbockers before de Gaulle, the Leader had added a true knight to his entourage. De Gaulle gave him a suitable reward: he sent him to Africa without delay.

Thus Leclerc escaped from the intrigues of Carlton Gardens, where a man so forthright would have come under attack from Right and Left. The Right would have produced witnesses who had seen him in his cadet days studying the sheets of *L'Humanité* pasted on the walls of St. Cyr (Communist sympathies); the Left would have nosed out his early reading of *l'Action Française* (*Cagoulard* sympathies) and discovered that he had once written: 'I faithfully read the *Action*, its principles are good!' When Leclerc, with a handful of followers, crossed the Wouri estuary in a pirogue on August 26, 1940, he not only made himself master of the Cameroun and opened the road leading to the Sudan and Tunisia, but he preserved his own integrity. He was remote enough from de Gaulle to be frank with him, as when he wrote in December 1941: 'Our national movement, Fighting France, contains some first-class men and also a goodly proportion of humbugs!'[8] or when he complained of having no ambulance aircraft, saying that the movement had turned from war supplies to politics, and kept French discord alive through its broadcasts and publications.

He did his best to keep out of the intrigues of Algiers, where pomp and parade did not attract him. On Bastille Day, 1943, he was seen dining alone with his Chief of Staff in a soldiers' eating-shop while de Gaulle, in great state, attended a gala at the Opera featuring Josephine Baker, the Negro singer, who was in the middle of *J'ai Deux Amours* when she was completely overcome by the arrival of the general. She pointed at the box and gasped out: 'I can't go on . . . HE is there!'[9] Then she collapsed upon the stage.

Those were the roaring days of Gaullism, but life in liberated France was less simple, even for the single-minded General Leclerc. He was made for the desert, for violent battles round the

71

oases and solitary hours of thought, and in France was heard to
lament the spacious days when 'there was no one to give him
orders and no telephone!' On November 22 he redeemed his
Crusader's oath and liberated Strasbourg, but had to share his
laurels with General de Lattre, whose 1st French Army led the
attack through the Vosges on November 14, breached the
Belfort Gap in one week and turned the German flank. General
Devers deduced from this that they could tackle the remnants of
the 19th German Army remaining in the Colmar area. But the
French lacked trained infantry replacements, their African
troops suffered terribly from the cold, and without the support of
VI U.S. Corps they bogged down in front of the Colmar
pocket. The Allied right flank was weakened, and when the
Germans struck back in the Ardennes Eisenhower considered
pulling the whole line back to the Vosges. A withdrawal from
Strasbourg, terrible for the inhabitants in danger of reprisal and
fatal to French morale, was prevented by the personal intervention of Mr. Churchill, and the French fought successfully to hold
the city. But after that there were bickerings between Leclerc and
de Lattre about two parachute battalions lent by the former and
not properly supported by the 2ᵉ D.B.[10] and going on through
crises of jealousy over the superior equipment of Leclerc's men,
who were treated by special arrangement as an American division.
Finally Leclerc refused to serve under de Lattre in the crucial
battle for Colmar, won with the assistance of XXI U.S. Corps
on February 3.

Outbursts of temper, of devotion, of jealousy and also of first-
class fighting were the normal accompaniments of Jean de Lattre
de Tassigny's work of liberation. Descended from country gentle-
folk of the Catholic province of La Vendée, there was something
of the Chouan of 1793 in his make-up and also something of the
bravura of the Napoleonic era. He had a turn for histrionics and
the trappings of rank, but there was nothing remote or disdainful
about his leadership. The man's affectations were excused by his
intense humanity.

One of the few French generals to win a victory in 1940 (at
Rethel, where he pushed the Germans back to the Aisne), General
de Lattre was loyal to Vichy until 1942, when he was imprisoned
for resisting the total German occupation of France. Escaping, he

was picked up by the R.A.F. near Mâcon and carried to London, joining de Gaulle at Algiers in 1943. It was not a record which especially endeared him to de Gaulle, who habitually spoke of both Juin and de Lattre in tones of critical patronage, but the latter was soon on excellent terms with General Alexander Patch, 7th U.S. Army, with whom he was to capture Elba and invade southern France. To a man like de Lattre, as sophisticated in character as in appearance — 'half prelate and half actor' — whose domestic life at Algiers was conducted with a pomp very different from the bourgeois standards of the de Gaulle ménage, there was something very soothing in Patch's panacea for the stormy conferences which preceded Operation Anvil: the summoning of an American soldier with an accordion, and the repeated playing of *Poet and Peasant*.[11]

General Patch had a sense of humour; General Devers, a few months later, was as little appreciative of de Lattre's qualities as Pershing had been of Foch's, but between the Rhône and the Neckar General de Lattre had to grapple with the serious problem of integrating the F.F.I. into the new army. The ragged levies straggled in during the autumn: 100,000 F.F.I. men signed voluntary engagements for the duration of the war in September, and after the *Gardes Patriotiques* were disbanded 75,000 more came in.[12] They were literally an army of *sansculottes*, ill-clad as the victors of Valmy in 1792; de Lattre had to appeal to the Americans for clothing,[13] and 6th Army Group's G-4 provided an emergency issue of trousers, while new agreements on their equipment and arms were being made with the U.S. Government. The new recruits were not easy to discipline, for few had ever held a lower rank than captain: de Lattre noted that colonel seemed to have been the preferred rank in the *maquis*. He also noted that Colonel Rol, the *ci-devant* commander of Paris, made an excellent soldier, who served with the 1st French Army during the whole of its progress into Germany.

The more politically minded the ex-*maquisards*, the more accustomed to hold democratic and lengthy debates on every plan of action, the more difficult it was to incorporate them as enlisted men, but the task was not beyond de Lattre. His strong sense of drama satisfied men whose lives *dans la clandestinité* had been all melodrama. As one of his veterans was to say: 'He led his lieutenants to victory in a storm of reproaches, flattery, angry scenes, pathetic appeals and curses, tremendous rows and brotherly *tutoiements*[14] — but he knew perfectly well what he was about: he was creating a legend of excitement, emulation and courage which would efface the memories of *la débâcle*.

All the four generals whose backgrounds and characters made up such a wonderful cross-section of French life knew how serious a problem in logistics must be solved before a shattered France could rebuild her army to even one-tenth of the 1939 strength. There was no reason to suppose that American subsidies would continue after the war, and the only hope for domestic budget allocations was that the Communists, usually opposed to military credits, were now posing as the godfathers of the new French Army. Maurice Thorez, a deserter in 1939, had returned from Moscow, where he had spent the war, and had been pardoned for his desertion under a special amnesty law.[15] He was now a highly vocal supporter of de Gaulle's plans for the army, and personally led a drive for recruits. Every Frenchman, the ex-deserter told a party rally at the Vélodrome d'Hiver on November 30, should be proud and eager to serve in the national army.

On the day after this egregious performance, General de Gaulle arrived in Moscow, accompanied by Georges Bidault and General Juin. He had been in transit for seven days, having halted at Cairo and Teheran, where he was received with the honours due to a chief of state, as well as at Baku and Stalingrad. This long eastward flight perfectly expressed his desire to leave the West behind, and to forget the snubs dealt him by Britain and America in the arms of Russia.

As winter approached, a curious attitude towards the Western Allies had been permitted to develop in Liberated France. Of the two, Britain was the less unpopular, which surprised many Vichy supporters who assumed that British aggressions at Mers-el-Kebir, in Syria and in Madagascar would never be forgiven. But the British, too, nursed some war-time grudges. In Scotland the sentimental tie of the Auld Alliance had been severely strained by the capture of 8000 men of the 51st (Highland) Division at St.-Valéry-en-Caux on June 12, 1940, when the surrender of the IX French Corps, without warning given, had left them with no time to fall back on Le Havre or Rouen.[16] Through the enterprise of Kemsley Newspapers Ltd. the mayor of St. Valéry paid a goodwill visit to Scotland in April 1945, but the relatives of the 6500 troops still held in German prisons thought him an inadequate exchange for the Highlanders. In London the ordeal of the rocket bomb had renewed earlier exasperations, for the launching platforms for the V-1s had been built along the French coast, usually by French forced labour. Stores of bombs had been deposited in the caverns of the Oise valley[17] and elsewhere in the Paris area.

The truth was that there were faults to forgive on both sides, and the French, who had been genuinely impressed by the British sacrifice and tenacity in the long struggle, were very willing to let bygones be bygones. Even before France was liberated, French residents in North Africa had been surprised to see the good feeling shown by the Fighting French to their British comrades of the Tunisian campaign. Unhappily, to be pro-British in North Africa also meant to be anti-American. The Gaullist commentators were eager to point out that the British had been through years of desert fighting, while the Americans came from safety at home or on British stations,[18] that British messes and canteens were open to French troops while the Americans lined up alone for soft drinks and candy bars at the well-stocked Post Exchanges, and so on. In Paris the abundance of food and drink supplied to the U.S. troops in the Communications Zone was the subject of jealous comment, and the liberated press, censored on domestic politics and troop-movements, might rail as it pleased at the Americans — the 'big kids' with the high pay, the Rainbow Corner, the U.S.O. shows and the deplorable habit of issuing German prisoners of war with the same rations as their own troops.

These details were played up, while the huge material contributions made by the United States to the rehabilitation of France were played down. Little had been made known of the Lend-Lease agreements signed by President Roosevelt, or the new agreement of February 28, 1945,* for shipments of food, petrol, machine tools, trucks and war matériel from the United States to France. Much more was made of the stimulus to the black market given by

* Value of supplies under this Agreement: $1675 millions repayable in 30 annual instalments at 2⅜ per cent per annum. Locomotives, trucks, machine vessels, $900 millions against a down payment of 20 per cent of the purchase price, 2⅜ per cent per annum on the balance.

75

the arrival of American troops. It was soon found that the G.I.s would sell anything from surplus clothing to penicillin. They did a roaring trade in cigarettes (sold in a package deal, one packet along with one or more tins of diced carrots or hominy), automobile tyres and petrol. Soon the fertile plain of the Beauce began to smell like a Middle East oilfield as the great invasion pipeline which ran from the Channel as far as Chartres was punctured at a number of points for the siphoning-off of petrol. Soon, at a big American garage near the Madeleine, Parisians began to assemble in the autumn dawns with their jerricans (petrol-containers also available on the black market) for the purchase of illicit petrol and oil. Some who lingered to watch had difficulty in reconciling the sharp traders of the sunrise with the *grands enfants* playing handball as the hour of inspection came round. 'That some sell their supplies, yes, that some play ball, yes,' said the bewildered civilians. 'But not both at once!'

★

The extent to which de Gaulle was driven by his personal daemon in the winter of the Liberation can be exactly measured by his determination to prove the independence of France and her continuing position as *La Grande Nation* by concluding a treaty of alliance with the U.S.S.R. The line he had followed for three years, and was to elaborate later, was that Russia and America, the two great Powers of the twentieth century, were diametrically opposed to one another, whereas the mission of France was to act as interpreter, to hold the ring and keep the peace between them. No man in Western Europe had received the news of Pearl Harbour with more sangfroid than Charles de Gaulle. He heard the news of the Japanese attack on the radio, after a long walk in the winter woods with his faithful Colonel Passy, and having meditated in silence for a time he announced to the latter that a great war between the Russians and the Americans was now inevitable.[19] For him to decide, as he did in 1944, to throw in his lot with the Russians, was to abandon the balance-wheel rôle he had anticipated for France; it was also a corollary of the scene in the wood near Portsmouth, where his antipathy to his Western protectors had been most clearly shown.

The most cordial diplomatic gesture which Russia had so far made towards France was to recommend her inclusion on the

European Advisory Commission, which was announced during the visit to Paris of Winston Churchill and Anthony Eden on November 11. It was not a very convincing foundation for a full-scale alliance, but de Gaulle saw in it the possibility of concluding a mutual assistance pact with Russia. The idea of a Franco-Russian treaty was not a new one; it had been tried in 1893, and esteemed as a potential weapon of revenge on Germany by nationalists like Paul Déroulède; it had led eventually to the imbroglio of alliances which pitted the Central Powers against the Triple Entente in 1914. Undeterred by this example, de Gaulle sought in Stalin's favour an equipoise to the misgivings of Roosevelt and Churchill; he was, moreover, well posted on the prevailing 'climate' of Moscow, for the head of the French military mission there since 1943 was his close friend and former chief of staff at Carlton Gardens, General Eugène Petit, who later sat in the Council of the Republic as a Communist fellow-traveller.

There were prolonged conferences and delays in the Kremlin which caused de Gaulle to put off an intended visit to the East Prussian front, but on December 9 the French delegation was invited to one of the convivial dinners at which only Mr. Churchill was really capable of matching drinks with the Muscovites. On this occasion the conviviality lasted until early morning. At 4.45 a.m. the Franco-Soviet Pact was signed by Vyacheslav M. Molotov for Russia and Georges Bidault for France. At 7 a.m., Stalin was complimenting de Gaulle on being 'the toughest negotiator' he had ever met. 'I like 'em tough,' he said.[20]

Read in the cold light of a Moscow morning, the pact contained no special indication of toughness. It consisted of a series of platitudes in which the High Contracting Parties pledged themselves to fight on side by side and with the United Nations until Germany was defeated, to enter into no separate negotiations for peace, to take all necessary measures against future German aggression, and so on. The only exceptional clause was

Article Five

The High Contracting Parties agree that they will not enter into any alliance or share in any coalition directed against either one of them.[21]

This meant that, if the Russo-American War anticipated by de Gaulle should ever take place, France was bound by treaty to refrain from fighting on the side of the United States.

This very important document contained no clause limiting the duration of the alliance, as had the Anglo-Soviet Pact of 1942. It was not dependent upon 'a common action to preserve the peace', such as an international security organization. It was essentially a bilateral treaty, for, although the British Government had let it be known that an Anglo-French-Soviet pact might be negotiated, de Gaulle rejected any idea of a tripartite document. All this Stalin reported to Roosevelt and Churchill while de Gaulle was actually in Moscow,[22] and the Marshal also described the objections he had raised to agreeing that the French frontier should be the left bank of the Rhine.

At a game of bluff de Gaulle was no match for Stalin, who concealed beneath compliments and flattery his intention to treat the French as a defeated nation, for although Stalin had recognized the Provisional Government he questioned their juridical right to sign international pacts.

If the Kremlin had taken de Gaulle more seriously the consequences might have been very grave for the West. A France truly neutralized by Article Five of the 1944 treaty would have been far more valuable to Stalin than any of the eastern satellites which the mistakes made at Yalta permitted to fall into the Russian sphere of influence. A France bound to refuse her ports and airfields to an American expeditionary force proceeding against Russia would have isolated western Germany and the Low Countries and pushed the Iron Curtain as far west as the Atlantic. As it was, considerable damage was done before half a dozen years were over by the rioting and sabotage of French Communists, taking their stand on this very treaty at Russia's instigation, when French ports and airfields were opened to American matériel and personnel forming part of the *cordon sanitaire* against Soviet aggression.

Had Stalin followed up his original gesture of goodwill over the French membership of the European Advisory Commission with more solid benefits such as inviting France to the Yalta and Potsdam Conferences and supporting de Gaulle in the dispute which presently broke out with the British over Syria, de Gaulle's period as head of the Provisional Government might have been both different and more prolonged, since the Communists would have continued to work with him as long as the honeymoon with Russia lasted. But the Russian dictator had summed up France as a nation materially and morally broken, which no *politique de grandeur* could raise up, and once the Frenchmen had gone away with their treaty he turned to something more realistic: the Yalta Conference and the concessions which should establish the geographical frontier of Communism in the centre of Europe.

The French delegation returned to Paris on December 16. On the same day, the break-through in the Ardennes began Germany's last offensive of the war. The threat to Strasbourg and the urgency of the whole situation took precedence of the Franco-Soviet treaty and de Gaulle's public analysis of its merits. It was not until February 5, when the Germans were in full retreat, that he spoke on the radio in defence of his policy of prestige and system of alliances.

> We are not so presumptuous as to suppose that we alone can assure the security of Europe [he said]. For that alliances are necessary. That is why we have concluded a fine, good alliance with powerful and valiant Soviet Russia.

And he added:

> We would like to make another some day, with dear old England — when she will agree to what we feel to be necessary for Germany, and when we have got rid of the vestiges of an old-time rivalry in certain parts of the world.[23]

But by the time that de Gaulle extended this hope of a consolation prize to England, events in France had taken a turn far from favourable to the policy of grandeur.

CHAPTER IV

LE RAVITAILLO ET LA RÉPARTITI

THE winter solstice of 1944 ushered in a new period of suffering and endurance for France. The news from the front was so bad that many people expected the Germans to break through to the capital, and only the control of petrol and transportation by S.H.A.E.F. prevented a new stampede of terror. German bombers got through to Paris again on the night of December 26 and to airfields near Brussels on the morning of January 1, while V-2 rockets were still falling on London. Jean Luchaire and Jean-Herold Paquis, collaborators now broadcasting from Radio Baden-Baden, consistently advised their countrymen to organize a new Resistance and take to the *maquis* against the Americans, who had brought the certainty of German reprisals upon them.

It was a miserable Christmas, without food or warmth. In Paris empty boxes and barrels, even ladders and stairs leading to disused attics, were chopped up to make a blaze for an hour or two on Christmas night. The shops in the poorer quarters were empty of nearly everything but the apples which the Food Minister, Paul Ramadier, had had brought, at a considerable waste of transportation, from Normandy. In the whole Place de la Madeleine, famed for luxury groceries and confectioneries, little was on sale for the Christmas table but tinned truffles.

The snow, which had fallen heavily during the battles of the Vosges and the Ardennes, began to fall in Paris early in the New Year. By mid-January it lay thick on the walls and rooftops of the capital, combining with the absence of traffic and the slow-down of the perimeter industries due to power and raw material shortages to give Paris back some of the aspect it wore in the Middle Ages. Palaces and churches, etched in snow, regained a purity of outline largely lost on citizens who had to pass from frozen streets to cold shops or offices and back to colder homes where the evening meal might consist of carrot purée and a few dry slices of rationed bread, served with a cup of meat extract or of low-proof wine. The coffee on which all French people depended as beverage and stimulant had become a vile *succédané* made from acorns, sweetened in cafés by a splash from a communal bottle of sugar-water. The January distribution of ration cards was the worst ever organized, and there were newspaper protests against the long wait of four or five hours which most persons had endured in the draughty courtyards of the *mairies*. These complaints, and the announcement that the class of 1943 had been partially mobilized, were among the few domestic news items carried in January by papers reduced on January 17 to tabloid format. Pierre-Henri Teitgen, Minister of Information, had ordered a 50 per cent newsprint cut, with allocations to be made proportionately among the political parties which controlled the press;* this remained operative until the defeat of Germany and caused French newspapers to become unsaleable in Switzerland, where there was no market for tabloids.

The housing shortage was keenly felt. For a long time before the war French urbanism had been extremely backward; 97 per cent of all towns lacked a complete sewage system and only 32 per cent of all tenants had running water in their dwellings. Rents were low, due to the rent controls imposed in World War I and still in force, but this meant that landlords were unable to modernize or repair their properties, which were patched up and in need of paint and plumbing even before war damage completed the disorder of the French housing system. Now over a million homeless families were billeted on their friends and relatives, and Raoul Dautry, an able engineer who was Minister of Reconstruction, estimated that 2 billion francs would be needed for repairs and rebuilding. Joseph Laniel, at the same ministry, thought that 20,000 million man-hours would be required to do the work.

The human problem was as serious as the financial for a country with nearly 2,500,000 citizens† held in enemy territory and

---

* An Algiers *Ordonnance*, May 6, 1944, had ordered the suppression of all Occupation newspapers, and political screening took place before a licence to publish was granted.

Newsprint tonnage consumed in the U.S. 1944-45, 280,000 tons; in France, 2,900 tons.

† *L'Année Politique*, 1945, gives the following breakdown of this total: 1,000,000 war prisoners, 780,000 workers conscripted through the *Service de Travail Obligatoire*, plus a small minority who volunteered; 600,000 racial and political deportees.

1,200,000 men now incorporated in the fighting services. The solutions propounded at Algiers had been doctrinaire rather than practical: they included the creation of labour-management committees (*comités d'entreprises*) as a means of increasing production. These committees, obligatory after February 22, 1945, in all companies having over 100 workers, were to have two non-voting members on every board of directors, oversee the general operation of the works, receive an annual report and statement from the employer and make suggestions on the disposal of the profits.

Statistics and works committees did nothing to meet the basic needs of the people, which were for trucks and barges to bring coal from the northern mines, increased herds of beef and dairy cattle, flocks of egg-laying fowls and tractors and seed for cereal crops. Above all, steps should have been taken to remove the basic source of irritation — the knowledge that where the many went hungry the few were feasting on the produce of the black market. Many sanctions were promised by the government against the black marketeers; few were ever applied. The nation, hungry and dissatisfied, turned in upon itself and fed on its own disillusion, of which the symbol, that winter, seemed to be the northern villages traversed by the Red Ball highway running from Paris to Brussels and the Dutch frontier, or the roads through the shattered townships of Alsace. There the shutters were closed before the early darkness fell; no children threw flowers at the endless convoys moving east, no laughing girls served wine and no smoke rose from the cold chimneys. The Liberation was over, and France, behind bolted shutters, was adding up the cost.

Although the physical needs of the country were so acute, Charles de Gaulle continued to give most of his attention to high-level diplomacy. From his pact with Stalin he had had little profit, except what might be represented by the support of Maurice Thorez, who had moved on from his recruiting drive to preach the dissolution of the liberation committees and the 'return to legality'. Stalin opposed French participation in the occupation of conquered Germany, which had been a topic ever since Mr. Churchill's November visit to Paris, and President Roosevelt was inclined to agree with Stalin. But — noted Harry Hopkins, Roosevelt's personal adviser and envoy — 'Winston and Anthony

Eden fought like tigers for France' and her right to have a full command in Occupied Germany; and in February 1945 France was given a place on the future Control Commission. But on the Yalta Conference Stalin was adamant; his 'tough' new ally Charles de Gaulle should not be invited there, and this meant a considerable loss of face for the *politique de grandeur*. Talking it over with Harry Hopkins, Georges Bidault tried to explain away the arrogance of manner which had lost the general so many friends and so many opportunities to be present at Allied conferences, great or small. 'He believes that Frenchmen always try to please the man to whom they are talking', said Bidault. 'The general thinks they overdo it and he adopts a different attitude.'[1] But the general was not asked to Yalta, and Bidault's suavities were wasted when he let it be known that de Gaulle would be delighted to meet President Roosevelt at any time or place he cared to choose on the return journey from the Crimea.

The general absolutely declined to go to Algiers to see the President, as the latter proposed. He evidently expected that the American President, whose failing health was obvious to anyone who saw the news pictures of the Yalta meeting, should make a detour to Paris and wait upon the head of the Provisional Government in his own capital; or else, as the British ambassador believed, he was piqued because the Emperor of Ethiopia had also been invited to greet President Roosevelt, as if a Haile Selassie could possibly be considered the equal of a Charles de Gaulle![2] Either way, the refusal was a diplomatic *gaffe* of the first order, and one which shocked Frenchmen nearly as much as the officials of the U.S. Embassy.

Stubborn in doctrine as in diplomacy ('You don't know how stubborn he is,' said Georges Bidault ruefully), de Gaulle lost no time in keeping his radio pledge to transfer the sources of wealth into the hands of the people. In a major speech at Lille, when he revisited his birthplace on October 1, 1944, he attacked the trusts — 'a concentration of interests as much out of keeping with the demands of our national economy as military feudalism was out of keeping with the needs of national defence' — and ten days later a government order suspended the presidents and general directors of the coal-mining companies in the northern departments. On December 13 the first nationalization brought into

83

being the National Coal Mines of the Nord and the Pas-de-Calais. The partial nationalization of the merchant navy was followed on January 16 by preparations for state control of the Renault works; the Gnome et Rhône air engine company was expropriated; the air lines known as Air France, Air Bleu and Air France Transatlantique were nationalized as a group. But popular discontent continued: for a textile worker in Lyons to be part-owner, under nationalization, of a coal mine at Lens might be good Socialism, but it did not put food in his mouth or stop inflation, and although the government had ordered a wage increase in September prices had risen to two and one-half times the pre-war figure. The Minister of National Economy, Pierre Mendès-France — a brilliant Jewish economist and former Deputy who had served in a Free French air squadron — advocated the policy of austerity and fair-share rationing which had brought Britain through the war, but this was an unpopular measure, like his proposals to tax illicit profits, call in high currency bank notes and block accounts. Instead of his Draconian ideas the government accepted René Pleven's old-fashioned formula of floating a loan, and the 3 per cent Liberation Loan was well enough subscribed by the end of the year. Nevertheless in rejecting the Mendès-France proposals the 'government of national unanimity' had lost its last chance to harness the generous impulses of the Liberation, to strike a blow at the black market and put the French currency on as sound a footing as the Belgian.

The housewives of France were the severest critics of the government's policy of *laissez-faire*. Slaves of their ration cards, those tattered sets of tickets from which morsels were clipped like confetti, they knew that the whole *service de ravitaillement* was worthless unless the *répartition*, or allocation, of each commodity was made at the proper time. In the confusion created when the new brooms took over from Vichy civil servants, the distributions were often in arrears, and confusion was worse confounded by announcements in the January papers that the December coffee was now available, or even the November issue of fats.

In this atmosphere of dissatisfaction de Gaulle went to the Luxembourg Palace on March 2, 1945, to address the Consultative Assembly on the programme of French reconstruction. The Assembly was growing impatient with de Gaulle's high-

84

handed attitude towards the advice it tendered. He left them in no doubt of his position, telling them fairly that he was not bound by the vote of the Consultative Assembly — even by its unanimous vote — and as for his government, it was responsible only to the voters of the country. Since it had not been democratically elected, this responsibility was a polite fiction, and the Consultative Assembly knew it; but de Gaulle's hold over them was still very strong, and at the beginning of his *exposé* he was loudly cheered. Before it was over he had heard for the first time the unmistakable sound of a large public meeting's dissent, and, during one part of his speech, something which came very close to barracking.

It was an omission rather than a declaration which drew the murmurs of the Left. De Gaulle had nothing at all to say about *la répartiti* and *le ravitaillo*. On the human problems of France he was silent, except for saying that 'twelve million fine babies' should be born in the next ten years. In the social sphere he merely repeated his theories on the state control of public utilities, and the main body of his speech consisted of variations on a familiar theme: congratulations to himself for having rejected Marshal Pétain's overtures at the Liberation, criticisms of Britain and America for having failed to give the needs of France priority over their own war effort, and a glowing tribute to the army. The occasion was his first public failure, and next morning the women in the food lines, who had breakfasted off the condensation of his speech in the shrunken newspapers, shrugged their verdict: '*De Gaulle est complètement dépassé par les événements*'* — a phrase that was to stick.

In the early hours of May 7 World War II ended in Europe, when the German surrender was made at Rheims, and at 3 p.m. on the following day bells pealed and cannon roared in Paris in celebration of the victory. Some days of bacchanalia followed, enjoyed in the same superb summer weather as had mocked the *débâcle* of 1940 and graced the liberation of Paris and Provence; once again crowds moved about the streets of the capital all day and half the night, and now the streets were fully lighted for the first time since 1939. Famous buildings were flood-lit. A victory V shone white over Les Invalides, another shone blue, white and

* Outdistanced by events.

red above the Arc de Triomphe. Water played in the dried-up fountains of the Place de la Concorde, and the summer dawns which turned the flying drops to rose and amethyst broke benignly over the exhausted revellers, Allied and French, as they slept enlaced on the grass-plots of the Cours la Reine.

The provincial celebrations were happiest where the Liberation had left the lightest furrow; in Paris the gaiety was brittle and quickly over. Since the previous year a great upsurge of national feeling had been diverted into too many stony channels, mean hates of the *collabos* who escaped the purge and the judges who set them free; of the B.O.F.s and their bedizened women; of the Allies who, it seemed, had contrived in one way or another to belittle France. The ally in worst odour was now the historic scapegoat, Britain, thanks to an unhappy sequence of events which took place in Syria within a few weeks of victory in Europe.

Both Syria and Lebanon had been profoundly affected by the Gaullist error of arresting the Lebanese ministers in 1943, and the French claimed that Brigadier-General Spears had done his best to keep the breach open while he remained in Beirut. He had now returned to England and had resumed his parliamentary career, but a British force, under the name of British Troops North Levant, remained in the area, which the British rightly considered vital to their whole strategy in the Middle East. The French, who had no Middle East commitments but who held the Mandate, also retained *troupes spéciales* in the Levant, and these troops were the cause of the deadlock, for early in 1945 the Lebanese let it be known that they would not sign any Treaty of Alliance to replace the Mandate while French troops remained in the area. They had been encouraged by the creation of the United Nations organization to believe that by presenting their case at San Francisco they could end the Mandate and obtain full autonomy.

The *politique de grandeur* required that so far from withdrawing the *troupes spéciales* these should be reinforced with others, and that a good deal of money be spent on cheers for de Gaulle at the time of the V-E day celebrations in Beirut. The wharf and slum population entered into the thing with great spirit, and at the height of the excitement pedestrians were even required to kiss the general's picture and cry: 'Long live the Liberator of Europe!'[3] No amount of bribery could have procured the same effect in

Damascus, where opposition to the French Mandate was led by the President of the Republic, Shukri el-Quwatly Bey, and his Foreign Minister, Djavid Mardam Bey, and it was agreed that Lebanese and Syrian representatives should meet at Beirut to discuss the future of the countries without any further reference to France. Two months earlier the Arab League had been formed at Heliopolis near Cairo, and Syria and Lebanon had joined it along with Iraq, Saudi-Arabia, Yemen, Transjordania and Egypt. The Moslem rulers of the Levant States rightly believed that here was a powerful weapon of coercion against any European element which attempted to fasten itself upon their territories: with this additional confidence, they faced the arrival of the French reinforcements on May 17.

The position of Britain had been stated by Mr. Churchill on February 27, 1945, when he told the House of Commons that his government stood by the 1941 decision to give the Levant States independence while preserving a special position for France, an attitude basically different from that of Russia and the United States, which recognized no French privileges in the Levant. It was all the more embarrassing, therefore, when, after advising de Gaulle that the dispatch of reinforcements might have serious consequences, the British were asked by the Syrian Government to restore order in the country.

This took place on May 28, eleven days after the arrival of supplementary French troops had caused an outbreak of rioting all the way up and down the Mediterranean littoral of Syria and Lebanon; after the riots had been handled aggressively by the French and fighting was general in Homs, Hama, Damascus and Aleppo. On May 29 fierce fighting broke out in Damascus, where the French made the parliament buildings their strongpoint — the marks of spilt blood were still pointed out three months later — and British Troops North Levant suddenly found themselves ordered to quell the disturbances, even at the risk of firing on the French. General Sir Bernard Paget, C.-in-C. Middle East, now took the situation in hand, and with a speed which the French called *brutale* obtained a truce and a cease-fire order from the French commander.

Unfortunately the text of a message, stiff enough in itself, which Mr. Churchill sent to General de Gaulle on May 31, was read to the House of Commons before it reached the general, and the delay in transmission, from which so many messages to Paris suffered at that time, was interpreted by the French as an intentional discourtesy. De Gaulle even considered the idea of sending the *Jeanne d'Arc* to Beirut as a further advertisement of *la présence française* in the Levant. When Ambassador Duff Cooper saw him on June 4, de Gaulle 'could not have been more stiff if he had been declaring war',[4] and said he had ordered French troops to fire on British and Syrian elements alike if any further force were used. But Georges Bidault told the ambassador later that it was all over, the *Jeanne d'Arc* would not go to Beirut; and on the same day in Damascus Shukri el-Quwatly Bey told the British minister, Terence Shone, that he was grateful for British intervention and would allow the French 'to keep their schools (if any Syrians still wanted to go to them) and their commercial interests; but neither the Syrian Government nor the Chamber nor the people could ever give them any privilege in the country after what had happened'.

So ended the French influence in the Levant States, with the French garrison at Damascus withdrawn to a camp outside the city, those at Homs and Hama dependent on the British for their food supplies, and those at Latakia going down to bathe in the Mediterranean with an escort of British other ranks, lest the debilitated and enervated populace should fall upon them. In Paris the best gesture of reprisal devised by de Gaulle, apart from a snub to high-ranking British officers and an order to certain French generals to refuse the British decorations which Mr. Duff Cooper had been empowered to bestow on them, was the order to Lady Spears to disband her ambulance unit, which from the beginning to the end of the war had cared for 20,000 French wounded, as soon as he saw its British flags flying[5] in his Eighteenth of June parade.

At the exact moment when the French were coming to blows with the British in Syria de Gaulle had embroiled them with the Americans. General Eisenhower had ordered elements of the 1st French Army to evacuate the Italian province of Cuneo, where he intended to set up Allied military government. General Doyen, commanding the French Army in the Alps, announced that he had been ordered to prevent this 'by all necessary means without exception'. This ominous language caused Mr. Churchill to write to President Truman, who had succeeded Roosevelt upon the latter's death in April:

Is it not rather disagreeable for us to be addressed in these terms by General de Gaulle, whom we have reinstated in liberated France at some expense of American and British blood and treasure? Our policy with France is one of friendship.

Once again Georges Bidault was called into the fray. Faced with President Truman's blunt statement that while General Doyen's threat that 'any insistence [on Allied Military Government] would assume a . . . hostile character and could have grave consequences' was allowed to remain, no more supplies would be issued to French forces, he explained that the whole matter had been a misunderstanding, to be put right at the highest level by a visit of General Juin to Field-Marshal Alexander. This was duly done, and so expired the last flicker of the *politique de grandeur* by which de Gaulle, in less than nine months, had embroiled his country with her liberators, involved her in an ambiguous connection with Russia, lost her the much-prized footing in the Levant and roused the whole Arab world, stretching westward through North Africa, against the French who had caused the killing and maiming of 2000 persons in the streets of Damascus.

★

In June 1945 the British people were too deeply engrossed in an imminent parliamentary election, the first for ten years, to pay much attention to the news from Damascus or Cuneo, and the French had a domestic preoccupation: the return of the prisoners and deportees.

The hundreds of thousands of Frenchmen who were then processed with the maximum of confusion through the reception centres at the Gare d'Orsay and elsewhere brought with them an equivalent number of personal problems. For some these problems were domestic: a bastard child might have been carried out of Germany to be handed over to a French wife who went in short order through all the stages of hysteria from indignation to acquiescence; or else return meant the revelation of a wife's fruitful liaison with a German soldier. For most, even if their domestic harmony were unruffled, repatriation meant looking for new jobs and listening to the sarcasms of the new Army about *les vaincus* of 1940.

It was a time of great personal confusion, but through it all the French were inching their way towards the balance which was one of the two constants in the national life. On the other constant element, passion, entirely too much stress had been laid for the past five years: the nation, weary of heroics and tirades, wished to regain the art of living through a balance of the senses and the intellect. They were well able to express this wish in a language perfectly constructed for the communication of ideas; for them conversation had long been an art as well as a pleasure, and one not neglected through the long dark evenings of the Occupation. The danger was that in restoring the sense of balance the French might become prisoners of their opinions, and allow the practical needs of reconstruction to bog down in a morass of talk.

Political leaders of the Third Republic, confined for longer or shorter periods in Germany, had been liberated by the Allies and were now back in Paris. Among them were MM. Daladier and Reynaud, whose total eclipse had been so confidently predicted by the 1940 *émigrés*. Prisoners since the Riom trials of 1940, they had come well through the ordeal — Monsieur Reynaud, who had used a skipping rope in his cell at Riom, had acquired a sun-tan in Germany, and declared that he had kept fit through a system of intensive physical culture. Both were eager to return to politics.

Léon Blum, the veteran Socialist leader, was in a more fragile state of health, while Édouard Herriot, the famous chief of the Radical party, had been liberated by the Russians and returned to Paris via Moscow. All professed admiration for de Gaulle and sympathy with the aims of his government, but they all represented electoral competition for the 'new men' of the Resistance.

Some weeks before this happy return Marshal Pétain had arrived in France. On April 5, at Sigmaringen, he had learned that he was to be put on trial *in absentia* and at once asked the German authorities to let him return to France via Switzerland. He was determined to answer his accusers in person: 'Only in France', he said, 'can I answer for my acts, and I am the sole judge of the risks I run.'[6] On April 25 he entered France, being arrested at the frontier by General Koenig, and was imprisoned in the Fort de Montrouge until his trial opened on July 23.

The trial of Philippe Pétain, Marshal of France, for deeds ranging from the signing of the armistice, plotting against the Republic, plotting against the safety of the State, losing the fleet, holding intelligence with the enemy and other acts of collaboration down to 'favouring the anti-Bolshevik crusade' was intended to be much the most important and sensational, as it was certainly the longest (three weeks) of all the Purge. Yet, in spite of the immense interest which it aroused, the trial somehow missed fire. Too many alleged traitors had been arraigned before the appearance of the Marshal: the public appetite was surfeited; and the long-drawn-out proceedings lacked the drama of the first condemnation to death — that of Suarez — and the challenge flung down by Maître Chresteil at the trial of Esteva. Constant Mornet was once again the Public Prosecutor, but a good deal of the limelight went to the Marshal's defenders, notably Maître Jacques Isorni, and to the extraordinary procession of witnesses who used the stand as a rostrum for their own political views. Ex-President Lebrun, General Weygand, Pastor Boegner, Pierre Laval, Léon Blum — each and all were a great deal more voluble than the weary old prisoner, now in his ninetieth year. Exhausted and apparently remote from the proceedings, he found only a few simple words to say, after a long silence, in his own defence. On the first day he had read a prepared statement, maintaining that by the armistice he had 'saved France' and that 'to condemn him was to prolong the discord of the country'. What he added, after a long refusal to answer questions, was precisely what he might have said in 1940, when he had most of the nation on his side:

My only thought was to remain with the French people on the soil of France, according to my promise, and to try to protect them and lessen their sufferings. Whatever happens, they will not forget this. They know that I defended them as I defended Verdun.

But the time had not yet come when such words could move an audience in Liberated France. The verdict of death, coupled with a recommendation for mercy, brought in at 4 a.m. on August 15, had been a foregone conclusion. The only human interest remaining was the attitude of de Gaulle.

At the Liberation he had managed to give the impression that he was indifferent to the fate of the Marshal. 'Send him to Switzerland'; 'Let him go and live on the Riviera',⁷ had been two of the views he had expressed to reliable witnesses.* But once again he had been 'outdistanced by events': the Left would have broken into open revolt if their arch-enemy, in extreme old age, had been permitted to go into exile in France, or in some pleasant climate overseas. De Gaulle, therefore, followed the pattern laid down by Marshal MacMahon as President of the Republic in 1873, when Marshal Bazaine was condemned to death for 'premature capitulation of a fortress' (Metz) and 'negotiating with the enemy before doing everything required by duty and honour'. MacMahon, himself in command at the crushing and decisive defeats of Worth and Sedan, commuted Bazaine's sentence into life imprisonment on the Île Ste Marguerite, near Cannes; de Gaulle raised the sentence of death on Pétain to commit him for life to an island off the coast of La Vendée. Bazaine, at 63, had soon escaped down the cliffs in a daring night rescue carried out by his 26-year-old wife, a feat hardly likely to be repeated by the elderly Madame Pétain and the 90-year-old Marshal, but in case of accidents Pétain was not only confined to the Île d'Yeu but to a cell in the Citadelle de la Pierre Levée.

With the Vichy Chief of State in jail and his premier, Pierre Laval, in Fresnes awaiting trial, the time had come to decide how the interregnum of their rule should be bridged. Was the Third Republic still in existence, or ought a new Constitution to be written for a Fourth? Was the Vichy Government illegal, or merely illegitimate? Had the votes of 569 Deputies been a lawful vote electing a Chief of State? These were legalistic niceties which had already earned a great deal of attention at Carlton Gardens and Algiers. One of de Gaulle's earliest advisers, Professor René Cassin, a Jewish legal expert, had gone to a great deal of trouble to prove that Vichy was *illegal*, for, as François Quilici later confessed in the National Assembly:

* Général de Lattre de Tassigny and Georges Duhamel, Secretary of the French Academy.

It was necessary to give to La France Libre, then only a few hundred men, a juridical basis. Because of Anglo-Saxon traditionalism, we had to make it appear to the eyes of the Allies that La France Libre was the real and legal representative of France . . . But the Vichy Government was only *illegitimate*.[8]

This statement showed a profound miscomprehension of the Anglo-Saxon mentality of that time, which was not in the least concerned with the juridical aspects of the case, but supported the Gaullists because they had declared for the Allied side and Vichy had not. But the 'juridical basis' supplied by Cassin was not permanent. In his Brazzaville declaration of October 27 ('WE have the sacred duty to assume the charge that has been imposed upon US'), de Gaulle declared that the Constitution of 1875, and by consequence the Third Republic, was legally in force and vigour; and he continued to emphasize his own position as a member of the last cabinet before the Vichy 'usurpation', and therefore entitled to preserve republican continuity. But after his concordat with the Resistance inside France, he was brought round to the position that both the Third Republic and Vichy were to be condemned: a new National Assembly must decide the country's destinies; and the Consultative Assembly afterwards went to the trouble of declaring the 1875 Constitution invalid. It was now decided to take the nation's opinion by means of a referendum held simultaneously with the parliamentary elections.

Answer Yes or No to the following Questions:

1. *Is the new Assembly to be constituent?*
[i.e. a *Yes* answer meant a new Constitution should be drawn; a *No*, that the Constitution of 1875 should remain in force.]

2. *Shall the new Assembly be subject to the sovereignty of the people?*
[i.e. a *No* answer meant that, as the Communists wished, the Assembly should be sovereign in itself.]

These two questions, by answering which — and particularly the second — France settled her fate for years to come, formed the main issue of the election. The Constitution took precedence over *la répartiti* and *le ravitaillo*, the provisions for social security developed at Algiers and since put into operation, the nationalizations and the *politique de grandeur*. For several months before the elections of October 1945 and for just over a year thereafter, the juridical and political charms of constitution-making wooed France from the vital economic problems waiting for solution. But there was another issue in the campaign, no less engrossing, but as yet hardly stated since the war — not much more than a rock showing in the middle of a violent river — and this hidden issue was the ancient quarrel between Church and State.

Since the days of the Occupation, when gigantic Vs for victory had been chalked and whitewashed on the walls of Europe, this simple slogan method had been much in vogue. In 1945, besides the traditional multi-coloured posters mounted on special wooden hoardings, on which candidates set forth their views with tedious prolixity, the answers to the referendum were spattered on all wall spaces. Oui-Oui; Oui-Non; Non-Non — quickly, the *oui-z-et-non* passed into Paris slang. De Gaulle was for 'Yes' to both questions; the Communists, who stood for a sovereign Assembly, for 'Yes-No', and the Radicals for 'No' in both cases. It was an article of faith with the Radicals that the Constitution of 1875 was still in operation, and for this, as well as for their equivocal attitude to Vichy, they were to be returned to the new Assembly with only a fragment of their pre-war strength.

Their place was taken, as the focus of Left-Centre opinion, by the *Mouvement Républicain Populaire* (M.R.P.) a Christian Democrat formation which was the most interesting major political group to develop after the Liberation, and incidentally the party responsible for bringing up the issue of Church and State.

The M.R.P., which the Communists translated as the *Machine à Ramasser les Pétainistes*, belonged by legitimate descent to the great liberal Catholic movement of Louis Philippe's reign (1830-1848), when Lamennais, Montalembert and Lacordaire had opposed the policy of enforced conformity which kept alive the fear of clerical rule in France. These men had been succeeded by the groups known successively as *Sillon* and *La Jeune République*, the latter being associated in the Chambre des Députés with the *Parti Démocratique Républicain*. All the *Jeune République* Deputies had voted against Pétain in the Vichy Casino, and shortly afterwards the Resistance network *Liberté*, headed by Pierre-Henri Teitgen and François de Menthon, became a rallying point for those of Christian Democratic principles. Gilbert Dru, shot by the Germans in July 1944, had drawn up a document which was to become the charter of the M.R.P., declaring the group's aversion to the old political parties, its determination to end the trust system, and also its willingness to collaborate with the Communists in the interests of national unity.

These were impeccable Resistance doctrines, and yet there was a modicum of truth in the Communist gibe: its Catholic background did make the M.R.P. a 'machine to pick up Pétainists', unless the latter preferred to abstain from voting. But the new party was also a useful 'machine to pick up Gaullists'. Maurice Schumann was one of its fervent leaders, and another was Georges Bidault, who had few illusions about de Gaulle but was loyal to him; and there was much to attract Gaullists in the anti-trust, pre-Marxian socialism of the M.R.P., which suited their economic theories. It was doubtful whether either Philippe Pétain, ex-pupil of the Dominicans at Arcueil, or the Jesuit-trained Charles de Gaulle would have subscribed wholeheartedly to the religious views of the M.R.P., describable as Lamennais-and-water, but for the mass of voters Catholicism had to be liberal in the extreme to win votes in 1945.

The Resistance had been predominantly anti-clerical, because the Church supported Marshal Pétain and his belief in regeneration through suffering. In Paris, Cardinal Baudrillart* had called Doriot's *Ligne des Volontaires Français* (L.V.F.) 'the best sons of France' because they were fighting with the Germans against Russia. In 1945 the Easter preaching honours went to priests who had either been in the Resistance or had suffered in concentration camps for the help they had given to Jews, and the most popular priest in Paris was the Jesuit Father Michel Riquet, who had been in the underground since July 1940 and was arrested by the Gestapo in January 1944 while saying Mass in the Oratory of the rue d'Assas. He had spent fifteen months in the prisons of Fresnes, Compiègne and Mathausen, and on his return to Paris had worn the hideous striped garments of the concentration camp instead of a cassock when he celebrated Mass before a huge open-

* Rector of the Catholic Institute.

air gathering on the esplanade of the Palais de Chaillot.[9] Father Bruckberger, the F.F.I.'s chaplain-general (and personal friend of Darnand), and Father Carrière, a member of the Algiers Consultative, ran him close in emotional appeal.

If this was the spirit inside the M.R.P., it was matched by the attitude of the opposing parties, whose anti-clericalism was expressed by tearing down all the structure created by Vichy on behalf of the Church communities. Led by the Freemasons, whose temples had been defaced and insignia exposed by order of Vichy, an attack was opened against subsidies granted to the Church schools (*les écoles libres*), amounting to 490 million francs, and stopped by *Ordonnance* on March 31, 1945. It was the first skirmish in a battle begun generations earlier and likely to last for years, and it was led, for the anti-clericals, by a Communist named Georges Cogniat, who sat on the Commission for National Education. When he declared: 'Secularity is a French tradition',[10] M. Cogniat was stating in the most succinct terms a belief going back to the Revolution, but championship of *la laïcité* was not confined to the Communist party. The Socialists were equally opposed to 'the entry of religion into the affairs of state', as one of their leaders, Vincent Auriol, had stated in a speech of January 1945. Auriol, a good human being who loved his fellow-men, believed and said that 'metaphysics and politics have nothing in common' — a phrase which, by substituting metaphysics for Christianity, only too clearly expressed the views of French agnostics.

The time was not yet ripe, however, for an open breach between the M.R.P. and the parties of the Left on the schools question, or any other point in the debate between Church and State. All were eager for a return to republican legality, as was shown by the large turn-out of voters (79.6 per cent) on October 21. Question one on the referendum — shall the Assembly be constituent? — was answered in the affirmative by the convincing figure of 96.4 per cent of the votes cast, and while a smaller number — 66.3 per cent — voted for the sovereignty of the People rather than the Assembly, the very definite majority permitted the new Chamber, elected for seven months only, to proceed at once with its task of drafting a Constitution.

The overwhelming response to de Gaulle's request for a 'Oui-

Oui' vote in the referendum had reaffirmed his leadership, and his triumph now appeared to be complete. Without presenting himself as the candidate of any party — for he held himself to be above mere party politics — he had seen his wishes endorsed by his countrymen, and on November 13 a massive vote of the new Assembly, joined in unanimously by all parties, elected him President of the Second Provisional Government. As it happened, he had seen Mr. Churchill that very day, and had listened with great courtesy to some rather long-winded war reminiscences;[11] but Mr. Churchill was out of office now, and sorely discontented thereby, while President Roosevelt had been for seven months in his grave. De Gaulle might have been forgiven for sketching a victory V of mild derision at the thought of both his adversaries, since after all their forebodings he had proved beyond a doubt that he commanded the legal and democratic support of France.

PART TWO

THE FOURTH REPUBLIC
1946, 1947

CHAPTER V

AT THE PALAIS BOURBON

O N November 6, 1945, the *Assemblée Constituante* held its first meeting at the Palais Bourbon, in the historic chamber which had housed the legislative body since the days of the Convention. Occupied from 1940 to 1944 by the secretariat of the Luftwaffe, the building had stood empty for over a year; now the *tricolore* was hoisted again over the classic façade which dominates the Pont de la Concorde, and the sovereign people began queuing up along the Quai d'Orsay for admission to the debates. In their area of the semi-circular public galleries they formed, with the spectators in the diplomatic and press sections, an integral part of the Assembly's décor. The rows of anonymous faces seen against red-draped walls, dimly lighted through a fan-shaped ceiling of bluish glass, seemed to have been supplied by the yard as part of the furnishings of a toy theatre.

To the new Deputies, young members of the Resistance for the most part, the *hémicycle* was indeed a theatre in which each hoped to create some fine dramatic effects. To the veterans it was the arena in which they had struggled all their lives, sometimes enacting the bull, sometimes the matador, and they metaphorically pawed the familiar sand and sniffed the blood as they found their seats to the Right and Left of the *fauteuil* of the President of the Assembly which stood refurbished and waiting on its tapestried platform beneath the great capitals spelling RÉPUBLIQUE FRANÇAISE. To Félix Gouin, elected to the *fauteuil* on November 8, to Vincent Auriol and to many others, the *hémicycle* was their natural element. The new Deputies, trained in the Consultative or the local liberation committees, quickly adapted themselves to it.

Only one man seemed ill at ease, as he took his place on the *banc des ministres* in front of the ten-tiered ranks of the Deputies. This was Charles de Gaulle, unfamiliar in blue serge — military uniform being forbidden in the Chamber — and obviously unaccustomed to be a mere unit of an audience. On the floor of the *hémicycle* he was available to all his supporters, condemned to endless perfunctory finger-shakes as they went up the stairways to their seats, but de Gaulle's unease did not arise from these familiarities, nor from the difficulty of adjusting his long legs to the narrow ministerial bench. As soon as the Assembly convened it was clear that his trial of strength with the Communists, implicit since his first moves against the *Gardes Patriotiques*, could not long be delayed.

In the weeks before the election his move away from the Left had been quite marked. His speeches contained no more allusions to the 'national insurrection' or the 'new France built by new men' but warned that 'reforms were needed but not complete upsets', and that the new France 'must be securely fastened to what she used to be'. At the Arc de Triomphe ceremonies of November 11 he had urged the French to 'walk the same road, to the same step, singing the same song' — undoubtedly the *Marseillaise* — and undoubtedly, as a *Sondages* poll revealed,[1] the sort of exhortation which attracted to him the women of leisure, the elderly persons, professional workers and small shopkeepers who had been warm supporters of Marshal Pétain; but what was intended as a call to unity had an authoritarian ring, and was interpreted by his unfriends as para-fascism.

The Communists, as the largest party in the Assembly, were eager for a test of their strength. The number of their card-carrying party members had increased from 385,000 in 1944 to one million in 1945, their morning paper *L'Humanité* had the largest circulation (400,000) in Paris and they had complete control of the *Confédération Générale du Travail*. Maurice Thorez felt entirely justified in demanding for his party one of the key Ministries of the Interior, Foreign Affairs and War in de Gaulle's new cabinet. He pointed out that besides winning a majority in the Assembly Communists could claim to have made major sacrifices during the war, in which 75,000 of their partisans had been executed by the Germans.*

De Gaulle, declaring that he could not form a cabinet under such conditions, offered to 'return the mandate' — an elegant phrase which some translated as 'resignation' and others as 'black-

* The *Direction de la Statistique Générale* gives the *total* number of those executed as 30,000.

mail' — and on November 17 he went on the air to explain that
France, which he persisted in seeing as a buffer between Russia
and America, was unable to take sides with either country. This
seemed like wilful ignoring of the Russian alliance which he had
engineered, but de Gaulle went on boldly to say that he could not
give the Russian-directed Communists any of 'the three levers
which control foreign policy: diplomacy, which expresses it, the
army, which supports it, and the police force, by which it is
covered'.

Next day he sent a message to the Assembly asking for a prompt
decision on his mandate. The forcing tactics worked: by 400 votes
to 163 the Deputies passed a motion appealing to the general
patriotism and calling on de Gaulle to resume his negotiations for
the formation of a three-party government.

He had won the first round, and in a more conciliatory atmosphere he was able to compose a cabinet, reserving for himself
the posts of Premier, Commander-in-Chief, Minister for War and
Minister of National Defence. But Maurice Thorez was a Minister
of State, and Communists were given the portfolios of Labour,
Armaments, National Economy and Industrial Production, which
gave them control of exports, prices, wages and personnel, and
which they celebrated by calling out two groups of workers
immediately — civil servants on December 12 and linotype
operators in January.

The problems facing the new cabinet, most of them unsolved
for over a year, were grievous indeed. The franc was devalued at
Christmas; bread rationing, ended as an election measure, was
resumed at the New Year. The Right-wing politicians began to
emerge from sequestration as a trade recession seemed to prove
that nationalizations and planned economy had failed, and
Joseph Laniel joined with Michel Clemenceau, son of the old
'Tiger', in founding a new conservative party, the *Parti Républicain
de la Liberté* (P.R.L.).

The cost of World War II, so far as it could be estimated a year
after the Liberation, had been sufficient to ruin France. The loss
of life had been very great — 170,000 military dead, including the
F.F.I., 150,000 civilian deaths in war operations, 280,000 deaths
of French retained by the enemy outside of France — although
the total of 600,000 was just over a third of the French losses in

World War I.[2] Twice in thirty years the country had been the main battleground of a war against German aggression, and the second ordeal, after the drainage of the Occupation, had ended with the destruction of all the principal ports, the communication systems, the sources of energy and food supplies, the invisible exports like tourism and high fashion and the means of industrial production. It was clear that only a people of extraordinary vitality could rise again from such misfortunes, and that as well as relief from internal strife they needed from their government such decisions as would give to every citizen a fair share of food and comfort while the work of reconstruction was begun.

At the Palais Bourbon they were tackling the budget, as was customary at the end of the calendar year. In 1945 the budget of each ministry was taken separately, and on December 31, with a holiday in sight, the Deputies passed the budgets of nine departments ranging from Algeria to civil aviation. In the small hours of January 1, they arrived at the vote on military credits, which belonged to de Gaulle's Ministry of National Defence.

The enthusiasm of the Left for the reconstructed defence services had evaporated as soon as the war was over, and nearly a year had passed since Maurice Thorez told young Frenchmen that they could help the glorious Red Army by joining the Army of France. Some of the Left genuinely believed in disarmament — a policy which the United States was also preparing to follow, in obedience to the general cry of 'Get the boys home!' — while others, especially those who had paid official visits to the headquarters at Lindau where General de Lattre's taste for pomp and circumstance was being indulged to the full, objected to spending money on the army which might go into housing or health services. It was a normal swing of the pendulum from the intensely militaristic attitude of the Liberation, and one experienced by all the Western belligerents; but, taken in conjunction with the military unpreparedness which had helped to bring about *la débâcle*, it was something which de Gaulle was prepared to meet head-on. When a Socialist Deputy, Jean Capdeville, proposed a 20 per cent cut in military credits on the ground of 'waste and muddle' in the administration, de Gaulle tried his former tactics of 'returning his mandate' unless the credits went through in full. But the manœuvre came too soon after the November friction to impress the combined Communist and Socialist ranks. Capdeville's amendment to the budget bill was allowed to stand, and the Assembly adjourned for a dozen hours of whatever rest might be possible for Deputies keyed up to hear the head of the government defend the army, on which so much of his 'policy of grandeur' depended.

Darkness fell early on the afternoon of New Year's Day. It had not snowed, but leaden skies hung over Paris, and Deputies making their way towards the Palais Bourbon before three o'clock, an hour when whole families should have been making merry indoors, saw lines of women still waiting at the icy street corners for their meagre ration of bread. It was at least warm inside the Chamber, and the temperature of the debate rose sharply as de Gaulle embarked on his defence of 'the French war machine, a thing of shreds and patches, built with vastly diverse elements'.

The previous night's debate had shown that the Left was going farther, in its opposition to de Gaulle's authoritarianism, than the matter of military credits: what emerged, as the day wore on to evening, was the first split in the ranks of the *Compagnons*. One of the most notable, André Philip — a man on whom de Gaulle had relied to bring French Socialists over to his side in the London days — led the attack on his leader,[3] sneering: 'We want him to acquire the habits of democracy!' It was a shrewd counter-thrust to de Gaulle's threats to the Assembly — 'You will feel bitter regret for the road you are taking now!' — and his trick of turning every opposition to his own wishes into a demand for confidence in himself. Again and again de Gaulle intervened in the debate, sometimes mounting to the tribune, sometimes rising in his place on the front bench to swing round on the Right and the Left like a bull with the *banderillas* in his neck. Then, as the murmurs and signs of dissent became louder, and by all indications the Assembly's confidence was about to be withdrawn from him, he cried: 'This, no doubt, is the last time I shall address you in this place!'

If he had expected a shocked silence, a sudden singing of the *Marseillaise* as the Deputies rallied to him once more, he was disappointed. He had learned, as painfully as possible, that the Palais Bourbon was a more exacting stage than the B.B.C. studio, where he had laid down his white gloves and his eternal cigarette so deliberately before facing the unargumentative microphone, while Maurice Schumann stood ready to breathe devoutly over his shoulder: '*Honneur et Patrie, voici le général de Gaulle!*'⁴

But the Second Provisional Government did not fall that night. The group of twenty-seven Deputies who formed the *Union Démocratique et Sociale de la Résistance* (U.D.S.R.) the only Resistance formation to be represented in the *Constituante* as a political party, apart from the M.R.P., came to his rescue with an amendment proposing that the 20 per cent cut in military credits should only become effective if the government failed to present its schemes for the army before February 15, one month after the Assembly met again. The U.D.S.R. contained a number of *Compagnons* whose loyalty offset Philip's defection, including MM. Soustelle and Pleven, Capitant, Baumel and Pierre Bourdan, and by their action they gave the general what a more experienced parliamentarian, and a more patient man, would have turned to good advantage: time to shift his ground a little, and regain control of the Assembly on some other issue. Spoilt by nearly six years of obedience from his Committees, and doubtless believing that the threat of his retirement would shock them into submission, de Gaulle refused to try another fall with the people's Deputies. On January 20, after a vacation on the Riviera, he gave his verbal resignation to the cabinet — a figure of speech afterwards corrected by his personal assistant, Gaston Palewski, who announced to the press: 'General de Gaulle does not resign; he leaves office — irrevocably.'

But the niceties of M. Palewski's diction were surpassed by the phrasing of the letter officially addressed by de Gaulle to Félix Gouin, President of the Assembly. In it he explained that he had only accepted the position of head of the Second Provisional Government to direct a period of transition. Now, he explained:

France is no longer in a state of alarm. Many sufferings still weigh upon the people and grave problems remain, but the essentials of life are assured. Economic activity is increasing. Our territories are in our own hands. We have regained a footing in Indo-China. The public peace is untroubled . . . We hold the Rhine. We participate as a first-class Power in the United Nations organization, and the first Peace Conference will be held at Paris in the spring.

106

If the general's abrupt departure from office had astounded the public, this lyrical summation of his achievements left them stupefied.

His opponents pointed out that after seventeen months of de Gaulle's rule, 'a dictatorship by consent',[5] the people of France were hungrier than they had been under the Germans. Production was hampered by nationalizations, go-slow tactics, strikes. The public peace was so disturbed that theft flourished in all forms from pilfering to armed house-breaking, and the black market was more thriving than ever. Syria and Lebanon had been lost as a sphere of influence; the 'footing in Indo-China' was the footing of an inadequate expeditionary force in a disunited territory already invaded by Communists in the guise of nationalists and destined to be one of France's chief anxieties for years to come.

By the time a reply came from Félix Gouin it may have begun to dawn on de Gaulle that New Year's Day, 1946, was the most important signpost in his political life since the famous Eighteenth of June, since by his reaction to the opposition he encountered on that day he had been led to put an end, perhaps for ever, to his career in government. For Monsieur Gouin's reply was purely formal: no invitation to reconsider so vital a decision, but polite regrets, good wishes, expressions of eternal gratitude from the men who were staying on at the Palais Bourbon. De Gaulle received it at his villa in Neuilly — la Résidence, as it was called to distinguish it from la Présidence at the War Ministry — where the comfort of his family was assured by the furniture, tapestries and carpets suited to the position of a provisional Chief of State, and the privacy of the general by an inner courtyard with a lawn beyond.[6] To de Gaulle's overwrought nerves a more complete solitude seemed desirable. Next day he left with Madame de Gaulle for a hunting lodge at Marly, sometime the appanage of the Presidents of the Republic.

Saint-Simon, in his Mémoires, describes 'the narrow low-lying valley between steep banks, made inaccessible by marshes and with no view' near 'an ugly village named Marly', where the caprice of Louis XIV transformed 'a den of serpents and carrion, toads and frogs' into a pleasure-ground. In the January dusks of 1946, when journalists haunted its environs and were rebuffed by the thin, shabby plain-clothes men of the Sûreté Nationale, the silent modern lodge against a background of bare trees, with a plume of wood smoke ascending from one chimney, recalled the *saint-simonien* depression rather than the extravaganzas of the Sun King. It was near enough to Paris for messengers from the Assembly to reach in a hurry, but although de Gaulle waited in this cool retreat for eight days, no messengers arrived with unanimous appeals for renewed leadership and other tokens of submission. All was silence — Vincent Auriol had blocked de Gaulle's plan to broadcast to the nation — until, on January 23, the news was received that Félix Gouin himself had been elected President of the Provisional Government.

The election of a Socialist president brought immediate cabinet changes. All the Gaullist ministers were out of office and the Communists held eight cabinet seats instead of five. Félix Gouin took the Ministry of National Defence himself; now his plump form and round face, with protuberant eyes beaming through bifocals, were to be seen where de Gaulle had sat stork-like on the front bench, and Gouin himself was replaced, in the daily procession when the bugles and uniformed files of the Garde Républicaine usher in the President of the Assembly, by another short, stout Socialist from the Midi, M. Vincent Auriol.

There was now an officially ratified tripartite government of M.R.P., Socialists and Communists, ready to proceed to its major task, the drafting of a Constitution — the fifteenth such instrument in one hundred and fifty years. The Constitutional Commission of forty-two members elected by proportional representation was presided over by Guy Mollet, a prominent Socialist who had come round to the Communist idea of a sovereign Assembly as the basic principle of the Fourth Republic. Both Mollet and André Philip, head of the Algiers committee on state reform, were opposed to de Gaulle's concept of a president on the American model, with the executive power kept apart from that of the Legislature.

By quitting the field at the first clash with the Communists over the military credits cut, a temporary measure revocable at the next budget debate, de Gaulle threw away the chance to fight them on the issue of a Constitution which was at least intended to be enduring. By alarming all those who dreaded presidential dictatorship, he was left to explain the merits of the American system, if he chose to do so, at public meetings held outside the

Palais Bourbon, where he was no longer able to influence the law-makers at work.

*

Two months of the seven allotted to the Assembly for its Constitutional labours had been spent on the budget debates and the reorganizations of the cabinet, and there was still a formidable body of other legislation to be placed on the statute book. Félix Gouin had a thrift plan for the army, designed to effect economies in manpower, arms factories and military supplies. André Philip had a project for nationalizing the 967 private insurance companies, which was carried on April 25. Marcel Paul, the Communist Minister of Industrial Production, brought in a bill for the nationalization of gas and electricity, prepared when de Gaulle was still in power, which became law on April 8. It was followed by the nationalization of mines in the Midi and Lorraine, and those not already under state control in the Nord and the Pas-de-Calais. On the same day, May 17, the nationalization of credit completed the financial regimentation begun with the banks and insurance companies; and to all this the only parliamentary opposition was provided by the rump of the old Right wing, which even with the votes of the twenty-four Radical Deputies could hardly muster one hundred votes.

These social changes were subsidiary to the great theme which preoccupied the Assembly and the general public — the statesmen of the Café du Commerce — which was the phrasing and voting of the new Constitution. It was a topic which combined the French love of argument and legal hair-splitting with their respect for the written word and their strong sense of history, and it engaged their attention for nearly twice as long as had been planned, because the first Draft, submitted to a popular referendum on May 5, was rejected by the nation.

This document began with a fine flourish of Jacobin trumpets in a

Declaration of the Rights of Man

On the morrow of the victory won by the free peoples over régimes which sought to enslave and degrade humanity and bathe the whole world in blood, the French people, faithful to the principles of 1789 — the charter of its liberation — proclaim anew that every human being is possessed of inalienable and sacred rights which no law can infringe, and these it decides, as in 1793, 1795 and 1848, to inscribe at the head of its Constitution.

The Draft contained 106 articles, of which 39 were concerned with the specific liberties and rights which this declaration guaranteed 'in the name of the Republic, to all men and women living in the French Union', but which did not include complete liberty of the press or 'free teaching', meaning the right of Catholic schools to subsidies granted by the State. The remaining 67 were concerned with the Executive, the Judiciary and the Legislature, the two former to be elected by the latter; with the setting up of a Council of the French Union and an Economic Council having consultative functions only, and with a single-chamber parliament, the National Assembly. The premier (*président du conseil des ministres*) and his cabinet were to be collectively responsible to the Assembly and the premier might not personally pose the question of a vote of confidence. The President of the Republic was to be a mere figurehead, every official act signed by him having to be countersigned by the premier and one other minister, while his public appearances, as Vincent Auriol disgustedly put it, were to be 'on the level of opening flower shows and charity bazaars'.

The Draft proved how much alarmed the Left had been by the aspirations of de Gaulle, but the result of the referendum proved that they had overplayed their hand. Food prices had risen by 20 per cent since January 1, and discontent with the government inclined the voters to throw out any measure it might sponsor. The peasant voters were anxious about the rights of property, for these had not been formally guaranteed in the Draft, and a bill introduced by René Coty to declare property a 'sacred right', above the law, was defeated by 296 to 232. Above all, it seemed to the adversaries of the Left that a sovereign Assembly controlled by its largest party would result in a dictatorship of the proletariat; the cry of '*Thorez au pouvoir!*' confirmed their forebodings, and on May 5 the Draft was rejected by 10.5 million 'No' votes to 9.4 million 'Yes'.

This meant new legislative elections, which took place on June

2 and returned the M.R.P. as the largest party in the Assembly (160 seats) with 28.1 per cent of the total votes cast. Georges Bidault, who became premier of a cabinet very little different from its predecessor, continued to hold the portfolio of Foreign Affairs.

One of Bidault's hopes was to get rid once and for all of what had come to be called 'the de Gaulle mortgage' and start afresh on the renovation of France. He was not optimistic, however, for he had summed up the general better than most of those who had wrangled with him in the past. Where others claimed to see the megalomaniac, Georges Bidault saw the schizophrenic. Where Churchill saw only one side of him — 'a remarkable capacity for feeling pain' — and Duff Cooper saw the same side — 'an ineptitude for happiness' — Bidault saw that there were two sides to the general. 'There are two men in him,' the Foreign Minister murmured to the British ambassador, 'the man of intelligence and the man of caprice!'[7] — and being himself of a scholarly turn of mind Bidault understood what those spring months in the political wilderness had meant to a philosopher manqué like Charles de Gaulle. Caprice and ill-temper had caused his resignation. Intelligence must come to his rescue if he were ever again to leave his modest property in the Haute Marne, near the tiny village of Colombey-les-Deux-Églises, for the political stage of Paris.

When de Gaulle reappeared on the scene, two weeks after the election of the Second Constituent Assembly, he set the pattern of his life for many years to come. A period of meditation and consultation with selected Compagnons at Colombey would be followed by a full-dress public appearance, a commemorative speech or press conference for choice, then he would return to his studies at Colombey. His calendar became studded with ceremonial dates: June 18; the fêtes of St. Joan and St. Louis; November 11; the death of Georges Clemenceau; the anniversaries of Koufra and Bir-Hakeim. It was one such which took him to Bayeux on June 16, 1946, the Sunday nearest to the anniversary of his visit on D-day plus 8.

The Provisional Government had already invited him to take part in the V-E Day anniversary rites on May 8, and the celebration of the Eighteenth of June; he had declined both invitations. The situation verged on the farcical: when they were at the Arc de

Triomphe he was at the tomb of Georges Clemenceau; when they were at the Hôtel de Ville he was at the Mont Valérien, where so many patriots (estimated at 1800) had been shot during the Occupation. Without him, the June 18 commemoration was like *Hamlet* played without the Prince of Denmark, but his invisible presence was strongly felt, for by that time his Bayeux speech had been delivered.

Surrounded by his *Compagnons* — Soustelle, Palewski, Schumann, Koenig, d'Argenlieu — he recalled his old symbol, the Cross of Lorraine, 'which overthrew the scaffoldings of a fictitious authority' and his successes as head of the Provisional Government, when he 'put the train back on the rails'* and declared that the future Constitution should define France as a democracy with power vested in the Executive.

De Gaulle's concept of a President of the French Republic bore no resemblance to the flower-show-opener of the rejected Draft. His President (and it was not too hard to guess who the first President would be) was the personal representative of the State, chosen by a much larger electoral college than the parliament and having the right to choose the premier as well as to preside at cabinet meetings. He should be able to dissolve parliament without conditions, and thereafter consult the people by calling for an election.

It was this last proviso, reminiscent of the plebiscites called by Napoleon III — elected President and self-made Emperor — which set the cat among the backstreet pigeons. In 1946 few British or Americans would have approached current politics by the light of 1851, or indeed knew much about the policies of Lord John Russell or President Millard Fillmore, but the French were always prepared to draw an historical parallel, and the women with the black oilcloth shopping-bags began to chatter about Louis Napoleon Bonaparte and mutter that de Gaulle was preparing another *Deux-Décembre*. That was the attitude of the rue de Buci and the rue de Verneuil, but farther west at the Palais Bourbon the groups in the corridors were less certain that de Gaulle had cooked his goose at Bayeux.

His views on the Constitution were spread in the country by a

* For the satiric weekly, *Le Canard Enchaîné*, Colombey-the-Two-Churches was thereafter to be Colombey-the-Train-on-the-Rails.

new party, the *Union Gaulliste pour la IVᵉ République*. He was not personally identified with it, having declared himself to be above party, but its founder, René Capitant, was one of his most fervent supporters. Capitant was not a *Compagnon* of London, but he had known de Gaulle before the war, and having gone to Algiers in 1941, where he was a professor of legal history, he had been an active helper in the Allied landings of 1942. He had been an Algiers Commissioner and Minister of Public Instruction in the first Provisional Government.

His *Union Gaulliste*, which set up a Paris bureau at 29 rue de Marignan, was one of the most exclusive political parties ever founded in France. A would-be member had not only to be a citizen of metropolitan France or of the French Union, but have maintained 'an irreproachable attitude under the Occupation'. He had to be introduced by sponsors and screened by the Union's departmental or national admission councils.[8] It was perhaps not surprising that this highly select group won only six out of the 629 seats in the November election, but it was a useful trial balloon for de Gaulle, for it claimed to be a 'rally (*rassemblement*) of all Frenchmen resolved to build the Fourth Republic in the spirit of June 18, 1940'. It was, in fact, the forerunner of the great *Rassemblement* of the following year, although it limped badly behind the general's current thinking when it quoted, in Article Two of its Manifesto, the vague principles of 'national renovation by democracy and in liberty' which he had stated in 1943. What de Gaulle wanted now was explained by himself in a speech at Épinal on September 22nd, the day the new Draft was passed by the Assembly.

At Épinal the general not only repeated the points he had already made at Bayeux on separate powers for the Executive, Legislature and Judiciary, but forecast a clash between two Powers which he regarded as equally bellicose, when 'the ambitious grouping of Slavs effected by a Power which knows no limits rises to face young America, brimming with resources and newly aware of the vistas which open to military strength'. With this clash in view he demanded one-party government for France, the intended buffer state, and a president who should be 'the guarantor of all treaties signed by France'.

These passages created an impression which could not be

effaced by ribald comment on those passages of the Épinal speech in which de Gaulle referred to himself by the royal We. 'WE greet with iron contempt the ridiculous imputation of dictatorial ambitions' — this was strong; but there was petulance in the allusions to the 'tactics' of political life, an 'obscure art' which WE did not practise at all. The enduring impression of the general's objections to the Constitution prevented a great number of M.R.P. voters, still faithful to the lost leader, from voting in the referendum of October 13. The electoral roll of 26 millions fell into three almost equal parts: those voting 'Yes' for the new Draft, those voting 'No', and those who stayed at home.

But the alarm felt by all liberals at the general's repeated demands for a powerful executive and a one-party government (construed to mean a one-party Assembly) drove just enough voters into the *Oui* camp to give the extra million votes which carried the Constitution. Balancing the *Ouis* against the *Nons* and the abstentions, it was a minority Constitution, voted simply to put an end to 'provisional' government and show that neither autocracy nor oligarchy was acceptable in France. The position was made clear in

Article Three

National Sovereignty belongs to the French people. No section of the people, nor any individual, may assume the exercise of it. The people exercise this sovereignty in constitutional matters through the votes of the Representatives and by Referendum. In all other matters it exercises it through its Deputies in the National Assembly, directly and secretly elected under a system of universal and equal suffrage.

The Constitution thus painfully brought to birth differed in significant ways from the rejected Draft of May. The Declaration of the Rights of Man was replaced by a preamble which added to the Declaration of 1789 certain new principles, including social security and the participation of workers in management. The sovereign Assembly was replaced by a parliamentary régime of two Chambers: a National Assembly (629 members), and a Council of the Republic (315) having a suspensive veto. The

Assembly was to make the laws, ratify international treaties, pass the budget and vote the declaration of war, while sharing in the election of the principal personages and organizations of the State. The President's powers were increased. He was President of the French Union as well as of the French Republic. He might suspend the promulgation of a law and demand its revision. He was commander-in-chief of the forces and President of the National Defence Committee.

When the Constitution was voted, no one in France looked forward with any enthusiasm to new legislative elections — the second in 1946, the third since the Liberation — following on three referenda and the municipal and cantonal elections of 1945. The cry of *'aux urnes!'* had lost its charm for Frenchmen who, in 1944, had thought an appearance at the ballot-boxes a most desirable privilege. They were not required, however, to cast votes for the second chamber of the parliament, which was chosen by pro-portional representation of the 'great electors', Deputies and can-tonal representatives, and the vote for the Conseil de la République gave the M.R.P. 62 seats, the Communists 61, the Socialists 37, so that *tripartisme* controlled more than half the votes in the second chamber. It was otherwise in elections held one month earlier for the National Assembly, where the Communists were once again the largest party with 169 seats to the M.R.P. 163 and the Socialist 101.

Thus, as the Fourth Republic was inaugurated, the Christian Democrat M.R.P., the 'party of fidelity' to Charles de Gaulle, still remained in place as the 'monolithic' party of the Centre opposing the equally monolithic Communist party, but with so nearly equal a number of votes that neither the one nor the other could form a government or raise either Bidault or Thorez to the premiership. The Socialists held the balance, and under the veteran Léon Blum, ill and living in semi-retirement since his German captivity, they took office as a caretaker government on December 16, with the understanding that they would resign after the election of the first President of the Fourth Republic.

A year earlier it had seemed inevitable that this high office would be filled by Charles de Gaulle, just as five years earlier it had appeared to his Resistance comrades that Jean Moulin, *dit* Max, was the obvious choice. What Max had lost by his heroic death de Gaulle had lost by caprice; but the vacuum was already filled. In a year when many political reputations had suffered, one at least had been enhanced, and Vincent Auriol, re-elected in November as President of the Assembly, was the favourite in January 1947 for the Presidency of the Republic.

CHAPTER VI

THE YEAR OF SCANDALS

THE year 1946 was a painful one for the people of France, and not only because of the prolonged distractions of the constitutional problem. Every material condition of life seemed to worsen: retail prices almost doubled between January and December, and at the end of the year were eight and a half times higher than in 1938. The production of coal was still only two-thirds of the pre-war output, and central heating in private dwellings, whether *chauffage ville* or *chauffage maison*, was a forgotten comfort for most families. Owners of the small shops in back-streets and markets, where cheap wine and spirits were sold along with bundles of wood and *boulets* of anthracite and coal dust, became significant figures in town life, for they would carry logs upstairs on their backs for a *supplément* added to the price, and for another would stack it in one of the *cagibis* or *remises* with which the ancient French tenements were well supplied. The grocer with a stock of candles was also a courted neighbourhood figure, for each urban sector had to submit to electricity cuts on two days each week (announced, with startling inaccuracy, in the daily press) and Paris by candle-light seemed to move back eight hundred years to the illuminations for the birth of Philip Augustus.

These shortages were a continued challenge to the women of France, who had to use all their talent for the 'rearrangement' of garments as the price of clothes rose higher and higher. Women who wished to keep up any sort of social life tried hard to create a gracious home atmosphere, although hospitality had to be limited to low-proof *apéritifs* and small bread rounds spread with anony-mous *pâtés* from the nearest tripe-shop. In all such domestic activities they succeeded admirably, for they had always been 'women of the interior', and their innate ability to cobble, mend, concoct, devise and calculate had been if anything sharpened by the Occupation. Outside the home their presence was less felt; they voted for the first time in 1945 and the idea of sitting in the

National Assembly was still a novelty. Nevertheless the crowds which filled the Grand Amphithéâtre of the Sorbonne on November 12, 1944, to hear a group of French and Allied women discuss the hazards and rewards of a political career — the speculations of so eminent a political scientist as André Siegfried on the advisability of gathering all the females in the future Assembly into a women's party — the energy of the Communist *Union des Femmes Françaises* — all these indications proved that the future of women in French politics was eagerly canvassed from the moment of the Liberation.

Thirty-three women were elected to the Constituent Assembly in 1945. Sixteen were Communists, some famous for their share in the Resistance. Marie-Claude Vaillant-Couturier, widow of an editor of *L'Humanité*, had suffered imprisonment at Ravensbrück, and in the Assembly usually supported Laurent Casanova, widower of Danielle, the chief Communist woman martyr and heroine. Another widow, Madame Gabriel Péri, was also the sister of André Marty; Jeannette Vermersch was described as the *compagne* (later the wife) of Maurice Thorez. All these relationships made the women's group of the Communist party something like a family affair. The Christian Democrats (M.R.P.) had ten women deputies in the *Constituante*, some of them having great talent, like Mmes Poinso-Chapuis and Peyroles, and Marie-Hélène Lefaucheux, a member of the French delegation to the United Nations Assembly. But the Frenchwoman whose name was most often in the news during the cold late spring of 1946 was Marthe Richard, a Paris municipal councillor and secret agent of World War I, who contributed to solving the housing problem by ordering the Paris houses of prostitution to be closed for business and reopened as dormitories for needy students. This operation, half-heartedly executed (for powerful forces of the underworld came out against it), earned Madame Richard some ridicule as well as unpleasantness, but it was a useful indication to French women that reforms could be carried out directly instead of by intriguing for masculine influence. This had never been the French way, for although society women would chatter politics by the hour they preferred to be the Egerias of some Deputy or Senator rather than demand the right to face themselves the heckling of the hustings or the baiting of the *hémicycle*. Nor had they any idea of forming and using the immense influence acquired by women's clubs in America. The family, not the club, was the Frenchwoman's unit, and her career, if she had one, was developed in conjunction with the family interests. The best of her working relationships was the one formed through laborious years with her husband, in politics occasionally but in commerce always; and in that respect there was no difference between the humblest *épicière* in the city, working at her husband's cash desk all day long and cooking their *bon déjeuner* at midday, and Madame Georges Bidault, who before her marriage in 1945 was Suzanne Borel, star graduate of the École des Sciences Politiques, *administratrice de première classe*, graded to ambassadorial rank, and now the accomplished hostess of the Quai d'Orsay.

Frenchwomen, of course, had always been free to pursue careers in the arts and exploit their first-rate talent for business, but they were increasingly aware that the post-war world demanded something more of them; not only a share in the disagreeable and contentious experiences of public life, but also that which came so hard to a nation of individualists: an attempt at *civisme*, communal effort, instruction of their children that life did not revolve round the inheritance of Cousine Bette's *lingots d'or* or the purchase of *une petite propriété* at Chailly-en-Bière.

The children of France presented a very serious problem at that time. Their health was bad, for lack of nourishment had opened the door to anaemia and tuberculosis, and their outlook on life was prematurely disillusioned because of the climate of disbelief in which they had lived among elders who had given up believing in Vichy, had no intention of believing in Germany and were waiting to be shown whether the 'Anglo-Saxons' could set them free. During the Occupation any form of clandestine activity, from sabotage down to petty pilfering had been praiseworthy as a means of harassing the enemy. It was not easy for youths who had been in the *maquis*, or even for schoolboys and girls, to re-adapt themselves at once to the disciplined ways of peace. *Dans la clandestinité*, that phrase which had stood for superb patriotism, daring and self-sacrifice, was debased to cover a multitude of petty rackets which seemed far more enticing to the children of war-broken homes than the discipline of the schoolroom. If a Frenchwoman could keep the family tie strong she could to a large extent defeat the baneful influences of the time, and it was for this reason that she saw her rôle in life as that of *la femme au foyer*, especially when, until the great army of captives returned from Germany, she had to be father and mother too.

To the statesmen who assembled in Paris for the Foreign Ministers' Conference in April and May, and the larger group of leaders at the Conference to discuss the peace treaties, held from July through October, this spiritual malaise was hardly apparent. Their position entitled them to material comforts *hors classe*; banquets and galas revived the pre-war elegance of Paris on their behalf, and if some of them went to see *La Folle de Chaillot* on a free evening, they went to admire the lines of Giraudoux, the acting of Louis Jouvet and the décor of Christian Bérard. Treaty-makers do not deal in allegory, and yet *La Folle de Chaillot* spread some of the truths of France before them: the four Madwomen (of Chaillot, of Passy, of the Concorde, of St. Sulpice) representing the half-crazed, half-lucid, wholly erratic Paris of the period, the *mecs* lured beneath the Passy cemetery in their greedy search for naphthaline representing the evil elements of the times. The scene in which the *mecs* were destroyed in the underground caverns while the true lovers, the scholars, the friends of animals and plants were spared was a grand display of wishful thinking; the play itself was a remarkable piece for the Second Provisional Government to have subsidized.[1]

Off the stage of the Théâtre de l'Athénée, the *mecs* were on the winning side — or at least, for they were sometimes haled to justice, on the profitable side. 1946 was the first year of the big scandals, which took the place of *l'épuration* as a public sensation. *L'épuration*, in fact, was becoming tedious: the supply of first-class traitors was running short, and from executing a Jean Luchaire the courts had to come down to inflicting 'national degradation' on his daughter Corinne, a very small minnow among the *collabo* pikes, who died soon after of tuberculosis.

The new planned economy, with its army of underpaid functionaries, gave many opportunities for bribery and corruption. There was constant temptation to illegal traffic in the bulk stores laid in by the various purchasing commissions, and to the favouring of political allies when points or goods were released. The Communist Minister of Production was accused of allocating

200,000 metres of fabric to the *Union des Femmes Françaises* and of distributing thousands of coupons for motor car and lorry tyres to the electors of Limoges. His political opponents, to make sure that the points were so much waste paper, sabotaged 9000 badly needed new tyres.

To obtain one French tyre by honest means demanded months of patient paper-work and visits to government offices, but this could be avoided by borrowing the certificate of ownership of a private car (the owner expected some recompense) and with it establishing the right to import four tyres from America, which would then be sold singly at considerable profit. As for the manufacture of false certificates, *cartes grises*, *S.P.*, and all the other *paperasserie* with which an administration-minded nation had encumbered post-war motoring, this was but one part of the racket. Everything to do with the internal combustion engine contributed to the black market, from the champagne luncheon which bought priority delivery of a new car to forged petrol coupons. Crowded public garages were liable to be raided by a gang in search of a new black Citroën *quinze, traction avant*, for their professional use. Street parking involved the adjustment of numerous anti-theft devices: a special clamp between driving wheel and gear lever, a locked cap on the petrol tank, a padlock and chain on the spare wheel. If women lived in fear of losing food tickets, men dreaded losing the four keys which set a car in motion.

All this was watched with grim amusement by those who got about on bicycles, and were able to carry their vehicles upstairs and indoors. Of more general importance were the black-market deals in food, clothing and wine which formed the provision scandals of 1946.

There were arrests of dried vegetable wholesalers, civil servants employed in the distribution of flour and cereals, and persons distributing foodstuffs to hospitals and Allied canteens. Company directors of three leading department stores — the Bon Marché, Galeries Lafayette and Galerie Barbès, were arrested for illegal possession of textile and hardware points.[2] Yves Farge, a Communist fellow-traveller who took over the thankless post of Food Minister in June 1946, unearthed a scandal in the allocation of import licences for Algerian wine,[3] by which the favoured dealers had sold the wine on the black market. Félix Gouin, premier from January to June 1946, was implicated in this transaction; he defended himself with great vigour, and M. Farge turned his energies to an attempt to place a price ceiling on meat (which resulted in a complete cessation of livestock deliveries at La Villette market), and started a quarrel between the wine growers of the Midi which only Monsieur Bidault, then premier, could compose. Meantime, the wine ration dried up for three months.

The provision scandals hungered the body, but the political scandals embittered the mind. The first to break was *l'affaire Passy*, a sensation of May, and one which gave Frenchmen a new idea of the Free French movement in London.

After the departure of Charles de Gaulle the Provisional Government had taken various steps to liquidate organizations too closely associated with himself: one such had been the group of eighteen *commissaires de la République* whom he had appointed at the Liberation. These men had at first wielded immense power, for they could arrest collaborators, suspend prison sentences and administer justice in all its forms within their territories. Since May 1945 their power had been reduced to advising and aiding the Prefects, and in May 1946, on the plea of all those who regarded them as Gaullist agents, they were disbanded. For the first time since 1940 (Vichy, too, had had its Regional Commissioners) the Prefects resumed[4] the full administration of the ninety Departments of France.

Within a month of his leader's withdrawal, Colonel André DeWavrin, *dit* Passy, resigned from the direction of the *Service de Documentation et de Contre-Espionnage*, which he had installed in a mansion on the Boulevard Suchet previously occupied by the Gestapo.

Upon returning to Paris with General de Gaulle, Passy had attempted to resign his commission, and although this had been refused during a state of war he was granted a year's leave without pay as from September 1945. The Ministry of the Army argued that it was therefore within its jurisdiction in ordering the arrest of Colonel Passy on May 2, 1946, and confining him to the fortress-prison of Metz for sixty days, on a formal charge of 'Grave negligence in the transfer of his accounts',[5] when his successor at the S.D.E.C.E., Henri Ribière, discovered that the provident Passy had been laying aside a fund in foreign banks, consisting of francs, sterling and dollars.

The supporters of Passy, while arguing violently that the army had no such rights over him, also declared that the government, notably MM. Gouin and Bidault, against whom he had nourished two of his antipathies, had planned the arrest for the eve of the election of May 5 to throw discredit upon Gaullism, whereupon Passy was sentenced to a further sixty days beginning when his first prison sentence ended, so that all the evidence might be brought in. This also gave time for several side-issues in the case, such as the reappearance of Lieutenant Lahana, the bully-boy who terrorized the merchantmen in Glasgow, as Capitaine Landrieu, *dit* Lahana,[6] a subordinate and accomplice of Passy in the illicit transfers. Landrieu-Lahana put himself beyond the reach of questioning by opening a vein in his wrist in his cell at Montrouge while Passy was in Metz.[7] Another and less sensational side-issue was the totally irrelevant polemic in which Passy engaged Maurice Schumann, who had attacked him in *L'Aube*, of an act of cowardice in failing to make a parachute jump over Brittany on the night of August 4, 1944;[8] and yet another development, quite in keeping with the general's probity in money matters, was de Gaulle's total disavowal of Passy's defalcations and his order that they be made good by the culprit.[9]

Passy himself frankly admitted having made such deposits — he put them at £10,000 to £12,000 in sterling, 7 millions in francs — but said he acted as a prudent and forward-looking executive. He had apparently taken de Gaulle's prediction of a Russo-American war to heart, for he seemed to expect another emigration to Britain, and this time, in case the British proved less open-handed, he meant the *maison* to have some cash in hand. So, he reasoned, what he did was no crime and could only be judged on the 'plane' of the secret service. But the Bidault government could not agree, even though Pierre-Henri Teitgen argued that 'you can't use choir-boys in counter-espionage',[10] that there was one law for secret agents and another for civilians. Colonel Passy was dismissed from the army, expelled from the Legion of Honour and the honorary Order of the Liberation, and property of his own was confiscated to cover the deficit in his accounts.[11]

After a time he went into private business and settled down to write his memoirs, which in 1948 admitted him to membership of the *Société des Gens de Lettres*.

The government handled a good case badly by not permitting an open trial for Passy, for if de Gaulle had appeared in the witness box he might have been able to stop, by mere force of personality, some of the attacks on his organization in the Left-wing press. Articles about *les tortionnaires de Duke Street* made interesting reading; and they were followed by the revelation that a Bessarabian scrap-iron merchant named Jovanovici, who made a fortune selling to the Germans and used the proceeds to buy arms for the famous network *Honneur de la Police*, had also been in league with the Gestapo and when challenged with this was able to escape from justice through his *relations* at the Préfecture de Police. There was a great upheaval at the Quai des Horloges, and Charles Luizet, the brilliant *préfet de police* who had come from Algiers to lead the Parisians to victory, was relieved of his functions. It was announced that there was no reflection upon his honour, since he was appointed to a high post in Africa; but this — and he died soon after — was the professional end of Luizet in the capital.

René Hardy, a leading Resistant, and the author of the so-called 'green plan' against the German communications system, was found guilty of having betrayed the first president of the C.N.R., Jean Moulin, to the Gestapo, as a result of his own arrest and admissions under pressure. The Hardy case was particularly dramatic, for he was acquitted at his first trial and accused again after new evidence had proved that he had in fact been in the hands of the Germans at the station of Chalon-sur-Saône on June 7, 1943, just before the betrayal and arrest of 'Max'.*

These three cases had a very bad effect on French morale. Always willing to believe the worst, the French now saw great cracks and flaws in the proud structure of the Resistance 'in and out of uniform'. If a Hardy were capable of betraying his leader, a Luizet of being hoodwinked by a Jovanovici, a Passy of mishandling public funds for some vague future purpose, then which of their new heroes could they possibly trust? It was a sad falling-

* Hardy, from prison, was re-tried in April-May 1950, and acquitted *à la minorité de faveur* by 3 votes to 4.

off from the spirit of true patriotism which had sustained the Resistance during its fearful adventures, and a denial of the faith of its martyrs whatever their politics. The true Resistants had France, and only France, in their hearts when their hour came; they had not expected to die for a Jovanovici, grown rich on the proceeds of selling rags, bones and bottles to the enemy, or that an executive of the Wine Control might have a chance to put through a good deal in Algerian *pinard*.

CHAPTER VII

THE MONNET PLAN AND THE OCCUPATION OF GERMANY

THE 1946 census revealed the existence of a French man and woman whose centenary celebrations had passed almost unnoticed in the terrible year 1940, and who had now attained the remarkable age of one hundred and six. There was a rush to interview *le doyen des Français* and *la doyenne des Françaises*, living in humble circumstances with attentive relatives, and who proved to be a little withered man and a little trembling woman, each previously unaware of the other's existence and inclined to be affronted on hearing of a rival.

Both were of peasant stock, but the old lady had been employed as a girl in a Paris glove shop and could remember running out on the rue de Rivoli, laughing and applauding, when the cannon announced the birth of the Prince Imperial in 1856. She had gone back to her village and married, and in 1870 had lost her husband in the Franco-Prussian War. *Le doyen des Français,* severely wounded in that war, had been handicapped as a tradesman all the rest of his working life. The hardships he and the old widow had then suffered had made them almost insensible to the two later German wars. Their clocks had stopped at 1870, and this was the one thing that the two oldest French citizens had in common, apart from an obstinate satisfaction in being still able to walk upstairs to bed.

Although such centenarians were rare, France had now the oldest population in the world. Due to the birth deficit of World War I, the country had the fewest numbers of potential parents and skilled workers between the ages of 30 and 35, while the 1,500,000 dead of that war had left a huge gap in the group of men aged between 50 and 55. The only bright spot in the demographic picture was the sharp rise in the rates of marriage and birth of first children during and after 1945. The birthrate in 1946, the highest ever registered in France, added 1,275,000 new citizens to a population established by the census of March 10 as 40,780,000.

This meant, however, that the country was heavily overweighted by the very old and the very young. The aged and infirm had to be cared for under Social Security, the pregnant women under the family allowance scheme, while the Liberation babies would in a few years need more schoolrooms and teachers and eventually more jobs.

More jobs postulated an expansion in production, which under the stagnant French economy did not seem likely. The French worker himself, by the modesty of his wants and the simplicity of his pleasures (the good meal, the digestion in the shade, the game of *belote*), failed to create a market for the kind of goods requiring enterprise and competition among producers, salesmen and advertisers. Content to live by the rules of his forebears, he was above all a craftsman, more interested in fashioning quality goods than in mass production, or, if he happened to be employed on an assembly line, in spending his leisure hours at the mending and improvising which he called *bricolage*. He had a horror of debt, and so would not buy goods on hire-purchase or time-payment plans, and he was not interested in keeping up with his neighbours in the possession of the kind of article which, like a car, a high-fidelity player, a television set, a self-defrosting icebox, a deep-freeze unit, can be turned in for a later model of the same thing. The French working man, even when descended from four generations of townsfolk, was imbued with so instinctive and so deep a love for the soil of France that his true ambition was to possess a few *ares* of it for his own, and where the *patron* planned to retire to a flowery *mas* in the foothills above Cannes, the *ouvrier* dreamed with an equal passion of the plants he would cultivate round some earwig-infested bungalow among the truck gardens at Argenteuil.

In one important respect the French worker's tolerance of antique conditions and equipment was very low. He and his family were weary of urban slum conditions just as farm labourers were tired of villages without piped water (which meant three-quarters of the villages of France), while town-dwellers were also weary of carrying water for all purposes from taps in the courtyard or on the landings (23 per cent of all houses), of using a common privy (50 per cent had no toilets), and doing without central heating (85 per cent, even without a coal shortage). It seemed as if the first reward which increased productivity should give in exchange for harder work under the proposed reconstruction plan, which required a return to the 48-hour week, should be better housing for all.

The stagnation of the market and the obsolescence of the methods were handicaps which, as even the Jacobins in the Provisional Government realized, could not be overcome by labour-management committees and nationalizations. In December 1945 it had called for the preparation of a Plan for Modernization and Equipment, prefaced by a summary of France's actual assets, which were few, and her liabilities, which were heavy. The Occupation had kept France economically helpless while the Allies, particularly the United States, enjoyed a war-time boom. The war damage had been enormous: out of the 477,200 completely destroyed buildings, almost none had been replaced when the *Commissariat Général au Plan* held its first meeting on March 16, 1946. Of the 1,363,000 partly damaged buildings certain groups had been repaired: 90 per cent of public buildings, 80 per cent of industrial premises, 50 per cent of farm buildings, 20 per cent of urban dwellings.[1] The work of wreckage clearance and mine removal was nearly complete.

The four key industries of agriculture, coal and coke, electricity and metallurgy all required renovation. The German pillage of livestock had left a dearth of horses, dairy cattle, pigs and sheep, and the animal husbandry of the whole nation had been stretched to give bombed-out or refugee farmers the beginnings of new flocks and herds when they returned home. There was a shortage of fertilizers and seeds.

The 30,000 tractors in use before the war were all worn out or beyond repair and 250,000 would have to be bought in the next five years. Milking machines, refrigerator plants, modern abattoirs and cellars specially planned for the maturing and storage of wine and oil were either unknown or existed only in rudimentary form. The machine tools were as obsolescent as the tractors.*

The man who assumed the direction of the *Commissariat Général au Plan* knew all about the traditionalism of the French

* Number of French buildings damaged in World War I, 927,600; in World War II, 1,840,200. Tractors, 1 to every 22 farmers in Britain; 1 to 43 in the U.S.; 1 to 100 in France. Machine tools, average age in Britain, 9 years; in the U.S., 7 years; in France 25 years.

worker and businessman, for he had been raised in that tradition in the charming western town of Cognac. Born in 1888, Jean Monnet began his working life in the family brandy firm; and when he started out as a salesman he received a solemn warning from his grandfather that 'any new idea can only be a bad idea'. In 1946, when the vast plan for modernization had come to bear his name, Jean Monnet and his technicians — there were never more than twenty full-time professionals on the staff — never forgot that resistance to new ideas might help to slow up a task chiefly handicapped by lack of funds.

The whole of Monnet's career in public life, which began soon after he formed an association to promote cognac sales, had been based on the importance of supplies, the pooling of resources and the grouping of men animated by the same ideas. At the age of twenty-eight he had been the permanent French representative on the Inter-Allied Supply Commission of World War I. At fifty-two, in 1940, he was back in London as chairman of the Franco-British Co-ordinating Committee for armaments, transport supply and finances. Between wars he had had a remarkable international training, being in turn the Deputy Secretary-General of the League of Nations, the economic adviser of Chiang Kai-shek, the financial reconstructor of Austria, Poland, Roumania, and the associate of a private bank in New York. In the dark hours of June 1940 he had proposed a Franco-British Union, whereby the two governments should declare France and Britain one nation, with dual citizenship, a single war cabinet, and joint organizations of defence, foreign, financial and economic policies. Enthusiastically supported by de Gaulle and assented to by Churchill, the proposal was declined by the French cabinet just prior to the surrender; and Jean Monnet at once returned to a more familiar field of operations: the accumulation of the massive supplies of material which he saw as essential to ultimate victory. Leaving his aide, René Pleven, to take the Cross of Lorraine and journey with Leclerc to the Cameroun, he went to Washington as a member of the British Supply Council, eventually becoming the only French representative on the Anglo-American war production committees. When the State Department was supporting General Giraud in North Africa, Monnet seemed the obvious choice as one of Giraud's technical advisers. After his arrival in

Algiers he resumed active collaboration with de Gaulle, and became in due course Commissioner (later Minister) without portfolio in the provisional governments of Algiers and Paris.

The *Commissariat Général au Plan* was set up in the tranquil backwater of the rue Martignac, opposite the false-Gothic towers of Ste Clotilde; and, still convinced of the need for the pooling of resources, and by consequence the grouping of men on a supra-national plane, Jean Monnet set out with Léon Blum for Washington in March 1946. Their mission, which presented the Plan as evidence that France would do her utmost to repair her own economy, was successful in obtaining the assent of the United States to the liquidation of debts incurred under Lend-Lease and reciprocal aid, plus a new credit of $650 millions at the Export-Import Bank. With these assets the experts of the Monnet Plan, as it was soon called, set production targets to obtain higher exports, with the peak year 1929 as the mark to be surpassed, and drafted modernization measures for the period 1947-50. Six basic programmes were established for modernization of equipment, increased exports and a larger labour force in coal mining, electricity, iron and steel, agricultural machinery and inland transport, these being 'activities [with] a paramount function, intended to open the way to the others'. Each separate programme was accompanied by a scheme of heavy capital investments, 'the direct result of the destruction, spoliation and neglect wrought by war, and imposed on France from the day of Liberation'.[2] New investments were mandatory, unless France wished to continue 'living on the savings of past generations'; but the success of the Monnet Plan did not depend entirely on French capital and labour, nor even on American credits. It was conditioned by two other factors: France's relations with her colonies, which were her most important export market since the loss of her pre-war outlets in central Europe, and with developments in post-war Germany, where she was one of the Occupying Powers.*

*

General de Lattre de Tassigny had been in tremendous form since the reduction of the Colmar pocket. De Gaulle had ordered

---

* France was also an Occupying Power in Austria, where the French Zone included Vorarlberg and Tyrol (joint pop. 486,400).

him to cross the Rhine at Philippesbourg 'even if the Americans are against it',[3] and later to take and hold Stuttgart, even when the Supreme Commander wanted General Alexander Patch and the 7th U.S. Army to occupy the city with a view to keeping future supply routes clear. Eisenhower had to threaten curtailment of American supplies to France before de Gaulle agreed that it would not be inconsistent with national prestige to modify his orders to de Lattre. There had also been trouble with General Devers about a combined operation on the Neckar; but such quarrels between Allied commanders were not new — as witness disputes between Montgomery and Bradley — and all ended well for de Lattre. General Devers was a delighted and to some extent a dumbfounded guest at the tremendous fête organized for him by de Lattre on the shores and waters of Lake Constance.

General de Lattre was already established at Lindau when the order came from Paris to proceed at once to Berlin and 'demand the same conditions' as a signatory of the ratification, on May 10, 1945, of the German surrender 'as those accorded to the British delegate',[4] Field-Marshal Bernard Law Montgomery. After a brisk discussion with the Americans over the air transport to be placed at his disposal, de Lattre arrived at Berlin, where he was irritated to find that nobody expected him, and that it would be regarded as only a courtesy on Marshal Zhukov's part to allow him to sign the document in the name of France. During the inevitable Russian delay before the ceremony, de Lattre discovered that no French flag had been included with the flags of the Allies. He and his two aides routed out a piece of blue serge torn from a mechanic's overalls, a white cloth and the red background of a Hitler flag, which women soldiers of the Red Army agreed to put together.[5] But the language difficulty confused the explanations, the strips of cloth were sewn horizontally and a Dutch flag was the result. There was time, however, for a second try, and the makeshift *tricolore*, right way up, took its place beside the Allied flags.

De Lattre continued to make his presence felt at the banquet which followed the ratification ceremony, refusing to eat or drink until the health of France (omitted from a lengthy toast-list) was drunk standing by the company; and generally redeeming by sheer force of personality a situation which illustrated both the

131

degree of esteem felt by the Russians for their new ally and the precarious footing France had won as an Occupying Power. De Lattre returned pensively to his headquarters at Lindau. For the next two months he kept his state in a villa set in flowers and lawns made of turf brought specially from Austria. He devised riparian pleasures which featured the fleet of speedboats he maintained on Lake Constance, and such fêtes as those for General Devers[6] and for General Guisan, commander-in-chief of the Swiss Army, were almost worthy of the court of Versailles. Pomp and circumstance, parades and reviews had an excellent effect on the Germans, who had been told by their propagandists that France was beaten for ever and had no soldiers in the field; but French visitors of Left-wing sympathies were less impressed, and André le Troquer, Jules Moch and Aragon, the Communist poet, were not likely to take back a charitable account of the expenditure and revelry.

After that, with the future reduction of military credits in the Socialist and Communist minds, it was only a short time before the dissolution of the 1st French Army was announced. De Lattre, who was present as an Allied commander-in-chief at the inauguration of the Control Commission in Berlin on June 5, had hoped to remain in Germany:[7] he felt that his place was there during the coming months, which, he foresaw, would be vital to the future of French relations with Germany. It was a shock to learn from a Paris broadcast that his mission to Berlin was 'only temporary' and to be obliged, a few weeks later, to take his leave of the 1st Army. He had not been able to surmount his double handicap in the eyes of General de Gaulle — of being an intensely popular combat leader, and of not being among the *Compagnons de Londres*. It was one of these, General Pierre Koenig, who became French representative on the Control Council and C.-in-C. of the French occupation force of eight divisions.* Koenig objected to Berlin as the meeting-place of the Control Commission, and went there as seldom as possible[8] between 1945 and 1949.

The conference held at Potsdam in July 1945 dealt a heavy blow to the prestige-policy of Charles de Gaulle. In spite of his efforts to impress the Powers, France was not invited to join them, and was left with the feeble consolation of declaring formally that

* 300,000 troops, including 100,000 Senegalese.

the nation was not bound by any international decisions taken without her representation and assent. The Potsdam Protocol reaffirmed and elaborated the Yalta decisions to democratize, reconstruct and pacify the Germans; to demilitarize and disarm the country; to dismantle the war potential and to decentralize the German political structure. The French heartily concurred, but could not agree with other points of the Protocol: to make of Germany a single economic unit, to create central administrative agencies under the State secretaries, and so on, because whenever the words *central* and *single* were used in connection with Germany the heart of Liberated France beat faster. The French knew what German singleness of a central purpose could do to them.

In the nineteenth century they had seen the *Staatenbund* become the *Bundesstaat*, the *Zollverein* joining the petty German kingdoms and grand duchies in a customs union which led to the domination of Prussia and the defeat of France in 1871. From Bismarck through the Empire of Wilhelm II and the Third Reich of Adolf Hitler the centralization of Germany had meant war and sacrifice for the French. Their attitude towards an occupation policy leading to centralization was bound to be different from that of the British, who had suffered on their own soil in only one German war, and then by air bombardment, or of the Americans, who had no experience of German invasions. Thus France, alone among the Powers, advanced an out-and-out policy of federalization for Germany, and this was behind General Koenig's objection to Berlin as a permanent Control Commission headquarters: regular moves from Hamburg to Düsseldorf to Stuttgart would have kept the seat of power shifting, and prevented the emergence of a central government.

Although the French used their veto frequently on the Control Commission, the first phase (1945-47) of their post-war German policy was by no means negative. France had positive demands to make apart from the parcelling-out of Germany, of which a *Sondages* poll showed 78 per cent of the public to be in favour. These were for international control of the mining and metallurgical industries of the Ruhr, for the linking of the Saar to the French customs and financial systems and for demilitarization of the Rhineland.

These were capital demands from a Power which for four years had taken no active part in the war against Germany, and which as a bargaining weapon had only the 600,000 German prisoners of war still detained for labouring work in France. By March 1946 the men in the larger camps were so well organized that they were in no hurry to return to the miseries of life in Germany, although the more intrepid did pay stolen visits to their homes, laden with American cigarettes and canned goods. The big depot at Trigny, near Rheims, was a case in point. The freight station at Châlons-sur-Vesle, six miles outside Rheims, was completely manned by Germans who forbade the French to enter. They had a thriving black market, winked at by their American guards, for whom the Germans had constructed a pleasure garden on the banks of the Vesle. At the motor pool the prisoners practised stunt driving, and French farmers short of petrol for their tractors watched in fury while the trucks and jeeps bucked and careered round the park within sight of their unploughed fields. When the prisoners became too arrogant on the streets of Rheims itself the U.S. authorities at last put a stop[9] to the saturnalia of Châlons and Trigny.

In August 1945, one month after the dissolution of Supreme Headquarters, the formation of German political parties, after due screening, was permitted in the American zone. In October the State Councils were allowed to function again. These small beginnings marked the trend which France feared and, to offset them, all she obtained was a settlement, 'in principle' only, of reparations payments on a percentage basis and a 'Definition of Restitution' of all art objects and valuables looted by the Germans, even when these had been taken from their French owners without force or duress.

When Britain insisted that France should be one of the Occupying Powers in Germany, the Russians had proposed that the French zone of occupation should be cut out of the British and American zones, and this was done, though in such a way as to give France control of an agrarian part of the territory, by contrast with the British and American zones, which were highly industrialized. In theory the Occupants were supposed to live off the country in an agricultural zone, but even in 1947 the famine conditions prevailing in the German cities were felt in the countryside and the prescribed daily level of 1500 calories was seldom reached. The costs of Occupation were therefore higher than had been expected, and increased when an army of French functionaries brought in their relatives[10] unto the second and third generation, all sworn to live as well in Germany as the Germans had lived in France.

The United States maintained a much smaller army of officials — 5000 in 1946 — but the community increased when American business men and industrialists moved in on the heels of James F. Byrnes's declaration at Stuttgart that 'the American people wanted to help the Germans to regain an honourable place among free, peace-loving nations'. By then the Nuremberg trials of German war criminals had become as tedious as the French *épuration*, the hardened American troops of the final battles had been replaced by youths whose chief interest was 'fraternization' or the black market, and who acted with malice toward none where former Nazis were concerned. The French deplored their attitude but wanted them to stay in Germany. Another of their fears, as early as 1946, was that the Allied troops would be entirely withdrawn from Europe, leaving them isolated before the reviving Germans and the watching Russians.

All through the year the French held fast to their three basic demands, advanced by Georges Bidault at every international conference and invariably rebuffed. In March an agreement was reached to limit German production to 50 per cent of the 1938 level, but in April dismantling of factories was suspended in the U.S. zone, and France, suspecting a revival of war potential,* retaliated by using her veto in the Control Commission when the question of central organizations came up again. Russia objected to a consortium over the Ruhr industries, fearing that preponderant Allied power in that vast arsenal might one day use its resources against Communism, and the British took up a compromise position: they would agree to economic but not to political control of the Ruhr. Seeing so many divergences among the Powers the Germans took fresh heart, and presently had the satisfaction of seeing Kurt Schumacher, leader of the renovated Socialist group, received by the British Labour Party with such

---

* German war potential was not completely destroyed by Allied bombing. Unserviceable: 10 per cent metallurgical works, 10-15 per cent chemical works, 15-20 per cent machine tool and textile manufactures.

honours as drew a protest from the French ambassador, René Massigli.

In the Rhineland, which France wanted under international control if not under a French Commission, the British took unilateral action on July 18. They announced the fusion of the north Rhineland and Westphalia, with an artificial capital at Düsseldorf. Two days later General McNarney demanded the economic fusion of the British and U.S. zones. To both of these actions France immediately objected. Here was the beginning of the end of any hope of federalism: the pieces of the German kaleidoscope had begun to fly together, and France had forebodings of what pattern they would make.

CHAPTER VIII

THE FRENCH UNION

AFTER two years of provisional government, France was more than ready for the *mise en place* of the functioning elements of the Fourth Republic.

Under the Constitution the electoral college for the presidency was composed of both chambers of parliament, in 1947 numbering 833, with an absolute majority of 442 required for election. The sovereign people thus exercised its will indirectly, by means of its representatives, and in avoiding a national referendum, along with the American-style Executive branch demanded by de Gaulle, had also avoided the dreadful tediums and six months' dislocation of public affairs caused by the party conventions and nation-wide campaigning which, once every four years, precede the election of an American President. The French President, elected for seven years, was eligible for a second term (but no longer) and in fact Albert Lebrun, the last President of the Third Republic, had just started on his second *septennat* when he was superseded by the voting of plenary powers to Philippe Pétain.

Monsieur Lebrun, nicknamed the Weeping Willow, was still alive, but having received as short shrift from Charles de Gaulle as from the Marshal was now out of public life. Three of the four aspirants for the presidency were politicians of little greater distinction than M. Lebrun at the time of his first election. Jules Gasser, who belonged to the *Rassemblement des Gauches Républicains*, was the oldest member of the Council of the Republic; Champetier de Ribes, who though very able was not the most eminent member of the M.R.P., was ailing, and died soon after; Michel Clemenceau (P.R.L.) was famous chiefly in his father's right. Their merits were precisely such as had been found among presidential aspirants of the Third Republic, when the fear of dictatorship had again and again defeated brilliant men and sent mediocrities to the Élysée. It was scant consolation for de Gaulle to reflect that other famous Frenchmen had also experienced a slip between the cup and the lip, though few had been at such

137

pains as himself to dash the cup away. Georges Clemenceau, so certain of his election in 1920 that picture postcards had already been printed to commemorate his victory, had lost to Paul Deschanel, a nonentity who suffered a mental breakdown and resigned his office within the year. Aristide Briand, equally famous as a man of peace and a would-be maker of united Europe, lost in 1931 to Paul Doumer, an excellent colonial administrator. Of the fourteen Presidents of the Third Republic, only four had finished their elected terms; two had been assassinated and eight removed by death or resignation, of whom one (Jules Grévy) had been implicated in a first-class scandal concerned with the sale of decorations. It was not an inspiring record, and it seemed to be a reversal of the law of averages that the President elected in 1947 should be a man of outstanding character and ability.

Jules Vincent Auriol had spent the whole of his working life in Socialist politics. Born in 1884, the son of a baker in Revel, a little village in the Black Mountains near Toulouse, he began by studying law at Toulouse University, went on to edit *Le Midi Socialiste* and married Michèle Aucouturier, daughter of the founder of the glassworkers' union. Elected to the Chambre des Députés in 1914 for the constituency of Muret (Haute Garonne) he was re-elected for the same district without a break until 1946, and in 1925 Muret also elected him mayor of the pleasant little town, where he had acquired *une petite propriété* called La Bordette, complete with seven fertile acres and an orchard of peach trees. Until 1940, Auriol's had been a conventionally successful political career, for he was one of those who quickly mastered the technique both of the *hémicycle* and the *coulisses* of the Chamber.

A worshipper of Jean Jaurès, he was in some sort the dead Socialist leader's spiritual heir; a representative of the old Republican *mystique*, he possessed a generosity of temper and freedom from sectarian bias which kept him from following the Leftist pipings when the Communist element in the Socialist party walked out of the Tours congress in 1920 and founded the French Communist party. He had an engaging dash of *Tartarin de Tarascon* and even, in his accent and eloquence, of *Numa Roumestan*, although unlike Daudet's hero he had no reputation for gallantries, and his solitary duel had been fought on nothing more romantic than a point of Marxist doctrine.

The war and the Liberation added an unexpected lustre to the modest political reputation of the Deputy from Muret. One of the eighty Deputies to vote against plenary powers for Pétain, he had spent six months in Vichy prisons and a long period in the *maquis* of his native region. Owing to an eye injury in youth he had never been in the army, but General de Lattre found him a good subaltern when they were together in the Aveyron underground; his son, Paul, was in the *maquis* too, and Madame Auriol was working for the Resistance in Lyons. Both remained in France when Auriol, *dit* Dr. Viard, was picked up by an R.A.F. Wellington on the secret airstrip near Mâcon — it was October 17, 1943 — and went to join de Gaulle's movement in London. From there he proceeded to Algiers, where he became a member of the Consultative Assembly with the future Constitution as his special subject.

Vincent Auriol's chief contribution to the politics of Liberated France was common sense, a quality not always found in its councils, and he was one of the few members of the Provisional Government who understood the aspect of public relations which is not connected with publicity. He got on well with nearly everybody. His experiences in the underground had added a needed breadth of charity to his doctrinaire formalism and sense of party discipline, and although as President of the Assembly through 1946 he kept the Deputies well in hand, his most important work was done as a backstage co-ordinator and conciliator in the long debate on the Constitution.

His own attitude to the position of the Executive branch was clearly defined. He had a horror of what he liked to call Caesarism, and was reluctant to put power into the hands of any one man by establishing a presidency on the American model. As he said:

> The temperament and carping nature of our people; a Bonapartist atavism which in time of crisis sometimes revives in certain sections of opinion; sentimental enthusiasm — always possible — for a fascinating or congenial man; vexatious memories of the past and the recent example of an old Marshal and his clique of rascals — these reasons will always make us shun the idea of a popular plebiscite and an all-powerful President.

For Auriol, the supreme authority in France was the sovereign people. He himself, the baker's son, was un enfant du peuple,[1] and the future President, whoever he might be, should function only in accordance with a programme defined in advance by the National Assembly.

On January 16, 1947, the electoral college met to elect the President of the Republic in the Congress Hall of the Palace of Versailles. It was a clear, sunny day, tempting a crowd of fashionable people to drive out of town for the luncheon and other social gatherings which to le tout Paris were part of the ritual of electing a President, but which were not prolonged on what might prove to be the first of several days of balloting. At 2 p.m. Auriol himself, as President of the National Assembly, declared the session open. As a candidate, he then turned over his gavel to the first vice-president, the Communist leader Jacques Duclos, whose party had decided to give him their votes. At 4.45 p.m. it was all over: on the very first round Vincent Auriol had obtained 452 votes, ten more than the required majority.*

Six years and three weeks earlier, President Auriol had had an odd experience of travelling under guard, when he made a painful cross-country journey from one Vichy prison to another on the sad Christmas Day of 1940. Now a more distinguished escort awaited him as the horses of the Garde Républicaine fell into place on either side of the official automobile before the drive from Versailles to Paris, along the classic highway down which the sovereign people had escorted Louis XVI and Marie Antoinette on a journey fated to end at the guillotine. The early winter darkness had fallen before he made his way down the Champs Élysées, but in the Place Beauvau the Ministry of the Interior was illuminated, and on the other side of the Faubourg they were preparing to roll back the courtyard gates, barred for more than seven years, and hoist the tricolore again over the Élysée.

The new President entered upon his carefully limited functions at a moment of exceptional gravity. One month before his election fighting had broken out in Indo-China; two months after, the Mouvement Démocratique de Rénovation Malgache led a rebellion against French rule in Madagascar. Almost before the new

* The figures: Auriol 452, Champetier de Ribes 242, Gasser 122, Clemenceau 60, Other Names 7.

Constitution came into operation there were strainings against the bonds of the French Union into which it had incorporated the overseas possessions of France (of which Union Monsieur Auriol was automatically elected President on January 23) by virtue of the

Preamble to the Constitution of 1946

France shall form with the peoples of the Overseas Territories a Union based upon equality of rights and privileges, without distinction as to race or religion.

The French Union shall be composed of nations and peoples who shall place in common or co-ordinate their resources and their efforts in order to develop their respective civilizations, further their well-being and ensure their security.

Faithful to her traditional mission, France shall guide the peoples for whom she has assumed responsibility towards freedom to govern themselves and towards the democratic administration of their own affairs; rejecting any system of colonization based upon arbitrary power, she shall guarantee to all equal access to public office and the individual or collective exercise of their rights and liberties hereinafter proclaimed or conformed.

'Equal access to public office' included representation in the legislative assemblies, including the new Assembly of the French Union, although as overseas representatives were completely outnumbered by metropolitan they were not likely to have a preponderant influence on the statute of government or possible change of status in each territory. The parliament also made laws for the political and administrative organization of overseas territories, and controlled the criminal code and public liberties, restrictions which galled some of the more advanced communities in the Union.

Restrictions against which Algeria, Madagascar and Indo-China were already chafing to a greater or less degree were justified in the eyes of the constitution-makers by the complexity of the structure of the old French Empire, whose 77 millions included peoples at many different stages of development, ranging from the primitive dwellers in Black Africa through the hardy fishermen of St. Pierre and Miquelon to the supple and indolent native aristocracy of Annam and Cochin-China.

The term 'French Empire' had been dropped in deference to the spirit of the times, which had turned the 'British Empire' into a 'Commonwealth' and only held the word respectable when used as 'newspaper empire' in New York or 'cattle empire' in Texas. But even before World War II the average Frenchman had never been empire-minded. One reason was that the French Empire had been built in two phases of endeavour with nearly one hundred years between them; there was no such irresistible and continuous colonizing movement as that which swept England, and later Great Britain, forward from the time the Cabots left for Newfoundland until the outbreak of World War I. In the age of exploration and conquest the French had established themselves in Canada, India, on the Gulf of Mexico, on the Great Lakes and elsewhere in the territory presently to become the United States, preaching the gospel wherever they planted the white flag of France. Their losing wars with the British in the eighteenth century had stripped them of their great possessions by the Treaties of Utrecht (1715) and Paris (1763): Haiti and San Domingo had been lost at the Revolution; in 1803 Louisiana had been sold. Very little remained but the *Anciennes Colonies* of Martinique, Réunion, St. Pierre and Miquelon, Cayenne and the Establishments in India.

The second and longer phase of French expansion began with a punitive expedition to Algiers in 1830 and ended with the establishment of the Morocco Protectorate in 1912. It included the annexation of Guinea and Gaboon in Africa, the Ivory Coast and the Gold Coast; the conquest of Madagascar (counterbalancing the loss of Mauritius to the British during the Napoleonic Wars); the acquisition of Tahiti and the Marquesas Islands in the Pacific; and it saw the *tricolore* moving across Africa to Jibuti and into South-East Asia on the banks of the Mekong. It was an impulse which sparked enterprises of the highest courage, like Captain Jean-Baptiste Marchand's epic journey across darkest Africa from the Ubanghi to Fashoda on the White Nile, but its basic motive was commercial, due to the need to find new markets and new supplies of raw materials. This had been true from the reign of King Louis Philippe onward, and just as it had been hard for young Frenchmen of the eighteen-thirties to find nobility in Guizot's get-rich-quick slogan — *Enrichessez-vous!* — so for many years after it was hard to remember, in the scramble for building concessions at Saigon or shares in the Algiers surface-transport system, that France's traditional mission overseas was a civilizing and Christianizing one — *gesta Dei per Francos*. The twentieth century was well advanced before proconsuls of the stature of Marshal Lyautey in Morocco or Paul Doumer in Indo-China taught a new generation of administrators that France must give her colonial peoples devotion as well as roads, schools and hospitals, in exchange for the riches contained in rice, vanilla, cocoa, timber, tungsten, oils and phosphates.

Another reason why the French were not Empire-minded lay in their innate satisfaction with all things French. They had never felt the urgency which sent a seafaring people, too numerous for their tiny, foggy island insufficiently equipped with foodstuffs and devoid of luxuries, to plant their flag at the four corners of the earth. In the rich and fertile land of France all the needs of the mind and senses had been amply satisfied, and although from 1914 onwards they had had much to complain of (and had eloquently complained) they had never at any time contemplated large-scale emigration to one of the colonies as a solution for domestic ills. Even in 1953, when the population of the overseas territories had risen to 79.4 millions, only 2.3 millions were French from Continental France. Similarly no special prestige attached to the colonial service, and *les colons* themselves, returning yellow and peevish to take the cure at Aix or Vichy, were not regarded as empire-builders but as people who had chosen to *faire fortune* in some locality disagreeably distant from France. The French, in short, had never been taught to think of themselves as members of a commonwealth, and Charles de Gaulle's frequent reminders that 'France has 110 million citizens' fell upon indifferent ears.

Imperialism was a necessary corollary of Gaullism, for the general never forgot how important a service he had rendered to the Allied cause by rallying a part at least of the Empire to his side, although the fact that the other part had stood firm for Vichy did nothing to promote harmony among the component parts of the Empire. De Gaulle was not dismayed because out of the 77 million inhabitants of the Empire only 8,850,000 had taken the Cross of Lorraine. He had established a Council of Imperial Defence as early as October 1940, and when the French National

Committee was formed in September 1941 he was bold enough to write his preamble to the *Ordonnance* 'in the name of the People and the Empire of France'.

Before France was liberated he had intervened actively in the territories receptive to his influence: early in 1944, for instance, he had published an *Ordonnance* 'emancipating' the Moslem population of Algeria. But his major contribution to imperial policy was the Brazzaville Conference (Jan.-Feb. 1944) organized by the French Committee of National Liberation. This gathering of Governors or Residents, drawn from the African colonies only, took it upon itself to formulate doctrines which were to influence the whole Empire, or French Union, in future years.

The Brazzaville Conference passed some excellent resolutions on the desirability of overseas representation in the metropolitan parliament, of local representative assemblies and the creation of a federal colonial assembly: all of which were in due course implemented under the Fourth Republic. But the Conference did lasting harm in the most important of all respects. It rejected categorically the idea of self-government for the component parts of the French Union. Instead, it decided in favour of assimilation for the colonies, meaning the extension of French citizenship and the transformation of all the territories into Departments of metropolitan France. It closed the door on any possibility of association on the model of the British Commonwealth, declaring:

> The aim of the civilizing work accomplished by France in the colonies excludes any idea of autonomy, any possibility of evolution outside the French bloc of the Empire. The constitution however distant of self-government in the colonies is to be dismissed.[2]

In the spirit of this resolution de Gaulle's Commissioners at Algiers approached the colonial question, although at Paris the Constitutional Commission, through its two attempts, finally evolved a preamble, already quoted, which softened the rigid no-self-government of Brazzaville into a promise that France would 'guide her peoples towards freedom to govern themselves' at dates and in ways unspecified. It was not enough to satisfy colonial populations, some already highly evolved, who had heard of the Atlantic Charter and the U.N. Committee on Non-Self-Governing

Territories, and who were caught up in the great movement — as irresistible as the European national movements of the nineteenth century — for the autonomy of Asian and African nations. No sooner was the Constitution promulgated than Ferhat Abbas, head of the Democratic Union of the Friends of the Algerian Manifesto, led his group of Deputies out of the Chamber, and within a matter of weeks there were unfavourable reactions all through the Empire. But the Provisional Government had set its feet along the path indicated by Charles de Gaulle, and for the next seven years the Brazzaville Conference brought forth its fruits in the form of riots in Algeria, rebellion in the Protectorates and Madagascar and a disastrous war in Indo-China.

Besides the Overseas Departments, regarded as a part of Metropolitan France, the French Union embodied a group of Overseas Territories,* two Associated Territories which were the old 'B' Mandates, Togo and the Cameroun, and the two Protectorates of Morocco and Tunisia. There was also the former Federation of Indo-China† in which, by the time the Constitution was voted, important changes had taken place.

★

In 1940 the French colony (Cochin-China) and protectorates (Annam, Laos, Cambodia) in Indo-China were governed by General Georges Catroux, who later, in the Syrian campaign, at Algiers and Paris, and as ambassador to Russia, was one of de Gaulle's most valuable *Compagnons*. It was not until the trial of Marshal Pétain in 1945 that his share in the surrender of Indo-China to the Japanese became known, along with the fact that he had joined de Gaulle after he had been dismissed from his governorship by the Marshal.

Catroux's own book of war memoirs began discreetly with his west-bound flight from Singapore on August 25, 1940, a date which served as an alibi for his connection with the Franco-Japanese Treaty of August 30. By this treaty Vichy gave Japan the right of passage through Indo-China and the use of bases in

---

* In order of population: French West Africa, Madagascar, French Equatorial Africa, French Establishments in India, Comores, New Caledonia, Oceania, Somali Coast, St. Pierre and Miquelon. Total pop.: 26,452,015.

† Later the Associated States of Viet Nam, Laos, Cambodia. Total pop.: 27,658,700.

the peninsula, eventual key points in the Japanese attacks on Singapore, Malaya and Manila, and Japan in return promised to 'recognize French sovereignty over Indo-China and respect its territorial integrity'. Rear-Admiral Jean Decoux, commander of the French Fleet in the Far East, who succeeded Catroux as Governor-General, was sufficiently fooled by this face-saving formula to repeat several times in his version of events that 'the essential rights of France' had been safeguarded; but he was also shrewd enough to report to Vichy that Catroux had left 'a Japanese mortgage' on the territory now confided to himself.

For between the start of *la débâcle* in France and his own departure to join de Gaulle, General Catroux had not been idle. When his transactions with the Japanese were revealed during the Pétain trial he stated to the Associated Press[2] that in order to forestall a Japanese attack on Indo-China he had voluntarily stopped, on June 16, 1940, the free transit of petrol and war supplies across Tonkin to China, which had been taking place under the Chinese-American barter agreement. He also permitted a Japanese transit control commission under General Nishihara, which arrived in Hanoi on June 29, to establish itself on the frontier, and he promised to revictual the Japanese army in Kwangsi and care for its sick and wounded on Indo-Chinese soil. For taking this initiative — he argued that he had consulted with Roland de Margerie, the French ambassador in Tokyo — he was rebuked by M. Lemery, Minister for the Colonies, and recalled from his post.

It appeared that, however wrong Pétain had been in collaborating with an ally of the Axis Powers, Catroux, as the man on the spot, had presented him with a *fait accompli*, and the only defence the latter put forward in 1945 was precisely the same as Decoux was to make a short time later: that he had attempted to save Indo-China by negotiation rather than lose to Japan in an unsupported fight. Catroux insisted that he had asked both Britain and the United States for aid in June 1940; Britain, he said, had replied that all her military resources were being devoted to the defeat of Germany in Europe, while the State Department had turned down a specific request for 120 aircraft and A.A. guns with the message: the United States Government 'did not believe that it could enter into a conflict with Japan and that furthermore it would take no action if this power attacked Indo-China'.

Such had been the beginning of Japanese power in Indo-China, an Occupation in all but name which engendered, as in France, a Resistance movement of decidedly Left-wing tendencies. As in the case of France, too, President Roosevelt had his own views on how the future government of the country ought to be decided. He wrote to Cordell Hull,[4] the Secretary of State, on January 24, 1944:

I saw [Lord] Halifax [the British Ambassador] last week, and told him quite frankly that it was perfectly true that I had, for over a year, expressed the opinion that Indo-China should not go back to France but that it should be administered by an international trusteeship. France has had the country — thirty million inhabitants — for nearly one hundred years, and the people are worse off than they were at the beginning.

As a matter of interest, I am whole-heartedly supported in this view by Generalissimo Chiang Kai-shek and by Mr. Stalin. I see no reason to play in with the British Foreign Office in this matter. The only reason they seem to oppose it is that they fear the effect it would have on their own possessions and those of the Dutch. They've never liked the idea of trusteeship because it is, in some instances, aimed at future independence. This is true in the case of Indo-China.

Each case must, of course, stand on its own feet, but the case of Indo-China is perfectly clear. France has milked it for 100 years. The people of Indo-China are entitled to something better than that.

The President was still of the same opinion in the following August, when the British asked the United States to agree to a French share in the liberation of Indo-China and offered to attach a French Military Mission to South-East Asia Command (S.E.A.C.) HQ at Kandy. The President negatived the proposal and went so far as to forbid American authorities in the Far East to make political decisions with the French or anyone else. How far his attitude was determined by anti-colonialism and how far by antipathy to de Gaulle is hard to decide; but it is certain that de Gaulle, by his own ambiguous attitude to Indo-China, helped on the work of diminishing French influence in the peninsula.

He had, of course, had his undercover men there for some time. Since the spring of 1943 Admiral Decoux had been well aware that General Aymé and General Mordant (*Pierre et Narcisse dans la clandestinité*)[5] had been in touch with Algiers, and after the Liberation a Malayan planter, Major de Langlade, arrived in Tonkin as the emissary of de Gaulle. What was more surprising was the order from René Pleven, Minister of the Colonies, which arrived as soon as the Provisional Government was established at Paris, that Admiral Decoux was to remain in office and 'maintain a façade'[6] permitting *Narcisse* to develop his resistance movement against the Japanese.

The reason for the general's most unusual forbearance towards a Vichy official was not the declaration of Indo-Chinese fidelity to the metropolis which Decoux had prudently published on the day after insurrection broke out in Paris, but the impossibility of getting his *commissaires* to a spot eight thousand miles away and in the heart of enemy territory. There was one means of communication, through the French Settlement of Chandernagore near Calcutta, where Colonel Passy's invaluable secret service had a branch office,[7] but while plans were maturing Manila fell, and de Gaulle at once ordered Decoux to proclaim Indo-China neutral if the Americans should attempt to disembark there. But there was no time for his old bogey of American military government to materialize in the Far East. On March 9 the Japanese threw off the mask of 'recognition' and occupied the whole of Indo-China.

In this crisis it was neither the French nor the Americans who proved effective against the invader. The Provisional Government took a number of bold steps: Admiral Thierry d'Argenlieu was named High Commissioner, an office intended to supersede the governor-generalship; his delegate, *dit* Cédile, parachuted into south Indo-China and alarmed French residents with such Resistance slogans as 'French blood has not yet flowed sufficiently in Indo-China!'[8] and 'Maurice Thorez is the second personage of France'. On June 17 General Leclerc was named commanding general of a French Expeditionary Force, although by a decision of the Potsdam Conference the task of liberating Indo-China was to be divided between British forces in the south and Chinese in the north. Arms were parachuted in, most of which fell into the wrong hands. But in spite of all this the most effective fighting was done by the followers of a new leader called Ho Chi Minh — 'He Who Shines' — who had founded a movement 'against French and Japanese fascism' which he called Viet Minh.

Ho Chi Minh had been for twenty years *dans la clandestinité*, preparing for an uprising in Annam, where he was born, and from where he had gone to study in Paris. A convinced Marxist, he had then gone to Moscow for indoctrination and had worked with Borodin and Chiang Kai-shek while the generalissimo was still a Communist. Now, profiting by the Japanese aggression, he had come into the open as leader of a 'nationalist' movement, sworn to free his native land both of its invaders and its suzerains, and within a few days of the bombing of Hiroshima and Nagasaki Ho Chi Minh proclaimed himself President of the Democratic Republic of Viet Nam. Bao Dai, Emperor of Annam, abdicated and became Supreme Councillor of Viet Nam, and French residents in the new state, then numbering some 20,000, suffered molestation, kidnapping and pillage.

Jean Sainteny, the *commissaire de la République*, had to depend on American transportation to fly him to Hanoi, where he arrived in August with Major Patti[9] of the O.S.S. M. Sainteny was confronted by the Viet Minh official slogan 'Independence or Death!' which made so favourable an impression on the Americans that they tended to ignore the Viet Minh's other war cry, which was 'Death to the French imperialists!' The *commissaire* averred that the representatives of the U.S. then at Hanoi 'played the game of Annamite nationalism'[10] and even supplied the Viet Minh *maquis*, through a misapprehension of the purpose of Ho's movement. Thanks to the decisions made at Potsdam, it was some time before any reinforcements could arrive from France.

General Leclerc was already on his way to Indo-China and had been the French signatory of the Japanese surrender aboard the U.S.S. *Missouri*. Always a *frondeur*, he had fallen foul of Admiral Mountbatten at S.E.A.C.,[11] but he found that the British had no designs on Indo-China and were anxious to hand over to the French and go home. It was quite otherwise with the Chinese, who were in no hurry to leave the country, and used their position in the north to establish contact with the Viet Minh.

Slowly some sort of order was restored, and on March 6,

1946, Ho Chi Minh and Jean Sainteny put an end to the hostilities by signing a treaty in which France recognized the Viet Nam Republic as a free state, having its own government, parliament, army and finances (though no powers were as yet formally transferred) and forming part of the Indo-Chinese Federation and of the French Union. General Leclerc and his Expeditionary Corps entered Hanoi on March 18.

Admiral Decoux had been in France for some months when this treaty was signed. He had been arrested on October 2 by order of the High Commissioner and flown to Paris, where after a rating from de Gaulle for his failure to join the Free French movement in London he was committed for trial by the High Court on the usual charges. He still maintained — and the High Court acquitted him — that he had preserved the allegiance to France of all the inhabitants of Indo-China, and could have pointed, if he wished, to the ephemeral nature of the peace which Ho Chi Minh had signed with his successor. The French colony of Cochin-China was a Naboth's vineyard to the new rulers of Viet Nam, who desired to add it to the State they had formed out of Annam and Tonkin, and they had stipulated that the treaty of March 6 should allow a plebiscite to be taken of the Cochin-Chinese to determine their future status.

Unfortunately Admiral Thierry d'Argenlieu anticipated the plebiscite.[12] While Ho Chi Minh was in France, negotiating a *modus vivendi*, the High Commissioner gave his sanction to the establishment of a Provisional Government in Cochin-China. To the more bellicose elements in the Viet Minh, led by the War Minister, General Giap, this was a sufficient *casus belli*. They did not take immediate action, for the French had about 60,000 troops in Indo-China — the original Expeditionary Force led by Leclerc having been reinforced by the 3rd Infantry Division and a brigade from Madagascar[13] — but they came very near it on November 20 at Haiphong, when the French seized a contraband Chinese junk lying in that port.[14] Shots were exchanged between Viet Minh and French troops, and the situation grew more tense. But the Viet Minh uprising, when it came on December 19, was unexpected. In Saigon the power station was seized and the roads mined: Jean Sainteny, speeding to the scene of action in an armoured car, rode over a mine[15] and was wounded in twenty places. Everywhere French troops and civilians were hastily thrust on the defensive as the Indo-Chinese War began.

This was the situation confronting the new President of the Republic and French Union, and it contained at least two disquieting elements beyond the normal anxiety of a war of rebellion, breaking out eight thousand miles from the mother country. In its simplest form the aggression of the Viet Minh was a nationalist uprising against an autocratic colonial power, which was how Ho Chi Minh had first presented it to the American military mission in Hanoi. Beneath and beyond that, however, was the Communist determination to enslave South-East Asia, which meant that unless the French could end the war very quickly they might find themselves at grips with a far more formidable enemy than Giap's guerrillas. And in the fight France had started with a double handicap: the quarrel between Vichy and de Gaulle which had brought about the arrest of Admiral Decoux and the consequent loss of 'face' for France, and the intransigent attitude of President Roosevelt towards colonialism in any form.

The naïveté, to use no stronger word, of Roosevelt's plans for the future of Indo-China — already shown by his confidence that Stalin's views on the future of the peninsula were quite disinterested — was extended to his plans for Britain. He believed that the British should 'return Hong-Kong to China, while China might in return immediately declare Hong-Kong a free port under international trusteeship'.[16] But Cordell Hull, the Secretary of State, although 'just a Tennessean mountaineer' to his crusty colleague Harold Ickes, held more realistic views on colonialism than his sophisticated chief. He pointed out that 'we could not alienate them [the British] in the Orient and expect to work with them in Europe'.[17] At the same time Hull snubbed a Texan critic, who wanted to see 'all colonies separated from their mother countries, and particularly to see the return of Hong-Kong to China', by reminding him that although Hong-Kong had been British longer than Texas had been part of the United States it was doubtful whether a proposal to turn Texas back to Mexico would be welcome.[18] But these snubs were not in keeping with the general American attitude to critics of colonialism, who, thanks to a basic misconception of the nature of the American Revolution, were sure of approbation from the Atlantic to the Pacific.

The very word *colony* had become debased in America. It had lost its real meaning of a land to be cultivated, tilled, developed, and now stood for a community to be oppressed. This was one outcome of the successful revolt of the Thirteen Colonies against Britain, a struggle for independence annually celebrated with immense gusto by persons whose ancestors had been nowhere near the Delaware in 1776, but located at some point between the Liffey and the Vistula. *Colony* and *colonial* had acquired an evil meaning except when applied to furniture or architecture, and were so used not only by a Democratic president, Franklin Roosevelt, but also by a Republican, Dwight D. Eisenhower, who wrote, while he was still the Supreme Commander, that:

Historically [America and Russia] had maintained an unbroken friendship that dated back to the birth of the United States as an independent republic. Except for a short period, their diplomatic relations had been continuous. Both were free from the stigma of colonial empire building by force.[19]

This was the concept which led the United States of 1946, or even of 1953, to suppose that all nationalist propaganda, whether from India, Indonesia or Indo-China, was the heart's cry of an oppressed people, brutally conquered and now struggling to be free. John Foster Dulles, after becoming Secretary of State in 1953, was to make a public statement on Indo-China in which he described it as '[once] merely a French dependency', now deserving special favour from Americans 'who also remember their struggle for freedom'.[20] Yet there was no connection between the American Revolution and the movement for Vietnamese independence. The revolutionaries of 1776 were not infiltrated by Communists. They were colonists, mostly of British stock, who rebelled against the policy of a British Government, and the native inhabitants of the liberated territory were not a penny the better for their success. The only Reds beyond the Alleghenies were Red Indians, and the emancipated Americans made short work of them. Indeed, the federal policy which drove the red man from his hunting grounds and sent him stumbling westwards along the Trail of Tears was more brutal than any policy ever devised by the British Crown.

The Americans themselves had become the most prodigious

colonists in the world, but — as André Siegfried once slyly pointed out[21] — they appeared to consider colonization respectable if it were carried out entirely on land; the 'stigma' only came when the seas were crossed. Moreover their own experience in a vast empty land where the white men always moved forward together had made them believe (as long as they kept their eyes shut to the Indian reservations) that the emancipation of a territory automatically meant civilization in conformity with the standards of Hometown, U.S.A.: the Community Chest, the Community Church, the lodge of the Brotherly and Protective Order of Elks, the branch of the Parent-Teacher Association and the free press attached to one of the most lucrative national chains. Only the medical and technical teams working in Asian or African areas knew how difficult it was to introduce these amenities to native populations.

It was hard to convince the average American that the French had poured public and private capital and an endeavour not to be reckoned in dollars into the countries of the French Union: it was so much more satisfying to picture the French colonist as a frog-eating Simon Legree (an attitude which assuaged American guilt in the matter of Uncle Tom), and this basic misunderstanding was a recurrent hindrance to good Franco-American relations. There was, besides, some jealousy in the matter. The Americans were not solely motivated by pity for the underdog, and not a little of their attitude to France and Britain as colonial powers was translatable by the French expression *Ôtes-toi de là que je m'y mette!** As Franklin Roosevelt said to his son Elliott just before the Atlantic Charter was signed in 1941:

> The British Empire is at stake here. It's something that's not generally known, but British bankers and German bankers have had world trade pretty well sewn up in their pockets for a long time, despite the fact that Germany lost in the last war. Well, that's not so good for American trade, is it?[22]

This admirably frank statement revealed that the Americans were as eager to open new markets and lay hands on new resources as the Elizabethan adventurers or the French in the days of

* 'You get up and let me sit down.'

153

African expansion, or the Germans in Damaraland, or the Belgians, or the Dutch; but having come too late to the scramble for overseas colonies they had to adopt new methods to get their share. Where others had opened trade routes by conquest and diplomacy the Americans now followed as champions of the peoples along the way, ready with good works and willing (in return for a few trifling oil concessions) to make the desert blossom as the rose.

PART THREE

FRANCE AND EUROPE
1947-1950

CHAPTER IX

THE R.P.F. AND THE COMMUNISTS

WHEN the lights went up again in the Élysée the new President's handsome wife set herself to restore dignity to the palace which had been shuttered for so long. Plate and plenishing of great value were brought from the *trésor national*, flowers were arranged with dramatic effect, the household servants were put into new liveries, and a first-rate chef in daily consultation with Madame Auriol planned suitable menus for the official and private meals, which had previously been sent in by a caterer. It was no longer possible to publish the time-honoured cartoons which showed famished guests hurrying from Élysée parties to the nearest restaurant.

While the necessary refurbishing of the presidential dignity was going on in the Faubourg St. Honoré, Charles de Gaulle was spending the winter — the worst since the first winter of the war — in his little stone manor on the edge of the forest at Colombey-les-Deux-Églises. He had now passed a whole year in brooding upon his position and his future, and although he had long believed that 'nothing heightens authority better than silence' and that 'prestige is inseparable from mystery, since familiarity breeds contempt'[1] he and his *Compagnons* had decided that he must make his voice heard once more.

In the spring of 1947 there were two paths open to Charles de Gaulle. He might re-enter politics alone, as the founder of a new group or movement, or he might associate himself with an established political group — the large and influential M.R.P., still his 'party of fidelity', being the obvious choice. Reinforced by the 'First Resistant of France', able to silence the critics of his authoritarian tendencies by pointing to his democratic position within the party, the M.R.P. might well have regained its leading position of June 1946 and become a truly powerful party of the Right. Such a party, reinforced by the votes of moderate Socialists, and by elements of the Independents, P.R.L., U.D.S.R. and others personally attracted to the general, might have opposed Communism with the same success as similar Christian Democrat movements in Italy and Germany and have carried Charles de Gaulle to a premiership like that of Alcide de Gasperi or Konrad Adenauer. But this would have meant a descent into the arena of the *hémicycle* on an equal footing with a Bidault, a Maurice Schumann and others to whom he had given commissionerships and ministries, and a denial of his faith in the *mystique* of the Leader.

For nearly six years de Gaulle had lived in such a blaze of publicity that it was sometimes forgotten that earlier in life he had spent twenty months in a German war prison. A period of captivity has often proved valuable to believers in the *Führerprinzip*: Adolf Hitler started to write *Mein Kampf* in prison, and Napoleon III, derisively *dit* Badinguet, to whom the Paris housewives were fond of comparing de Gaulle, had worked out his *Idées Napoléoniennes* while a political prisoner at Ham. Although de Gaulle did not publish *Le Fil de l'Épée* until 1932, it undoubtedly embodied many ideas arrived at by him in 1917-18; what his advisers of 1947 had to do was temper the tone of these ideas to the necessities of the times.

'How are states founded? Through the personality of brilliant leaders and through a people which deserves to have the crown of laurel bound about its brows!'[2] The words were Hitler's; the thought approximated closely to de Gaulle's, for 'nothing great', the general believed, 'can be accomplished without great men, and men are great through resolving to be so ... Weapons have tortured but also shaped the world ... Men cannot do without being directed, any more than without food, drink, or sleep ... To dominate events, to make an impression, to accept the consequences — this, above all, is expected from the Leader'.[3]

With such a determination to be great, to dominate and to direct, it was inevitable that de Gaulle should believe, as he said in a speech at Strasbourg,* that to enter the party game would 'diminish without profit the kind of national capital which events had led [him] to represent'. He therefore prepared, soon after the new government took office, to contribute something new and different to the politics of Liberated France.

The new premier, Paul Ramadier, had been Keeper of the

* April 7, 1947.

Seals in Léon Blum's caretaker government but was not a dynamic figure. Like President Auriol, he was an elderly Socialist Deputy of Third-Republican origins who had voted against Pétain in 1940 and dragged his ageing self up and down the *maquis* of the Aveyron; but there the resemblance ended, for Ramadier had taken the step considered suicidal by the politicians of the Liberation: he had accepted the Ministry of Food. He had even held it, for six months of the first Provisional Government's régime, and the shortages and restrictions which increased during that time had put the new word *ramadiète* into current slang.

There were still five Communist members in the cabinet, four of whom, MM. Thorez, Billoux, Tillon and Croizat, had held office under General de Gaulle. The same group which had eliminated de Gaulle with hardly a struggle now advanced to a trial of strength with the undistinguished Paul Ramadier, for as 1947 moved on to the month of March and the Conference of Moscow Russia made a decisive move away from her war-time alignment with the West.

A few days before the Moscow Conference opened, the Treaty of Dunkirk was signed between France and Britain, an instrument based on the belief expressed by Ernest Bevin that 'the danger still came from Germany rather than from Russia'. The treaty, effective for fifty years, contained five clauses promising the mutual aid of the contracting parties in the event of a new German aggression: it was thus an extension of the Entente Cordiale, defining the military alliance which, to the steady regret of the French, had not been included in the treaty of 1904.

The new treaty called for consultations between Britain and France if Germany should transgress against her economic obligations. This did not prevent the British from failing to side with France in the economic discussions at Moscow: correctly observing the letter of the Dunkirk agreement since no actual infraction by Germany was in question, the British delegation headed by Ernest Bevin failed to implement its spirit, for Bevin and Molotov made common cause for an increase of German steel production, fixed one year earlier at 7.5 million tons, to 10-12 million tons. This was done against Bidault's plea for the definite limitation of this source of war potential. General Marshall, for the United States, and Molotov supported the establishment of central administration in Germany against Bidault's arguments for federalism and the attachment of the Saar to France.

Thus France left Moscow unsatisfied, but Britain and the United States departed with the knowledge that on many important details they had been opposed by the Russians, and American opinion at least was beginning to harden. It was the moment of the Truman Doctrine, when the American President's promise of economic aid to Greece and Turkey reversed the long-lasting doctrine of President Monroe, and as the world began to split into two camps the United States emerged from its own continent to share at last in the concerns of all the others. There was a corresponding stiffening of the Communist attitude, and in France the whole group of Communists in the Assembly abstained from voting on the motion, otherwise unanimously passed, to open a credit of 3000 million francs ($2.5 millions) for the French Expeditionary Corps in Indo-China, now enlarged from 65,000 to 115,000[1] troops.

On March 30 Charles de Gaulle was due to speak at Bruneval in Normandy, at a ceremony commemorating a joint Commando-Resistance operation in 1942, in the presence of the British and Canadian ambassadors. It was an important occasion, thoroughly prepared by the *Compagnons*, whose technique had improved considerably since the early Carlton Gardens days, and who had recruited a first-class propaganda expert in André Malraux, the only man of world-wide reputation who ever took the Cross of Lorraine.

It was appropriate that de Gaulle, who had followed Chiang Kai-shek's example in progressing from co-operation with Communists to militant anti-Communism, should have won the allegiance of the author of *Man's Fate*, although that brilliant study of the Kuomintang belonged to an earlier phase of Malraux's career. He had since moved from Communism to nationalism by way of solidarity with the Spanish Communists (*Man's Hope*) and the German Communists (*Days of Wrath*) and a rupture with French Communism in 1939. As 'Colonel Berger' he had been a resourceful *maquisard*; he fought well in the 1944 campaign in Alsace, and his *Walnut Trees of Altenburg*, the first volume of a trilogy, contained a moving account of the sufferings of French soldiers of *la débâcle* in their war prison at Chartres. The double

capacity of Malraux as man of action and man of letters made a
strong appeal to de Gaulle when the two men met at the Liberation, and in the Second Provisional Government the writer was
appointed to Soustelle's old place as Minister of Information. He
held it very briefly, until the general left office in January 1946.

At the same time, the character of de Gaulle made a profound
impression upon André Malraux. Like many converts from Communism he was in search of a substitute for authority, and what
others found in the Catholic Church the dictates of his genius
drove him to seek in human kind. Before the war he had been
fascinated by the character and achievements of Lawrence of
Arabia, describing him as 'the forerunner of a new human type
developing in the world: the Liberal Hero'. Now, as a successor to
the young British officer whom his Arabs had called 'Prince Dyna-
mite' and who had altered the map of the Middle East within
three years, he had de Gaulle as the object of his admiration,
although the general conformed more nearly to the Carlylean
idea of the Hero as Commander. A leader with a taste for the
liberal arts and the Nietzschean doctrine of aristocratic anarchy is
not always at his best when appealing to the masses, and Malraux,
well aware of the general's handicaps, began to coach him in an
easier platform style. The good effects were easily discernible in
the two speeches delivered by de Gaulle just before the launching
of the French People's Rally.

At Bruneval he launched a scathing attack on the government,
the 'heroes of the Fourth Republic' and the 'sterile games' of their
political system; predicting that 'the day would come when the
immense mass of the French would be reunited (*se rassemblera*)
with France'. It was an unusual attack to make in the presence of
foreign dignitaries, and the government was shocked; Monsieur
Ramadier was driven to a spirited denial that the greatness of any
one man could be the salvation of France. 'There is no supreme
deliverer, neither Caesar nor People's Tribune!' Such was the
Roman exhortation of Paul Ramadier, and, when it was spoken,
battle was joined between de Gaulle and the government representing the sovereign people.

Until his appearance at Bruneval the new government had kept
up a polite fiction of admiration and deference towards the 'First
Resistant', accepting his snubs as its predecessors had done and

acquiescing in the honours accorded him on his various journeys. But before his next public appearance he was personally warned by Paul Ramadier that he would thenceforth be treated as exactly what he was, a retired brigadier-general, with no title to military honours; the use of radio for political speeches would be reserved for members of the government; and no official delegates might attend any of de Gaulle's political declarations. The warning was obeyed to the letter. At Strasbourg on April 6 de Gaulle was present with Generals Juin, de Lattre and Koenig at a celebration of the second anniversary of the city's complete liberation. On April 7 he strode out alone, with neither generals, ministers nor *corps préfectoral* by his side, and stood on the balcony of the city hall, preaching to the crowd which packed the Place de Broglie a new rally, *le rassemblement du peuple Français*, which should transcend party politics and restore the greatness of France. Seven days later he announced that the French People's Rally (R.P.F.) was now open to all comers except former collaborators, with the dual aims of liberating the State from the party régime and establishing a strong presidential régime. Within twenty-four hours Soustelle claimed that 12,700 applications for membership[5] had been received in Paris alone.

The national organization of the R.P.F. had been carefully planned. On Departmental level a 'committee of provisional initiative' was set up in each *chef-lieu*, directed by a Departmental delegate. On the professional level an 'economic group' included artisans, agricultural workers, commercial and industrial employees and professional men, and a 'social group' including youth organizations and war veterans.[6] An executive committee, notable for the youth of its members, directed the whole structure and was presided over by the general himself. As in Italian Fascism, there was no women's group, but it was announced that the new equality of the sexes made this unnecessary.

André Malraux, Director of Culture and Propaganda, devised a number of too literary slogans like: 'The R.P.F. has killed fear!' and 'The R.P.F. proclaims the priority of the general interest!' but few good songs were forthcoming to add to the *Marche Lorraine* and the *Chant des Partisans*, and for its party rallies the R.P.F. was badly in need of a few good marching songs. Boulanger had had his Paulus to sing of him as 'General Victory':

Regardez-le là-bas! Il nous sourit et passe
Il vient de délivrer la Lorraine et l'Alsace —

but *le brav' général* of 1947 was living in another world, and it was not easy to picture an Yves Montand or a Charles Trenet rousing a music-hall audience to frenzy for the disdainful and melancholy de Gaulle.

The ambiguity of de Gaulle's position as a man above politics, inimical to the party system yet heading a 'group' which intended to present its candidates at all elections, took a good deal of explaining, and this M. Malraux left to M. Soustelle, who defined the president of the R.P.F. in a kind of Gaullist litany as the

Man of the Eighteenth of June*
Denouncer of the infamy of Personal Power
Constructor of a France based on Liberty
Liberator of the Territory

in a brochure published on July 27.[7] This began, amateurishly enough, with a depressing list of negatives:

What the R.P.F. is Not
A political party.
A league.
A friendly society.
An armed militia.
A parliamentary group.

and went on to declare the following aims:

State reform by separation of powers, with a Chief of State who shall be truly chief, an arbiter above party.
Economic and social renovation.
Defence of the French Union on a federal basis.
Protection of French independence by decentralization of the Reich, guarantees for the Rhineland, coal from the Ruhr.

This was not the official programme of the R.P.F., for it had none; its principles were always described, in its own sibylline

* Reproductions of de Gaulle's best-known broadsheet ('France has lost a battle. She has not lost the war', etc.) were now overstamped with the date of June 18, 1940, to convey the impression that this, instead of his actual broadcast, was what de Gaulle had said on the B.B.C.

language, as *les idées-forces*. Similarly, all the members were now called *les compagnons*, their congresses *les assises* and their Communist opponents *les séparatistes*. The members of the cabinet were invariably *les gouvernants* and their constitutional procedure *le système*, a word often qualified by the adjective *stérile*. It was just the right mixture of esoteric dialectics and medieval tournament to attract the floating vote left over from Vichy days, and this was important, because the R.P.F., although not a party, sought votes in the same way as other parties, and proposed to present its candidates at all elections.

There was a good deal that was amateurish in the early propaganda of the R.P.F. The district headquarters were badly chosen, being installed in vacant shops in obscure streets, where the stickers of the Cross of Lorraine flapped loose on dusty windows and announcements of group meetings were allowed to become out of date. This was partly due to lack of funds, and one money-raising device attempted was the sale of specially priced stamps for use on letters or postcards bearing messages of encouragement to the general. It was estimated that three and a half million stamps were bought and two million messages dispatched to Colombey-les-Deux-Églises, not all of them complimentary.

André Malraux was more successful with poster campaigns. 'We cannot set the style of a grocer selling pickles', he decreed. 'These are not what the general has to offer', and his posters, in the early days of the R.P.F., were original and artistic. The most successful was a reproduction of Rodin's statue of the aroused Republic, with the Cross of Lorraine added to show who was doing the arousing; the most dramatic, the gigantic Lorraine Cross fashioned from barbed wire. This was intended to represent France crucified, but allowed the opposition to inquire if the R.P.F. proposed eventually to set up concentration camps.

It was something new for a French political group, whether party or above-party in inspiration, to use such varied forms of advertising media, and there was the same originality in Malraux's preparation of the personal appearances of de Gaulle. They were not quite as well done as Hitler's Nuremberg rallies or Mussolini's emergences on his Roman balcony, because the French genius is not suited to such things: but *Compagnons* like

Rémy who had had theatre and cinema experience helped out with the stage settings at the Vel' d'Hiv' or the Hippodrome de Vincennes, where there was space to display the tall masts from which drooped giant Crosses of Lorraine, and to instal a battery of projectors with their beams focused on a vast *tricolore* draped from the battens. A *service d'ordre* of young men in leather jackets stood grimly ready to deal with interrupters (a formal period for questions was seldom accorded) and to raise their arms whenever they heard the slogan Malraux had chosen for the Rally: 'We fight with bare hands!' Malraux himself was very often among the speakers chosen to work up the audience to the appropriate pitch of excitement; he was as effective as in the days when he was one of the best orators in the Communist party, for he had the genuine spell-binder's touch; but he always knew that the big moment would only come when the *tricolore* blazed with added light, the crowd reached the apex of suspense, and the general entered to the strains of the *Marseillaise*.

It was all very different from the usual *réunions contradictoires* of French electioneering — those earnest schoolroom meetings where the air grew thick with chalk and argument — and it made a strong appeal to an increasing number of the French during 1947. The R.P.F. had been fortunate in the timing of its first campaign. The Kominform, or Communist bureau of liaison and information, had been recently set up at Belgrade, and when the French Communist Party joined it along with Russia and the Balkan satellites the average Frenchman saw through their pretence of being a national party, and agreed with de Gaulle that they were entirely under the control of Moscow. Criticisms that the general had used Communist help in his rise to power, given his approval to fellow-travellers like General Eugène Petit, his ambassador to Moscow, and Pierre Cot,[8] and had concluded an alliance with Russia, were met by the general's own apologia. In a speech at Rennes on July 27 he grasped that particular nettle boldly, declaring that national unity was now imperilled

by a group of men whose leaders place, above all else, the service of a foreign State. I say this all the more forcibly because I myself attempted, up to the limits of the lawful and the possible, to attract them to the service of France. Yes! at the Liberation I judged, with the entire Resistance movement, that these *séparatistes* should be given a chance to integrate themselves with the nation ... I played that game, I played it up to the hilt. I introduced men of that kind into the government, which then united representatives of all shades of opinion.

This frankness allowed him to attack Russia with conviction; it was just the kind of manly confession about to be made by several leading men in other nations, who had regarded Russia as a comrade and the Communists as patriot nationalists until the scales fell from their eyes. To the crowds, ranging from 30,000 to 60,000, which cheered him at all his appearances that summer, de Gaulle seemed to justify his own claim to be part of the national capital, or at least to represent their best hope of internal security.

But while the crowds in Brittany and his native Lille shouted '*De Gaulle au pouvoir!*' the harassed team of elderly politicians who formed the cabinet had succeeded where the general had failed. They had met the Communist challenge to government stability and emerged intact from the head-on clash.

When Paul Ramadier became premier in January he had announced his intention of continuing the experiment of price cuts, which though difficult to apply had met with some success under the Blum caretaker government, and of attempting to increase production rather than wages. The Communist-dominated trade union (C.G.T.) then intimated that the hardships of the winter made a pay-raise essential. Ramadier countered with a second price cut of 5 per cent, effective on March 1, but this was unsupported by increased productivity and wholesale and retail prices continued to mount.* By the end of April the Communist ministers had withdrawn their support from the official wage-freeze policy and were manœuvring to get the government out.

On May 4 Ramadier's policy won a vote of confidence by 360 to 160 in the National Assembly. Thereupon the premier took the bold step of dismissing the five Communist ministers

* The *actual* production of the French worker rose, but owing to shortages of power, labour and raw materials the *industrial* production was deficient, e.g. production of coal. Taking basic production figure for 1938 as 100, then production at the coal face in 1947 was 109, industrial production 85.

who had been appointed to cabinet rank, on the grounds that they had voted against the government's policy previously approved by the National Assembly. This decision cost him more than one debate with his own party, for the Socialists found his action arbitrary, and had to accustom themselves to the idea of governing without Communist support. It was the end of *tripartisme*, the three-party coalition which had lasted since the Liberation, and also of the idea that the two parties of the Left should support one another. The separation of the Tours Congress of 1920 was repeated in 1947, and on May 6 the Communist party found itself, for the first time in three years and for many years to come, in opposition.

The dismissal of the Communist ministers did nothing to alleviate the increasing social unrest in the country. The news that Daniel Mayer (Soc.) was to be Minister of Labour instead of Ambroise Croizat (Com.) did not prevent the recurrence of strikes, ranging from the 'spot strikes' involving workers in apparently unrelated occupations from banking to laundering, to the *grèves perlées*, which stopped the *métro* or the buses for short unannounced periods. In the provinces there were demonstrations against the Food Ministry and its local employees. A shortage of corn, which closed the bakeries on Sunday, May 11 — a step calculated to shorten the life of any French government — was followed by a strike of journeymen bakers. Railwaymen, gas mechanics, powerhouse operators came out one after the other during a summer heat-wave which followed the bitter winter. The famous Eighteenth of June passed almost unnoticed, and on June 23 the Palais Bourbon was surrounded by 15,000 Communist-led demonstrators moving in angry waves against the police cordons. Under such continuous pressure the experiment of price cuts was abandoned for good. Milk and butter now cost more, the bakeries were closed on two days a week instead of one, and a shortage of grain for sowing promised another poor harvest in 1948. No petrol coupons were issued during the month of September, and in October a general transport strike reduced Paris to the immobility of the Liberation.

This strike was the last touch required by the R.P.F. for the success of their first public test, fixed for the municipal elections of October 19. For six months the Rally, with no established position to defend, had been able to maintain the offensive, and make election capital out of every weakness or failure of the government. Now, over a week-end of early frost, foreshadowing yet another winter without the elementary comforts of warm rooms and hot water, the strike of bus and subway workers pointed up the kind of paralysis which might overtake a country not led by a strong executive. The Parisians went on foot to the polling stations, wrapped in garments which had seen much hard wear, and warmed by an inner glow, mistaken by many for honest indignation, which was in reality their irrepressible stimulation at the advent of a novelty in politics. Boredom at that moment was far from them (but Lamartine, as well as Taine, had left a warning: *La France s'ennuie!*), they recorded their votes for the novelty and woke to find next morning that the R.P.F. had swept not only the capital but the municipalities of the whole country. Algiers, Besançon, Bordeaux, Brest, Lille, Marseilles, Metz, Nancy, St. Étienne, Strasbourg had all put their municipal councils in the hands of the R.P.F., which in its great 'tidal wave' had piled up 40 per cent of the total votes cast, against 30 per cent for the Communists and 30 per cent for all other candidates put together. Five months later the Paris municipal council, where the R.P.F. had won 55.9 per cent of the votes, elected the general's brother, Pierre de Gaulle, to be its president.

In the first frenzy of triumph it seemed to the Gaullists that their municipal success implied the overthrow of the legislature. André Malraux prematurely announced that the leader would only accept power if called on to do so by a national referendum, and although his colleagues had the sense to issue a denial (for they knew the danger of evoking such words as *plébiscite* and *Bonapartisme*) de Gaulle himself did not hesitate to throw down an ultimatum: dissolution of the National Assembly, the holding of new parliamentary elections and the revision of the Constitution.

There was discord in the Assembly, for the R.P.F. victory had been won at the expense of the M.R.P., and the purely technical question of the diminished M.R.P.'s right to remain in the coalition led to a vote of confidence from which the Ramadier cabinet emerged in a weakened state. This was the only positive result of the R.P.F.'s *raz de marée*. Otherwise de Gaulle's ultimatum fell upon indifferent ears, for not even the most obscure Deputy intended to give up his seat in the Chamber, with the rewards and prestige thereof, until the five years of his constitutional mandate had elapsed. Not even the bogey of the country's liability to invasion, evoked by de Gaulle in a speech on October 27 (though without details of the expected invaders' nationality), succeeded in persuading the Deputies to vote themselves out of office because a majority of municipal councillors were sporting the Cross of Lorraine.

CHAPTER X

FROM THE MARSHALL PLAN TO N.A.T.O.

FRANCE at the end of 1947 had reached the nadir of her post-war fortunes. The Communists, rising to the challenge of the R.P.F. and supported by the new Kominform network, embarked on a series of conflicts which brought danger and discomfort into every large town in the land. They had made full use of the eighteen months during which they had held some of the key ministries, handed to them by de Gaulle in November 1945, and at the Ministries of Labour, Industrial Production and National Economy had been able to make blueprints of the industrial organizations and zones where strikes could do most harm. Now, in co-operation with the C.G.T., they prepared for mass stoppages of work.

In June General George Marshall, the American Secretary of State, had made a speech at Harvard in which he promised financial aid from the United States to all European countries, excluding Germany but including Russia, if they would take the initiative of drawing up a common programme of economic reconstruction. General Marshall emphasized that his country made this offer from the highest motives, to fight 'hunger, misery, despair and chaos' and that it was not directed against any people or doctrine; but he also recognized that the gesture was not entirely disinterested, since the restoration of the European economy was necessary to the stability and peace of the world.

The announcement of the Marshall Plan (hereafter referred to as E.R.P., for European Recovery Programme) completed the acceptance by the Truman Administration of the world responsibilities of the United States. The Truman Doctrine was the first step, E.R.P. the second, which took the United States back to the European continent, from which it had been over-hasty in withdrawing its seasoned forces in 1945, and where it was now represented only by the organizations and green troops which it maintained in Occupied Germany. Inevitably, E.R.P. meant a realignment of the relationship between the United States and

France. It revealed the dependence of the latter on the resources of the former, which most Frenchmen not actually on the management side of industry had previously been able to ignore. It was possible to overlook a line, in a tabloid newspaper concerned with condensing all the events which might have taken place during a week-long printers' strike, to the effect that France had borrowed a given amount from the Export-Import Bank. It was not so easy to ignore the whole machinery of borrowing when its headquarters, the European Co-operation Administration (E.C.A.), were imposingly visible in the rue St. Florentin, with the Organization for European Economic Co-operation (O.E.E.C.) in a building at the west end of the Quai d'Orsay.

As soon as General Marshall's proposals were made known, France prepared to assume her traditional rôle in Europe by taking the lead in the required appraisal of the countries' needs. President Auriol in a speech on June 17, and Monsieur Bidault before the Assembly on June 20, laid stress upon the vital importance of American aid to their own country, in which the economic deficit could be only too clearly stated. In June 1947 the dollar gap had shrunk only a little since 1946, and in external commerce the debts exceeded the credit by $1,746,000,000. One month earlier France had borrowed $250 millions from the International Reconstruction Bank. By the end of August $220 millions had been spent on raw materials, machine tools and transport charges, and the $30 millions remaining, plus $210 millions borrowed from the Export-Import Bank, represented the whole of France's dollar credits[1] for the last four months of 1947. Restriction of imports as well as of public utilities was envisaged.

Any hopes that Russia might agree to share in American aid, inspired by Molotov's participation in a conference to discuss the Marshall Plan, were dashed. At a four-power conference at the Quai d'Orsay Russia remained faithful to her line at the Moscow Conference, and declined, with the proffered help, the principle that any other Power or Powers might study the balance sheet of the Soviets. The satellites of Russia — Poland, Czechoslovakia, Jugoslavia, Roumania, Hungary, Bulgaria, Albania and Finland — perforce declined help under E.R.P. On July 12, 1947, only fourteen European nations, which included Western Germany, accepted the invitation of France and Britain to discuss their needs round the table of the Quai d'Orsay.

It was this attitude on the part of Russia which caused the French Communist party to speed up and intensify its provocation of strikes and social disorder, and gave to the disturbances of early winter the name of 'the Marshall Plan strikes'.

These broke out furiously in the middle of November. At Marseilles on November 10 a demonstration against increased surface transportation fares led to a march on the City Hall and a brawl in which the new R.P.F. mayor was wounded. After a night of street fighting and looting, a general strike of 80,000 workers paralysed the city. In the Nord 70 per cent of the miners went on strike, the C.G.T. brought out the dockers and automobile workers, and the works committees instituted during de Gaulle's régime proved lively centres of disaffection. In the Paris area schoolteachers and civil servants decided to proclaim a sympathetic strike. Letters lay uncollected in mail boxes, while the contents of many sacks of mail were destroyed. There was a delay of hours in communication by telephone with London, by radio-telegram with the United States. Trains between Paris and the Channel ports were held up by pickets of *cheminots*, and those travellers were fortunate who could complete their journey by private transport. The Paris-Tourcoing express was derailed with many casualties. Garbage lay uncollected until the piles in the courtyards and narrow streets resembled medieval kitchen middens. For the first time in the long history of French industrial unrest the strike committees did not arrange for the safeguard of plant and tools. Maintenance squads deserted, and while pumps were neglected so that water seeped into mine workings and fires died out in furnaces, emergency gangs of soldiers and sailors were drafted to man the gas works and power stations. Communist posters, warning housewives that the work of the amateur gasmen might produce explosions if stoves were used incautiously, were responsible for a series of cold meals eaten in rooms chill with November fog and smoky from the *ligots* and *margotins* carried painfully upstairs from damp cellars.

The Ramadier cabinet could not survive the double attack of Communist strikes and Gaullist demands. On November 20 the premiership passed to Robert Schuman. Monsieur Schuman, a member of the M.R.P. and therefore a Christian Democrat in the new European international tradition, was a target for Communist sneers, for besides having very briefly held an under-secretaryship at Vichy (but he had spent most of the war in the underground), he had actually been born in Luxembourg of Lorraine parents while Lorraine was a German province after 1871, and was constantly issuing denials that he had fought in the German Army in World War I. He was a thin, bald man with a sceptical expression, an inquiring nose and a downward smile: well fitted, by his deprecating appearance and supple manner, to represent the political 'Third Force' now in process of evolution between Gaullism and Communism.

The Communists led an attack on the Schuman ministry which lasted through four days and five nights of Assembly debate, using every known weapon of filibustering, gerrymandering, irrelevant points of order and vulgar abuse to wear down the new premier's proposals for increased family and tax-free cost-of-living allowances to satisfy the needs of the strikers and increased policing to restrain their demonstrations. Schuman, by weathering this storm and passing his measures by 413 to 183, proved that he could fight the Communists on their own ground without retreating. The non-Communist trade unions plucked up heart and came out on the government side. The *Force Ouvrière*, organized by Léon Jouhaux, accounted for one million trade unionists who were ready to resume work. The *Confédération Française de Travailleurs Chrétiens* (C.F.T.C.) accounted for another million. Finally, support began to ebb away from the mighty C.G.T. as women began to urge the strikers back to work and wages, and conferences between the government and the employers' and workers' organizations, fixing a new minimum wage for a three months period, brought the strikes to an end* on December 10.

The government, besides its 80,000 special constables and its reorganized shock troops, the *Compagnies Républicaines de Sécurité*, had an imponderable strike-breaking weapon at its command. This was the Emergency Aid which had been voted by Congress following a request tabled by Secretary Marshall at the time (November 10) when the social unrest in France became aggra-

---

* After much damage had been done to French production, e.g. coal production for October 4,625,000 tons, November 2,550,500 tons.

vated. Pared down during the passage of the bill through Congress, interim aid to France was fixed at $280 millions of merchandise against a counterpart payment in francs into a special fund for redemption of the debt. The ratification of this agreement by Georges Bidault and Ambassador Caffery on January 2, 1948, marked the start of a revivifying blood transfusion into the desiccated veins of the French economy.

The widespread strikes had not officially ended when a day of national mourning plunged the capital into deeper gloom.

For General Leclerc 1947 had been a year of anti-climax. As commander of the French Expeditionary Corps in Indo-China he had found the complexities of Asian politics and the nature of the pacification fighting in the Delta to be very different from the action which had carried him from Alençon to Berchtesgaden, and when, after the Viet Minh attack of December 1946, he was offered the High Commissionership in place of Thierry d'Argenlieu, he hesitated. He took the road to Colombey-les-Deux-Églises, which the *Compagnons* were beginning to know by heart, to ask for guidance from General de Gaulle. There he was roundly told that he knew nothing at all about politics and if he accepted would be merely a pawn in the hands of *les gouvernants*,[2] to whose address de Gaulle was then preparing his Bruneval speech; so that in the event Thierry d'Argenlieu, whose Indo-Chinese policy had ended in disaster, was replaced by Monsieur Émile Bollaert instead of by General Leclerc.

There may have been some jealousy in the case: it was certainly obvious later in the year, when the two generals appeared side by side on the third anniversary of the liberation of Alençon. De Gaulle, who made a regulation R.P.F. campaign speech, was well received by a crowd of 20,000. But it was Leclerc's day, for the people of Alençon thought more of the general who had certainly freed them from the Germans than of the leader who might possibly save them from Maurice Thorez, and the loudest cheering was for the fighting Leclerc. De Gaulle showed his resentment publicly[3] and only Leclerc's determined goodwill saved the situation.

Instead of going to Indo-China as High Commissioner Leclerc was appointed Inspector-General of land, sea and air forces in North Africa. There the aircraft in which he was flying on a tour of duty crashed on November 28, and Philippe Leclerc met death in the desert where other crusading de Hautecloques before him had fought for the honour of France. On December 8 his coffin was carried in procession through the streets of Paris and consecrated to the Invalides, near the graves of Turenne and of Foch.

The holiday season could scarcely be gay, and there was little temptation to *réveillonner* when the traditional delicacies, from Christmas Eve *boudin* to Epiphany *galette*, could only be found at ransom prices; although housewives had a chance to work off their frustrations on the garbage collectors who, as soon as their strike was over, boldly appeared at service entries with requests for Christmas tips. Only the *midinettes* and saleswomen of Christian Dior, pouring champagne for a crowd which filled the first platform of the Eiffel Tower, were in gay enough spirits to enjoy the biggest publicity party of the season, organized by the house which had given employment to the unheard-of number of 800 workers. After all, they were associated with almost the only French success of the winter; the creation of a style of dress employing increased fabric yardage and graciously feminizing its wearers, which had become known throughout the world as the New Look.

★

The Economic Co-operation Act (E.C.A.), passed by Congress on April 3, 1948, was followed by an agreement with France providing goods in kind, or dollar credits for the purchase of goods in the United States, against which grants the value in francs was to be deposited by French importers in a Counterpart Fund. Of the francs in this fund, over 75 per cent were released by the United States Government in 1948 towards the financing of the Monnet Plan. In return, France had to agree to convertibility for American private investments, and to the rule applicable to all countries receiving aid under E.R.P. that half the goods received should be transported to Europe in American vessels. In the first two years of E.R.P. this Counterpart Fund reached 584,000 million francs, reallocated to twelve different sectors of French and North African economy.

The dollar purchases represented by the counterpart funds were nearly all of consumer goods at the start of E.R.P., and by June

1948 the economic situation of France showed a marked improvement. Agricultural equipment, nitrogenous fertilizers, wheat and edible fats improved food supplies and general husbandry, while coal and liquid fuel, non-ferrous metals and rubber were imported to supply some of the basic needs for increased production. The Communists, still describing the Marshall Plan as 'a Western trap', lost face when confronted with evidence of returning prosperity.

Many French members of non-Communist parties had adopted a grudging and suspicious attitude towards E.R.P., under which France was allotted a total sum of $626 millions between April 1 and September 30, 1948, plus $478 millions' worth of procurement authorizations for purchases in the dollar areas. They declared themselves unimpressed by the amounts involved, for they had an ingrained belief that it was America's duty to aid France in 1948 after having done nothing to help her in 1940.

For other reasons American aid to France was taken for granted by a large section of the people. The first was the jealous awareness that the American homeland had emerged unscathed from a war which had laid France in ruins. There, undevastated fields produced an abundance which gave superior energy to the American worker who, stuffed with steak, homogenized milk and enriched bread, could easily produce more than an undernourished Frenchman: therefore let him share his abundance with France without expecting very effusive thanks. The second was that every French person who had ever been in the vicinity of a U.S. Army camp or supply depot during the war had seen the trash-cans piled with half-loaves, rejected vegetables, half-sucked oranges, half-worn garments and all the stuff discarded by the most pampered army in the world, and had come to the conclusion that the Americans, besides being unbelievably wasteful, were all egregiously rich. Envy, a sin seldom checked under the Third Republic, had returned to choke the generous impulses of the Liberation, and it was now mingled with French resentment at becoming a 'Have-Not' nation looking to a 'Have' for aid.

Frenchmen who reasoned on a higher plane were not immune from fears that the vitally important relief might carry with it some hampering conditions. Already in the debates on Interim Aid in the American Congress Robert Lovett, acting Under-

Secretary of State, had proposed that aid to France and Italy should be suspended if the Communists came to power in these countries, a discriminatory attitude which, though opposed by Senator Vandenberg, revealed the effect which the refusal of Russia to accept American aid might have on the division of the world into two camps. Other conditions were adumbrated by Paul G. Hoffman and Averill Harriman in their declarations that 'the Americans would only aid a united Europe'; and by the brothers Dulles: John Foster threatening that 'if Europe did not succeed in uniting, the U.S. might return to isolationism', and Allen stating that 'the success of [American] aid to Europe depends on the re-establishment of the economic life of Germany'.[4] This was in line with the dictum of General Marshall himself that the restoration of Europe presupposed the restoration of Germany.

The French Government therefore understood that in accepting aid under E.R.P. they were morally bound to fight Communism, although the Communist Party was not outlawed in France; to work towards some form of European union and to reverse their entire policy regarding Germany. For two years, ever since the Potsdam Conference to which France had not been invited, Georges Bidault had been advancing at every international meeting a French viewpoint which was consistently overridden by the Western Allies. There had been no ambiguity in French policy between 1945 and 1947:[5] a confederation of German states, an internationalized Ruhr and a permanently occupied Rhineland had been, with a Saar attached to the French economy, the objectives for which France had striven in vain. Now another period of two years was about to begin in which French policy was rather negative than positive, suspended between the dream of punishing Germany and the dream of a united Europe with Germany reintegrated at its core.

This is not to say that French policy was static, although the great daring sweeps of the Coal and Steel Plan and the European Defence Community were still maturing in the brains of Jean Monnet and Robert Schuman. It was redeemed from static opposition by the actions of the Russians on the one hand, and the determination of France to resume the leadership of Europe on the other. Through 1947, the French reactions to British and American policy in Germany had consisted of a series of negatives, deploring the creation of a Bizonal Economic Council of fifty-four German members empowered to issue general directives on reconstruction; the proposed adoption of the Deutschemark as currency; the raising of permitted levels of German production and the indication that (without prior consultation with France) the mining and steel industries would eventually return to German, even to ex-Nazi, ownership. On October 11, 1947, the British and American Occupation authorities published a new list of 713 German factories and works to be dismantled: this was less than half the original number (1600) and was part of the August plan for increased German production. On January 24, 1948, all this came to a head with the French Government's *aide-mémoire* to the Powers, warning them that Bizonia meant the beginning of a powerful centralized government in Germany.[6] But within three months the Russian blockade of Berlin had begun, and with it any pretence at co-operation between Russia and the Western powers in Germany came to an end. General Lucius D. Clay announced to his countrymen in the United States:

If we withdraw, our position in Europe is threatened. If America does not understand this now, does not know that the issue is cast, then it never will, and Communism will run rampant.[7]

The French Government understood the position equally well. In the long months of crisis, during which the Russian blockade was challenged and defeated by the freighting of supplies and passengers from the West into Berlin by air, they tacitly withdrew their objections to the system of unification and prepared for a new orientation of policy.

The Berlin blockade, and the absorption by Russia of the East zone of Germany into the ranks of her satellites, marked the real declaration of the 'cold war' threatening for some time, and the Powers of the West began to close their ranks in self-defence. There already existed the nucleus of a *rapprochement* between them, and on more grounds than one. During the war the governments-in-exile of Belgium, the Netherlands and Luxembourg had exchanged views in London on a future money convention and customs union, and these proposals, ratified on November 29, 1947, were the basis of the 'Benelux' organization. The Treaty of Dunkirk had brought Britain back into an alliance with France, and on January 21, 1948, the two Powers proposed to meet the Benelux group for the discussion of a political pact on collective self-defence. The Foreign Ministers of the five countries met in Paris without delay, and on March 15 the Treaty of Brussels, valid for fifty years, was signed by Britain, France, Belgium, the Netherlands and Luxembourg two days after the opening of the second Paris Conference between the sixteen E.R.P. beneficiary nations, which on this occasion decided to add West Germany to their number, and sixteen days before the beginning of the Russian blockade of Berlin.

With the signing of the Brussels Treaty, which created Western Union, France found herself deeply committed to a European policy in which the reintegration of Germany had to be taken for granted. The Russians, when they blockaded Berlin and left the Allied Control Commission, had completed the process begun at the Moscow Conference one year before and declared a 'cold war' upon the free nations of the Western world. Western Union was the first answer to the challenge, and from the modest beginning of five countries, one of them (Luxembourg) having a population of only 300,000 and an area of 999 square miles, great developments were to come.

The first of these belonged to the military sphere. One month after the treaty was signed discussions had been opened on the creation of a permanent defence organization, and by October 1948 this had taken shape at Fontainebleau, rousing the charming French town from the calm in which, with but a few interruptions, it had basked since Napoleon, on his way to exile, had taken leave of his troops in the Cour des Adieux. The headquarters of Western Union, set up in the nearby Château de Fougères, now resounded to the tread of France's dynamic de Lattre de Tassigny, now Inspector-General of the French Army. De Lattre became commander-in-chief of the ground forces of Western Union, Vice-Admiral Robert Jaujard of the French Navy was appointed flag officer of Western Europe with Air-Marshal Sir James Robb of the R.A.F. in command of the air forces, and Field-Marshal Viscount Montgomery became the permanent military chairman of a defence organization which was otherwise represented only by the small staff of 120 officers and 200 n.c.o.s from the five member nations who started work in November on the blueprints for '*Uniforce*'. It was well for Europe that the temperature of the 'war' remained cold, for the forces represented by Western Union were quite inadequate to cope with a Russian attack, if this had followed the Berlin blockade; but the names of Montgomery of Alamein and de Lattre, hero of the Rhine and Danube, were in themselves warlike enough to alarm the body of French opinion shaping up to what was to be called neutralism. It was in 1948 that Garry Davis, the son of a wealthy American bandleader and himself an ex-soldier of World War II, started a campaign for world citizenship which, in spite of its well-publicized one-man demonstrations (Citizen Davis pitched a little camp at the gates of a United Nations meeting in Paris, from which he gladly gave interviews and argued his rights with the police), attracted a great many of the more intellectual elements of the Left-wing Resistance, eager to mark their refusal to 'be led to the great slaughter now being organized'. In December Garry Davis attracted a crowd of 3000 to a meeting in the Salle Pleyel presided over by the vacant chair of Albert Einstein (who wired his approval) and sponsored by Vercors, the author of *Le Silence de la Mer* (*in absentia*), the writer Albert Camus and Claude Bourdet of the *Combat* underground and publication.[8] These men were avowedly pacifist in their dread of the ultimate functions of Western Union; but criticism of different kinds, tending to the same stultifying ends, was also heard from Charles de Gaulle and the Communist party.

At the invitation of Great Britain, the five ambassadors of the Western Union countries met in London on March 28, 1949, and were joined by the ambassadors of Denmark, Eire, Italy, Norway and Sweden. The result was the Statute of the Council of Europe, a document of forty-two articles which declared the desire of the signatory nations to 'safeguard and promote the ideals and principles which are their common heritage'. The Council was to have a Committee, composed of the Foreign Ministers, and a Consultative Assembly, which was to meet first at Strasbourg in August, with membership proportionate to the population of each country. This gave France eighteen seats in the Assembly, the delegates voting as individuals and not *en bloc*, and, it was hoped, sufficient influence to defeat Mr. Churchill's proposal—discreetly supported by the American Secretary of State,

Dean Acheson — to admit Germany to immediate membership. But the machinery of rehabilitating Germany had turned too rapidly to be reversed by French misgivings. On May 23, less than three weeks after the Statute was signed, the Federal Republic of West Germany was proclaimed in Bonn, the provisional capital, with a constitution and a two-chamber parliament of its own, a president, Theodore Heuss, and a chancellor, Konrad Adenauer. Soon afterwards the Allied High Commission announced an Occupation Statute forbidding Germany to rearm and revive totalitarianism, but curtailing the dismantling of war potential, and on July 19 West Germany became an associate member of the Council of Europe. From that time forward West Germany had to be taken into consideration as a potential ally in war hot or cold, and this, thanks to Russian aggression, meant a complete reversal of the situation in the short two years which had passed since Britain and France signed the Treaty of Dunkirk as an instrument of mutual defence against Germany.

Finally, from the wings, a formidable and much-courted prima donna joined the anxious little group on the European stage. America at last added to her rôle of public benefactor and oracle that of an active participant in the scenes from which she had fatally withdrawn after her intervention in World War I. Her European Co-operation Administration had met with its deserved success; during the period from 1947 to 1949 all the countries receiving help under E.R.P. had increased their production by large percentages* in all branches. Now the desired participation of the United States in the defence of Europe, always envisaged at Fontainebleau as indispensable, took the form of a North Atlantic Treaty Alliance (N.A.T.O.) signed on April 4, 1949, and holding its first Council meeting at Washington on September 17. The member nations were the five which had formed Western Union under the Brussels Treaty, with the addition of the United States and Canada, Denmark, Norway, Iceland, Italy and Portugal. Thus aligned for the defence of the West beside her Allies of the Liberation, France was confirmed in her desired position as the leading nation of Continental Europe.

* Increases: Coal 18 per cent, Electric power 16 per cent, Steel 56 per cent, Mechanized industries 30 per cent, Chemical industries 25 per cent, Textiles 35-40 per cent, Cereals 37 per cent, Potatoes 24 per cent, Sugar 46 per cent, Dairy produce 30 per cent.

CHAPTER XI

CHURCH AND STATE

D URING the radiant Whitsuntide week-end of 1948, when all the strikes were over and France was on the verge of receiving aid under E.R.P., the visit of Princess Elizabeth and her husband, the Duke of Edinburgh, aroused more than common interest in Paris. The recent marriage of the royal couple and the rumours of an expected heir gave a romantic flavour to a visit not without its political significance for the inheritors of the Entente Cordiale, but beyond this Paris was flattered and gratified at being once again the scene of royal progresses by road and river, and turned out with all its own verve to scream, a little prematurely, '*Vive la reine!*' as the young lady made the very short journey from the British Embassy to the Élysée, to dine in state with President Auriol.

It seemed like old times come back again, but with a younger generation rising out of the ruins of the past; and in the same way a younger generation of French people began that Whitsuntide to enjoy the beauty and grace of a land where life had been for too long a mere struggle for existence. Devotees of *le camping* set off on their *vélos* with an excess of equipment on their backs, for a canoeing weekend on the Seine at Samois or exploration of the surrounding belt of forests; more automobiles were seen at the star-shaped Gates of Paris. Deauville, liberated by Belgian and American troops in 1944, had reopened as a pleasure resort in 1946, and once again welcomed café and theatre society to its luxurious settings; but even in the shattered towns of Normandy, along the Voie de la Libération running inland from Avranches, it was possible to find fair accommodation and superlative food.

At Mortain, devastated in August 1944 during its capture by VII U.S. Corps, its recapture by 47 Panzer Corps and its ultimate liberation, the Grand Hôtel de la Poste had re-opened in an army-barracks-type hut, with a Whitsun menu of sorrel soup *à la crème*, veal *à la crème*, chicken *en cocotte à la crème*, Camembert cheese and chocolate *mousse à la crème Chantilly*. On the other side of Paris, at Compiègne — the scene of brutal imprisonments and executions during the Occupation — the members of the Société du Sport de Compiègne played tennis, drank tea and leafed through out-of-date copies of the *Illustrated London News* in the mild imitation of English customs practised there since the Entente Cordiale. All over the land France forgot poverty and demagoguery and the shadow of the cold war for a hard-won moment of peace and relative plenty, which oddly enough seemed to have an irritant effect on some of the foreign visitors who shared it with the French.

In 1948 genuine tourists had begun to reappear, although British visitors were fewer than before, due to the meagre travel allowance of £25 then permitted by the Socialist government, and lacked the style of the traditional *milord anglais*. The Americans were arriving in appreciable numbers, thanks to superior publicity by the Commissariat Général au Tourisme and the transportation companies, though most visitors from the United States were hag-ridden by fears of the sanitary conditions in a country they had been conditioned to regard as a mixture of graveyard and pest-house. They had been inoculated against all possible maladies and carried large supplies of potions and pills. As a rule the medicines most in demand by tourists were remedies for indigestion.

The British, whose shrunken stomachs were quite unable to cope with menus of the Mortain kind, suffered not only from 'tourist trouble' but from jealousy. In their austere lives nothing had been served *à la crème* for eight years (instead there had been an equit-able distribution of milk) and therefore, by force of puritan logic, to enjoy cream was wrong. The Americans were not interested in *la grande cuisine*, and greatly preferred their own bland dishes, rapidly prepared and served, to the subtly seasoned, patiently cooked and ceremoniously offered French fare. They thought the menus too copious and the French too spendthrift on food for a nation receiving the bounty of E.R.P.

It was unfortunate for France that this impression of plenty, essentially superficial, should be the first and most frequent to be recorded by the tourists of 1948, as by the liberators of 1944 and the refugees of 1940. It was true that the French paid more for food than for rent and clothing and regarded good cooking as an art of life; but the disproportionate interest in eating was due to the post-war uncertainties which turned a good dinner into an investment — something which could never be devalued, requisitioned or stolen.

It was even more unfortunate that during this summer of increased contact with foreigners unconnected with official or military circles — the first of such contacts for nine years — France should have been in the throes of a political crisis of the kind fated to earn her a dismal reputation for instability.

Faced with the opposition of the Communists and of an R.P.F. parliamentary intergroup of 72 members — for the R.P.F., having no elected Deputies, was boring into all parties whose members could be persuaded that it was ethical to be elected on one ticket and later support the non-party Rally — Robert Schuman had begun the Assembly year on a line of strong government. The Finance Minister, René Mayer, was responsible for a supertax or forced loan, the withdrawal from circulation of 5000 franc notes and the repatriation of foreign holdings, and a new devaluation of the franc. The Minister of the Interior, Jules Moch, had retaliated against the social conflicts of the winter by creating eight super-Prefects, or *Inspecteurs-Généraux de l'Administration en Mission Extraordinaire* (I.G.A.M.E.)[1] with a mandate to reorganize the security forces round the eight French towns where the army had established a command headquarters. The official reason was the need to reinforce the *corps préfectoral*, some of whom had found themselves at a disadvantage during the Communist troubles, but unofficially I.G.A.M.E., like the C.R.S. shock troops, proved useful to the minister during that spring's clashes between Gaullists and Communists. These became more frequent as the Italian legislative elections drew near: André Malraux was convinced that the Communists would win in Italy and that it would then be the sacred duty of the R.P.F. to save France from the Red horde which would presently burst across the Alps: there were a few rehearsals of the work of salvation in places like Grenoble. But the Italians had listened attentively to the warnings of such men as Robert Lovett and John Foster Dulles. They elected the Christian Democrats and kept their place in E.R.P., and in France the Communist-Gaullist brawls died down to mere fisticuffs between street sellers of *L'Étincelle Ouvrière* and *L'Humanité*.

The financial measures and the restoration of order were well

enough received in the country, but in 1948 the French Government was in the same position as an American administration in
the Congressional election year which comes midway in a presidential term. The cantonal elections and those for the Council
of the Republic were due in October, and a vigorous Gaullist
campaign made it possible that the R.P.F. would repeat its
municipal successes of 1947. The R.P.F. intergroup, with growing
assurance, began to put pressure on the government. But the
split came, during the early summer, within the Third Force
itself.

Once again, as in January 1946, the question of military credits
divided the cabinet and brought the Socialists out against the
M.R.P. to which the premier belonged, and this was the ostensible
reason for Robert Schuman's fall from power on July 19. But
the Third Force was split by something far more permanent in
French politics than a credits vote,[2] or than the Socialist opposition,
which had been strenuous, to the reorganization of nationalized
industries, the reduction of administrative personnel, and other
elements of the Mayer Plan. This was the quarrel between Church
and State, which had broken out again in the month of May, in its
perennial form of subsidies to the Catholic schools.

Three years had passed since the Vichy subsidies had been
ended on a Communist motion, and the M.R.P., although it had
reached its apex and begun its decline since those days, felt itself
strong enough to take its stand, particularly in Alsace-Lorraine,
on the *loi Falloux* of 1850, which permitted any qualified person to
open a school and guaranteed that public education should have a
religious content. Of the five million children receiving primary
education in France,[3] 18 per cent were enrolled in private
schools (*les écoles libres*) which apart from a few crammers' establishments and boarding-schools for the backward invariably meant
Catholic schools, and although the largest percentage of such
schools were to be found in the West and the Massif Central there
were also a good many in the mining areas of the Nord and the
Pas-de-Calais. The nationalization of coal mines carried with it
the transfer of such schools to the State, ratified by an Assembly
vote (297 to 267) on May 15, 1948.

One week later the M.R.P. Minister of Health and Population,
Germaine Poinso-Chapuis, brought in a bill for the grant of sub-

sidies to families 'having difficulty in educating their children'. For the Communists, this was the restoration of subsidies to Catholicism in an oblique form, and although their motion for annulment was defeated by 405 to 192, they succeeded in persuading the Socialists and the whole anti-clerical faction (whose members might be discovered in any party, always excepting the M.R.P.) that Monsieur Schuman and his adherents were tampering with the glorious principle of French secularity. Every man in the country who for his own reasons of personal conviction or atavism or frustration was a 'priest-eater' could be counted on to rally to the side of the Left on such a challenge. It was the Poinso-Chapuis decree of May, far more than the military credits vote of July, which caused the fall of the Schuman cabinet.

Clearly there were undercurrents in French political thinking which cut across party barriers and kept alive theories and prejudices which went back to the Revolution and even to the Wars of Religion.

There were in France, and had been ever since 1789, two spiritual families almost equal in number: the Catholics and the unbelievers. Their conflict was the secret drama enacted behind the scenes of the great secular decisions and disturbances, and it was also a tragic drama, because it took place in a country where nonconformity had never found a foothold, so that the bitterness of religious schism was never dissipated through a number of minor sects. The Protestants, though great in character, were few in number — about 800,000 in the whole of France — and they were established at some distance from the *bassin Parisien*.[4] Strasbourg had the largest Protestant community in France (50,000) and was the centre of a Protestant church system running through Alsace, the Bas-Rhin and Montbéliard; otherwise the congregations were clustered in the Cévennes, the Vivarais, Dauphiné — 'the most ungrateful soil of France'[5] — and the members were simple pastoral people, whose offspring, if they migrated to the towns, were chiefly anxious to become teachers. Thankful for the immunity from persecution granted them by the Édit de Tolérance of 1787, the Protestants as a community had nursed few political ambitions. In World War II they made excellent *maquisards*, and their most distinguished pastor, Marc Boegner, the minister of the parish of Passy, had made his wartime headquarters at Nîmes a centre for helping Jews and other persecuted citizens, in the same way as had Monseigneur Feltin, Archbishop of Bordeaux, who became Archbishop of Paris in 1949. But when all was said and done the Protestants were outsiders in the great religious and anti-religious controversy which was still smouldering in France. The gulf lay, not between Catholic and Protestant as in Scotland and Northern Ireland, but between Catholic and unbeliever.

There were, however, many shades of unbelief, ranging from the mild agnosticism of the *bourgeois* who went to church only when the daughters of his business friends were married, to the paganism of the slums round the *fortifications* of Paris, where *le respect humain* obliged free-thinking working men to *boulotter du curé*, as it had done ever since the Paris mob, singing the *Carmagnole*, had enthroned the Goddess of Reason in an unfinished neo-classical building later known as the Church of the Madeleine. The Liberation, for the Resistance, had come in on a wave of anti-religious feeling due to the reaction against Pétain, a devout Catholic, and the ties between Vichy and leading members of the hierarchy. Apart from the conventional service of thanksgiving in Notre Dame and the Te Deums sung for Charles de Gaulle at Lille and Strasbourg there were no religious celebrations on the grand scale; thereafter the place allotted to organized religion was small. Children were sent to confession and to recite their Catechism until their first Communion, at which point their religious life ended in an agreeable flurry of white-fringed brassards or long white veils, a copious family luncheon and the distribution of small pious pictures among the first-Communicant's friends. A christening or a burial by the rites of the Church took place to the tune of complaints about the fees; a wedding might bring out a fashionable crowd which gossiped in church, appraised the bridal dresses and paid little attention to the gabbled Latin of the Mass, but must certainly be registered beforehand at the *mairie*, after a busy *maire-adjoint* in a shabby *tricolore* sash had recited Articles 211 to 217 of the Code Napoléon. For most of the children of the Eldest Daughter of the Church, the Church offices seemed to represent a mere convenience or form of insurance against fatality. Nothing could have been more superficial than their occasional religious observances; no *monuments* were more obvious tourist attractions than the great churches of Paris, of Chartres, or of Bourges.

But beneath that tarnished surface, a variety of religious experience lay concealed. The Society of Jesus, the Dominicans, the Carmelites were still active in the anti-clerical land. The little chapel of Notre Dame Consolatrix Afflictorum in St. Germain des Prés was never empty of working women telling their beads by candle-light; the great *trompe l'œil* Nativity in St. Roch received the genuflections of many Christians every day. Beneath the mask of indifference, violent feelings lay concealed; nearly all political manœuvres were examined in the light of religious belief or anti-clerical prejudice. A great man might be defeated for a great office if he leaned too far to the one side or the other: Georges Clemenceau might have won the Presidency if he had accepted the divinity of Christ and so gained the support of the Right's *bloc national*; Georges Bidault's practising Catholicism might keep him for ever in the position of a visitor at the Élysée.

The most interesting development in the Church had taken place during the Occupation. Inspired by Abbé Henri Godin,[6] a leader of the *Jeunesse Ouvrière Chrétienne*, and sponsored by Cardinal Suhard, the *Mission de Paris* had been instituted to carry the message of the Church to the proletarian masses living on the fringe of the capital, who in the words of Fr. Loew, one of the *missionaires*, were little better than 'pagans with Christian superstitions'. The priests enrolled for this task — fifteen in number at the beginning — were trained at the Lisieux seminary, and then went to live as workers among the workers, some at the Renault plant, others in the slums of the 20th *arrondissement*, plying some trade like that of shoemaker, but prepared to baptize, to marry, and to serve Mass at the little portable altar they carried with them. The worker-priests made some converts among Communist sympathizers not completely indoctrinated with the idea that religion is the opium of the people: the same idea of universality which attracted such individuals to a world movement of so-called comradeship also attracted them to the idea of a Church Universal; and others, in their turn, felt easier in approaching a priest who wore no cassock, nor lived apart from the world in his presbytery, but worked at the factory bench with the people of the same parish and when the whistles blew returned to the same narrow room, the same mess of *haricots blancs* and *pinard* as formed their evening meal. The movement spread: from the *Mission de Paris* it became the *Mission de France*; Fr. Loew himself went to Marseilles and worked as a docker, and in other cities the worker-priests continued a mission no less valuable than those of St. Francis Xavier and St. Vincent de Paul in other centuries. There were, however, premonitory rumblings from the Vatican, where opponents of the idea dreaded the influence of Communism in the worker-priests.

The Catholic hierarchy in France was fighting on two fronts; first against apathy and militant anti-clericalism at home, which could only be fought by such small movements as the *Mission de France* and a similar mission to unfortunate women, led by the *Travailleuses de l'Immaculée* — young women who had taken the vows of religion but went about their work of healing in ordinary clothes. Secondly, they were engaged, and had been engaged for five hundred years, in preserving the liberties of the Gallican Church against the pretensions of the Holy See.

The Church in France had always maintained a greater independence of the Pope than the Church in Spain, Italy or Germany. National rights and distinctions, emphasized by the liberation from English authority after the Hundred Years War, had developed an independent spirit which found expression at the great Council of Constance, at Bourges in 1438, and by the actions of the Valois kings who, while strictly orthodox and eager to suppress heresy in the form of Huguenotism, were as determined as Henry VIII of England to be free of the suzerainty of the Pope. In the reign of Louis XIV an assembly of clergy, led by Bossuet, met at St. Germain[7] and resolved, *inter alia*

That a general council is superior to the Pope.
That the power of the Pope is subject to the regulations and canons of councils, and he cannot decide anything contrary to the rules and constitutions of the Gallican Church.

From this declaration of constitutional rights it was an easy step to one of the most important decisions of the Revolution: the reaffirming of the existence of a Gallican Church, not subject to the disciplines of the Catholic Church, by the Civil Constitution of the Clergy of 1790. The refusal of a great majority of beneficed ecclesiastics to take the required oath to observe this constitution caused a schism within the Church in France which was only partly healed by the Concordat signed between Pope Pius VII and Bonaparte, then First Consul, in 1801, which gave the latter the right to nominate all bishops and the Pope to invest them. The Concordat, while never satisfactory, endured after a fashion until challenged by the dogma of papal infallibility in 1870; and under the Third Republic the Law of Separation of 1905 had liquidated the State Church as a temporal power in France, following on the dissolution of the religious orders.

However briefly recorded, this history of nationalism within the Church and republican anti-clericalism without illustrates the schismatic tendencies of the French as a people: tendencies which some commentators on the France of the Liberation have erred in believing to be exclusively secular in nature, and to date only from the period of the French Revolution. To such short-sighted viewers the high Communist vote in Liberated France was proof of the 'undigested Revolution', although Marx and Lenin had both lived since 1789, and it was their theories, not those of Robespierre, which influenced the residents of Kremlin-Bicêtre and the dismal area which surrounds the renamed *métro* station of Stalingrad.

Champions of the 'undigested Revolution' theory* were no doubt misled by the successful struggle of the Assembly in 1946 against the constitution of a strong Executive, the repetition of a similar struggle waged in 1791, when the individual whose power was dreaded, like that of de Gaulle later, was the ineffectual Louis XVI. But the religious conflict went back farther and did more to undermine the solidarity of the national life than any inadequacy of secular politics. Also, and much more than the competition of the R.P.F., it undermined the power of the Christian Democrats.

The *crise* of July 1948, which followed the defeat of Robert

* Examples of American thinking on this point:
'For the past 160 years, France has been trying to digest the French Revolution . . .' *Time*, April 2, 1951.
'To understand the French crisis of today [we must go back to] that great revolution which is still unfinished.' *World*, February 1, 1954.
'France Needs a New Revolution' — title of article in *Collier's*, January 22, 1954, containing this outline of the requirements: 'No bloodshed, no reliance on a single strong man, *nothing the Communists can seize upon and use*' (author's italics).

Schuman, lasted for two months less one week. For five days there was no premier; then André Marie, a pre-war Deputy suffering from the effects of imprisonment at Buchenwald, received the Assembly's vote of investiture. It was the first time that a Radical had been considered for the premiership since the Liberation, showing that the Third Republic's powerful party was coming out of eclipse at the same time as the Right was regaining some of its influence. MM. Daladier and Reynaud had both been back in the Assembly since 1946, contrary to the expectations of simple British people who had read the tirades written to their address in London; M. Daladier as *l'homme de Munich* had had to run the gauntlet of some well-aimed overripe tomatoes at his first return to the hustings, and a protested validation at his reappearance in the Assembly; but the 'Bull of the Vaucluse' was now a fixture on the fight-card of his old arena. As for the energetic Paul Reynaud, he had reached cabinet rank again, and took the Finance Ministry under André Marie. It was he who brought the short-lived cabinet to grief,[8] for, having got the Assembly's assent to the passing of decree-laws giving the government a free hand on financial measures, he refused to compromise on the proposed wage increase which Socialists and M.R.P. wanted to see raised above 10 per cent. His intransigence broke up the coalition after Marie had been in office for little over a month.

President Auriol began his tour of the *pressentis*, or party leaders being sounded out on their capacity to form a government; Paul Ramadier failed once and Robert Schuman twice* before another Radical, Dr. Henri Queuille, succeeded in forming a stable ministry on September 11. This troubled interlude in the government of France, lasting from mid-July to mid-September, was the longest series of *crises* since the Liberation and caused some unfavourable comment both inside and outside France. Some believed that the instability of successive cabinets could be traced to over-emphasis of the vote of confidence required for the investiture of a premier, who instead of taking office on a simple majority had to bargain with the smaller groups to scrape together the 311 votes then required for an absolute majority. For those who looked at the matter in an ethical light, the weakness lay in an

* Ramadier failed to *form* a cabinet, Schuman to *establish* his; so technically there were two Schuman ministries at this time, one lasting from August 31 to September 3, the other from September 7 to 10.

element of the French character not peculiar to Deputies; a blend of self-interest and indiscipline which meant, in the Assembly, that every man was serving his own ends first, those of his party second, and — no matter how often *la Patrie* was invoked from the tribune — those of the country third. Party discipline as practised by the Whip system in the House of Commons could never be completely obtained in France, where a splinter group could cause the downfall of a cabinet. This was the essence of *la combinaison*, and the *combinaison*, not the *Système D*, was the really base moral element in French public life.

The literature on 'the fall of France' had contained many references to the D System, which stood for *débrouillez-vous* (get disentangled; muddle through; use your contacts), the motto of the old army in Algeria. In the literature it was usually described as the root of French corruption, but this was an overstatement: a similar system in England was elegantly known as 'having friends at court', in America more succinctly as 'graft'. Every Frenchman, in politics or not, was by instinct a *débrouillard*; and even a bedridden old lady was said to *se débrouiller* when she arranged with a neighbour's child to fetch a litre of milk for her cats.

La combinaison was another matter. It went all the way down, from the government through the civil service, into legitimate trade and the black market and into private life. It was responsible for the paradox of the most complete individualists in the world for ever seeking to form *combines* with other individualists and believing that no independent action could succeed unless supported by *des bons tuyaux* and *des coupe-files sérieuses*. It meant that, since every *combinard* kept a strict mental tally of the help he gave to others and expected exactly the same value in return, *la combinaison* was fatal to altruism and public spirit.

The power of *la combinaison* was illustrated by the carrousel nature of French cabinet reshuffles, which again and again brought the same men back to office (though not always to the same office) and restored the Premier Schuman of July as the Foreign Minister Schuman of September, with six out of fourteen ministries and seven out of eight secretaryships of State filled under Queuille by men selected by Schuman. France had the right to say of these and succeeding governments that *plus ça change plus c'est la même chose.*

One constant factor of political life was the Purge, which went on through 1948, 1949 and 1950, until the Courts of Justice, trying cases of general collaboration, had sentenced 7000 persons to death (5000 *in absentia*), 3000 to life imprisonment and 37,000 to prison terms of varying length.[9] The civic courts had imposed 48,000 sentences of *dégradation nationale*, 25,000 of which were still in force. Only in 1949 had the High Court finished its work and declared itself at an end, having tried 58 cases and imposed 18 death sentences, most of which had been commuted to life imprisonment. Marshal Pétain still lived in his lonely prison on the Île d'Yeu. One prison for collaborators, Poissy, had been emptied and closed, but Drancy and Fresnes still held their wretched tenants fast, and the great sounding-board of Paris echoed rumours of cases still untried, dossiers lost and charges long forgotten. It was a state of affairs which angered those who argued that since the Assembly contained men who had had to be cleared of their Vichy loyalties by the *Jury d' Honneur* — since Roland de Margerie, Vichy Ambassador to Tokyo, was back at the Quai d'Orsay and André François-Poncet, once a Vichy national counsellor, was French High Commissioner in Germany — there ought to be an amnesty for petty offenders still in jail.

The rising generation saw no objections. In the short period of relative prosperity between the start of E.R.P. and the Korean War, there were many signs that the nation was weary of horrors and eager to forget suffering on its rare occasions for pleasure. Picnickers discussed ham sandwiches and *pinard* in woodlands where a few years earlier *maquisards* and *miliciens* had played a deadly game of hide and seek. The mill-workers of Lyons, baring most of their sun-starved bodies in bacchanalia which erupted all over the pretty lakeside town of Nantua in the *congés payés* of 1949, were not cast down by the recollection that on December 13, 1943, one hundred and sixty hostages had been murdered there by the Germans. Nor did the schoolboys of Passy, pounding along the rue de la Pompe on their way to the Lycée Janson de Sully, waste many thoughts on the infamous private 'Gestapo' of that street, or remember that the little *librairie* almost opposite the school buildings had been the underground headquarters of Pierre Brossollette.

The memorials erected in the fervour of the Liberation were

being neglected or conventionalized. The flowers stuck in wall brackets under the plaques at Paris street corners (*Ici est tombé/ Jean Dupont/le 24 août 1944/Mort pour la France*) were renewed at longer and longer intervals. The best known of them all — the tablets marking the place where a group of young men and a Red Cross nurse had fallen beneath the wall of the Jeu de Paume — had been stylized into a series of funerary urns, graceful and remote as the classical statues in the Tuileries just beyond. The scars in the trunk were being covered as Paris added another ring of bark to the two-thousand-year old tree.

Only the Communists, and those of other parties who had been most active in the Resistance, were still tracking down collaborators in the beginning of 1950. For them any suggestion of an amnesty was 'an insult to our dead'. It was therefore all the more striking when Gilbert Renault, *dit* Rémy, first and greatest of all the underground leaders, published a strong plea for an amnesty in *Carrefour*, the Gaullist weekly, on April 11.

Shortly before, General de Gaulle had declared, on the subject of Marshal Pétain, that it was 'a disgrace to keep a man nearly ninety in prison'.

Rémy revealed that during the war de Gaulle had spoken to him about the Marshal in terms quite other than those he employed on the B.B.C. from the summer of 1940 onwards.

'Remember' [the general had said] 'France must always have two strings to her bow. In 1940 she needed the Pétain bowstring as well as the bowstring of de Gaulle.'

Ten years ago [continued Rémy] — I would do the same thing again if we were back in the 'climate' of 1940. I haven't changed; but what I have learned since the Liberation has sickened me. I see too many innocent French people suffering, I get too many distressing letters from despairing families, exactly like those which used to reach me secretly from those imprisoned by the Gestapo. I have seen too many of my countrymen whom I know to be blameless attacked in their personal dignity and in their duties. I have met too many pretenders and listened to too many proclamations inspired by falsehood, covering greed, hatred, and the most sordid ambition.

This outburst was attacked by nearly the whole of the Paris press, disavowed by the secretariat of the R.P.F. (from which Rémy at once resigned), and drew from General de Gaulle a stately expression of his high regard for Rémy, his conviction that nothing could ever justify collaborationism or the Vichy policy.[10] To the 'bowstring' conversation he discreetly made no reference at all. Yet the 'bowstring' theory was exactly what Maître Isorni had advanced in his defence of Marshal Pétain: that in 1940-44 Pétain and the Resistance had served France in two ways: the Marshal by a policy of safeguard, defence, acquisition of material advantages at the price of moral concessions, the Resistance by the moral advantage of their acceptance of sacrifice.

Rémy, expelled from the *Association des Français Libres*, had had the courage to say what many others thought about the excesses of the *épuration*. In November the Deputies began where he left off, and in the course of a lengthy and embittered debate listened to many of the wartime plans for 'national insurrection' published by Resistance men who wanted 'the instant arrest and execution' of all their opponents 'in the short lapse of time between the departure of the Germans and the arrival of the Anglo-Saxons'.[11] It was this kind of wholesale punishment which, the Right believed, had gone on too long. They carried the Amnesty Law by 316 to 269 and, when it became operative on January 1, 1951, France seemed at last to have a hope of closing the worst of her divisions.

CHAPTER XII

TOWARDS REARMAMENT

THE Queuille cabinet made post-war history by remaining in office for thirteen months. A general wage increase of 15 per cent, becoming law at the end of September 1948, was accompanied by a successful attempt to stabilize prices, which fell slowly but consistently from January to July 1949. The hated ration tickets disappeared at last, the street markets began to fill with the fruits of land and sea, and as a final proof of returning prosperity it was possible anywhere in France to buy not only long golden crusty loaves of good household bread, but milk rolls, *croissants*, *pistolets* and *brioches*.

No one now was interested in the white, 'enriched', but tasteless American bread, thankfully devoured at the Liberation by all who could obtain access to U.S. mess halls, but the black traffic in butter, sugar, coffee beans, rice and cigarettes was carried on via food parcels sent from the United States and purchases made at the American PX or commissaries. The early months of the Queuille ministry were good ones for the American residents in Paris, who simultaneously enjoyed the excellent French produce on free sale, the American brand-name goods sold in the commissary of their affiliation and the advantageous black-market rate of 518 francs for a dollar legally valued at 214. While bemoaning French 'corruption' and lack of public spirit, Americans were ready enough to contribute to the general lowering of standards by dealing on the *marché parallèle*, as it was politely called, and that without any hole-and-corner work in back street cafés, tourist fashion: their transactions took place in well-furnished offices, where after compliments and refreshments a dollar cheque was written to the order of an unknown individual in America which the *trafiquant* would immediately cash at the black rate; and the French Government was cheated once again.

Although the black-market dollar rate fell from 518 to 335 between January and April 1949, it was the dollar which indirectly brought down the cabinet of Dr. Queuille. In autumn food prices began to rise again, and at the same time Britain, after four years of the costly experiments of a Socialist government, was compelled to devalue the £ sterling from $4 to $2.80. A realignment of the franc* immediately followed, which started the scare of another increase in prices and an automatic demand by the labour unions for another wage increase. At this point Daniel Mayer, the Socialist Minister of Labour, was charged by his party's executive committee with the defence of labour interests in the cabinet, and decided that these were not consistent with the government programme of price reduction and arbitration. He publicly 'reserved the right not to maintain cabinet solidarity' on this issue, and in the face of a preposterous disciplinary situation Dr. Queuille resigned.

The *crise* which followed lasted for twenty-seven days and saw the rejection of Jules Moch and René Mayer by the Assembly before Georges Bidault came back as premier on October 27. Henri Queuille was still in the cabinet (as vice-premier) and eight other ministers held the key positions which had been theirs in the previous government.

The affairs of France, on the national and European plane, had been so absorbing since Georges Bidault had last held the premiership in October 1946 that many Frenchmen tended to overlook the fact that for the whole of that time, less two months, France had been fighting Communism in Indo-China. It was, from the very beginning, a punishing guerrilla war staged in swamps and paddyfields against a highly mobile enemy.

After the surprise attack of December 1946, the French campaign in Indo-China passed from the defensive to the offensive, to such purpose that on May 7, 1947, Paul Coste-Floret, Minister for War, returned from a tour of inspection to declare: 'There is no longer a single French garrison in a state of siege in Indo-China. The roads are all in our hands. The cities are entirely cleared. I think the desired result has been obtained.' On the political side the French attitude was equally aggressive. Émile Bollaert, the new High Commissioner, was certain that 'France will remain in Indo-China and Indo-China within the French Union' and that

* Exchange rate of the franc	*1914*	*1944*	*1945*	*1948*	*Sept. 1949*
£1 = Frs.	25.22	200	480	864	980
$1 = Frs.	5.16	50	119.10	214.39	350

'the conscience of civilized peoples will not tolerate the determination of State status by the kidnapping of important persons and the suppression of the opposition'.[1] His tone was all the more firm because the Communist champions of the Viet Minh rebels were out of the home government, and it convinced one hearer, Bao Dai, ex-Emperor of Annam and titular Supreme Councillor of the Democratic Republic of Viet Nam.

Since February 1946, Bao Dai had been absent from Indo-China, Ho Chi Minh having invited him to lead a mission to Chungking with a view to getting him away from possible followers. Three months later the ex-emperor, temporarily known as plain Mr. Vinh Thuy, appeared at Hong Kong, from which retreat he opened negotiations with the French Government 'in order to re-establish peace in an independent Viet Nam'. Like Ho Chi Minh, Bao Dai had an eye on the French colony of Cochin-China, the status of which had contributed to start the war, and when he met M. Bollaert aboard the *Duguay-Trouin* in the Bay of Along on June 5, 1948, the ex-emperor signed an agreement to return to Indo-China as chief of state in a Viet Nam *independent within the French Union*, to which Cochin-China was to be united.*

With the cession of Cochin-China, French colonialism came to an end in Indo-China. What remained was the principle of affiliation, which it would have been more prudent to establish under the Constitution, and which created the Associated States of Indo-China, as Laos in July 1949 and Cambodia in November signed treaties guaranteeing their independence within the French Union on the same lines as the French agreement with Bao Dai. What remained also was *la présence française*, that authority of a Western power in an Eastern land against which the peoples of Asia were everywhere rebelling, and against which Ho Chi Minh kept his so-called 'nationalist' armies on the move throughout the year.

When the Indo-Chinese Federation had officially ended, the French Government began a gradual transfer to the new Associated States of some of the services common to all three, including

---

* Letters exchanged at the Élysée on March 8, 1949, between Bao Dai and President Auriol on the Bay of Along agreements were ratified by the Assembly and became law on June 4, 1949.

justice, security and public instruction, and on December 30, 1949, an agreement was signed which created, on paper at least, a Vietnamese National Army, 'charged with the maintenance of order, internal security and the defence of the country' — bolstered, for defence purposes, by the troops of the French Union. In view of the military situation — the Viet Minh were now established on the Chinese border, on the eastern seaboard of Tonkin, and round Saigon — it was agreed that the French High Commissioner should continue to be responsible for the conduct of operations, and the French command to incorporate into native armies the irregular forces of Viet Nam.

While the details of Vietnamese independence were being worked out in Saigon, a first-class political scandal had broken in Paris. On September 18 a soldier back from Indo-China, by name Thomas Perez, 2e classe au l^{er} Régiment de Marche du Tchad,[2] became involved in a squabble with two Vietnamese in the unlikely setting of the 91 bus, and all three were haled to the nearest police-station. There it was discovered that one of the Vietnamese had in his brief-case a copy of the future plan of campaign in Indo-China, prepared by General Revers, chief of the general staff of the French land forces, after a tour of inspection made in the early summer.

Investigation revealed that this was one of several copies of the Revers report which had been sold to a Vietnamese called Van Co by a French adventurer named Roger Peyré, already accused of national indignity in the civic courts, who since 1947 had been involved not only with General Revers, but with General Mast, an officer who had won General Mark Clark's and Eisenhower's praise for the services[3] he had rendered the Allies at the time of the North African invasion. Peyré had not been able to satisfy General Revers's ambition of becoming a five-star general, nor General Mast's of succeeding Émile Bollaert as High Commissioner in Indo-China, but he averred under examination that it was on their behalf that he had sold the Revers report to Van Co.

At first it seemed as if the affaire des généraux could be hushed up. Revers and Mast told their version of the story to MM. Queuille, Moch and Ramadier at a dramatic dawn meeting on September 24, and on giving their word of honour as soldiers that they had not touched a penny of Van Co's money were dismissed with a non-juridical verdict of Not Proven. Revers lost his post as chief of the general staff and Mast was placed on indefinite leave of absence, and these sanctions might have satisfied the parliamentary opposition if Roger Peyré had not been allowed to leave — not punished and not penniless — to begin a new life in Brazil. Then the fat was in the fire and a year later Jules Moch, the Minister of the Interior, was still under attack by the Communists for the alleged irregularities of his methods of investigation, and narrowly escaped being arraigned before the High Court.

By that time — November 1950 — Jules Moch was Minister for National Defence, and an attack on him meant an attack on the government's rearmament policy, as the Communists had calculated. But long before then, for the *affaire* Revers-Mast had been discussed in the French press since the beginning of the year, it had had an adverse effect on the war in Indo-China as seen from France. The war, so far from being settled in six months, had dragged on for three years, and had taken a serious turn with the advent of the People's Republic of China, which meant that Ho Chi Minh now had Communist allies due north of the border and already infiltrating south. Every French soldier fighting Ho Chi Minh and his millions of Chinese allies was a volunteer, whether he came from Continental France, Metropolitan France (including Algeria and the *Anciennes Colonies*) or any other part of the French Union, thanks to a law of 1950 preventing conscripts from being drafted to serve in the Associated States. It was scant comfort for the family of a volunteer to reflect, as many of them did, that if the Revers report had indeed passed into enemy hands, their son had been *vendu* to gratify a general's greed for gold. *Vendu* (sold) had long been a favourite verb, or expletive, of the French public; it had been in constant use in the summer of 1940, and now the feeling began to spread that the war in Indo-China was a gigantic sell, as well as a drain on the motherland which the importance of the territory did not justify. This feeling was fully exploited by the Communists. With China in Communist hands and the United States at last ready to give technical aid and military equipment to the Associated States the French Communists felt that the time was ripe for sabotage of the war effort at home. In February there were strikes at the arsenals of

Lorient, Brest, Toulon; a mob of 2000 at Nice threw war material into the Mediterranean; the Marseilles dockers came out for forty days over the loading of arms and equipment for the Expeditionary Corps. There was a mutiny aboard the troopship *Pasteur* and a fight between the police and a mob, 1500 strong, outside the Clignancourt barracks in Paris when a new detachment was leaving for Indo-China. President Auriol denounced attempted sabotage, and Premier Bidault's cabinet remained obstinately determined to pacify the whole area of Viet Nam.

★

When South Korea was invaded from the north in June 1950, and President Truman took unilateral action in ordering General Douglas MacArthur to support the South, France was again without a government. While the U.N. Security Council vainly ordered a cease-fire, and thirty-three nations, including France, answered the United Nations' appeal for help to the South Koreans, the indefatigable President Auriol was making another *tour d'horizon* in search of a successor to Georges Bidault. This time the ministry, after a civil service debate enlarged to include the eternal schools question and the status of the French Union, collapsed on a technical point in the reclassification of civil servants, so abstruse that even the editors of *L'Année Politique* for 1950 could only observe that it 'put to flight the most sagacious spirits'.

On July 12 René Pleven was elected premier by a vote unanimous except for the Communist bloc, a choice considered satisfactory by the U.S. Government, which in a crisis of such gravity was glad to deal with a man who spoke excellent English, had worked in London, knew America and was a business man by training and instinct. This instinct had led him to leave de Gaulle, one of whose first *Compagnons* he had been, when the general founded the R.P.F., and proceed, after some abortive attempts to reconcile de Gaulle with the Third Force, to make his own career in the U.D.S.R. To this record of Resistance fervour and practical sense, René Pleven added the ownership of a newspaper, *Le Petit Bleu des Côtes du Nord*, and a physical appearance encouraging to Anglo-Saxons, for he was tall, florid and possessed of the toothy smile of a Theodore Roosevelt.

In Washington those Allies who spoke in the Western idiom were being eagerly and critically counted in 1950, a year which brought the sharp realization that huge global responsibilities could not be met by dollar grants and technical aid alone. That detestation of a doctrine meant fighting it with weapons as well as with words was a hard principle for the Americans, basically a humane people, to accept twice in ten years; it created widespread distress and tremendous emotional reaction to the departure of American troops for Korea, where from first to last they bore the brunt of the fighting. In such a mood it was inevitable that the Americans would require every country in the free world to attack Communism both on the battlefield and in the investigating committee-room, and the position of the French Government, which had only just dismissed a card-carrying Communist, Professor Joliot-Curie, from the direction of the national atomic energy commission, seemed to verge on the equivocal. But the French did not see the matter in that light. They pointed out that they had been fighting Communism in Indo-China for nearly four years, and could only send a token contingent to the United Nations' forces in Korea.

The battalion which left Marseilles aboard the *Athos II* on October 25, under the command of Major Le Mire, distinguished itself at Wonju three months later;[1] but the staff rejoicing in the disproportionately grand title of the *État-Major des Forces Terrestres Françaises de l'O.N.U.* (it was commanded by General Magrin-Vernerey, *dit* Montclar, one of Passy's aversions in the early London days) received a number of complaints about the lack of sleeping sacks, the non-arrival of mail, the allowances for soldiers' families. There had been similar complaints in the Delta; but a strict censorship kept them out of the dispatches.

It is no reflection on the courage of the *F.T.F. de l'O.N.U.* to say that in American opinion by far the most important contribution which France could make to the war against Communism was to increase her national defence effort and agree to the re-armament of West Germany, towards which, as France well knew, American policy had long been tending. The fusion of the zones, the halt in dismantling, the permitted increase in production and the formation of the Federal Republic had been successive stages on the road, and France, while objecting to some of them, had yielded to pressure on the others. Now, in the middle of 1950, the government was inescapably faced with a situation preparing ever since the Potsdam Conference: the reintegration of West Germany in Europe in the hope that this ally, whose military temper no one could doubt, would provide effective resistance against Russian aggression. Chancellor Adenauer had profited by the Korean situation to ask for an increased, armed, Federal-controlled police force, promising, as an inducement, that he was ready, as soon as authorized, to contribute two or three German divisions to the projected N.A.T.O. army. Mr. Truman and Mr. Churchill thought that the West Germans might quite well contribute ten, which as it happened was the size of the expected contingent from France.

So strongly marked an attitude on the part of the Western allies might well give France pause. The reintegration of West Germany with Western Europe was almost an accomplished fact: only the Occupation Statute remained as a barrier to sovereignty, and the French leaders of 1950 would have done well to ask themselves whether the simplest solution might not be to permit the inclusion of West Germany in N.A.T.O. and of a German contingent in the Atlantic Army, in which a chain of command including the United States and Canada could act as a check on renascent German ambitions. The stumbling-block was that the creation of a German *national* army was anathema to France. The only possible way to utilize German soldiers was to integrate them in some military organization having a supra-national authority, and this concept happened to accord with the thinking of the men whose aim was to 'make Europe' by a system of fusion.

Six weeks before the Korean War began, Robert Schuman had proposed a plan to which his name, as Foreign Minister, was afterwards given, but which in fact was largely inspired by Jean Monnet, faithful to his belief in the group system of planning. The Schuman Plan envisaged the creation of a single European market for coal and steel to eliminate the opposition of France and Germany by allowing the Saar, the Ruhr and the French basins to work together as one, and, in so doing, to advance the ideal of a united Europe. This plan, weakened at the start by the refusal of Great Britain to share in it, on the grounds that it would separate her from her Commonwealth, did away with customs duties and quotas for coal and steel within the area in which it would operate, and by creating a common market was expected to lower prices and allow free access to all the sources of production.

The machinery of the Schuman Plan, although not ratified by the National Assembly until April 18, 1951, of course existed in the blue-print stage when the rearmament topic became urgent. It was expected to consist of a High Authority of eight members drawn from the governments of the participating nations, plus one elected by the eight; a Special Council of one member from each government; a Common Assembly of seventy-eight delegates appointed on a proportional basis by the national parliaments. The Assembly, in which, as in the Assembly of the Council of Europe, France was to have eighteen seats, was to be the organ of democratic control of the European Coal and Steel Community, destined in due course to take its place beside the Council of Europe, a political fusion, as the supra-national economic fusion of the Continent.

The existence of these two examples of supra-national planning inspired Christian Democrats like Pierre-Henri Teitgen to go one step further and declare that it was necessary to *'faire l'Europe* at all levels — including the military level' and M. Schuman to persuade the government of the day that the machinery set up might be used in the delicate matter of German rearmament. The result was the Pleven Plan for a European Army, basis of the European Defence Community, an abortive birth which divided the chancelleries of the free world while the Communists consolidated their gains elsewhere.

The idea of a European Army had been propounded in other quarters before M. Pleven made his proposals to the National Assembly on October 24. The Assembly of the Council of Europe had recommended such an establishment in August, and some months earlier General Billotte, a leading Gaullist, had advocated a European Army, including West Germany, Italy and Spain, as an integral part of Atlantic strategy. Billotte's proposals were supported by General de Gaulle, later a bitter antagonist of the European Defence Community, at a time when both Britain and France were criticizing the declaration of John J. McCloy, American High Commissioner, that the Germans must be given the means of self-defence.

The Pleven Plan, abandoning the use of national units in the defence of Europe, proposed 'an Army of a united Europe, composed of men from the various European nations, realizing in the greatest possible measure a complete fusion of the human and material elements that it brings together under a single European military and political authority'. This army would be under the control of a European Minister of Defence 'responsible, in a manner which remains to be determined, to those who would designate him [the participating governments] and to a European Assembly . . . either the Strasbourg Assembly or an agency proceeding from it . . . or specially elected'. Its financing would be 'guaranteed by a common budget'. The participating countries would 'maintain their authority over that part of their existing forces not integrated into the European Army'.

Just as the proof of French energy given by the Monnet Plan had encouraged the United States to go ahead with E.R.P., so the Pleven Plan was France's proof of *bona fides* in her request for more financial aid from America in carrying out the work of rearmament. It met with great approval in America, where it was supposed that to 'make Europe', to unite nations with hundreds of years of independent sovereignty, of different languages, religions and wars, would be as simple as to promote good relations between Wisconsin and Michigan; and Americans felt that the French meant business when they promised to have ten divisions on the Continent at the end of 1951,* twenty in 1953, and to increase the period of compulsory military service from twelve to eighteen months.

These were measures which could not and did not wait upon the Pleven Plan, which would come up for ratification by the National Assembly in due course; and meantime the Korean War took the same turn for the worse as the war in Indo-China. The American troops cleared the invaders out of South Korea and were moving northwards when the Chinese Communists rendered even more massive aid to their North Korean allies than they had given to the Viet Minh. What had been a conquering 'police action' turned into a war of attrition, and the angry despair in America was

* On December 31, 1950, France had five divisions on the continent, eight in Indo-China, two in North Africa, two distributed through the French Union. Peacetime effectives 635,000; maximum mobilization 1,100,000.

matched by extreme apprehension in France. From midsummer onwards timid people had anticipated a Russian attack on Europe — an atomic bomb dropped on Paris, or at the very least a tank attack across the Rhine — because French pessimism refused to be lightened by Moscow's promise of non-intervention in the Korean War. Although Garry Davis, the 'world citizen', had long since returned to America, the neutralist movement had gone on, supported by some eminent intellectuals and the equally eminent *Le Monde*, and the Korean War had roused them all to deplore a French alignment with the West which could only bring upon her the sanctions of the East. It was an ostrich-like policy which paralleled, though in a negative manner, de Gaulle's old concept of France as the arbitrator between Russia and America; and it was equally effective. For France the die was cast; aspiring to the leadership of Europe she had thrown in her lot with the free world, and after a debate on military credits lasting as long into New Year's Day as the struggle of 1946 which had ended the leadership of de Gaulle, the government — the febrile, much-maligned government, *la combinaison* in all its splendour — remained faithful to its pledges to the West and passed a Rearmament Law calling for the expenditure in 1951 of 740,000 million francs, or two and a half times the military budget for 1948.

PART FOUR

FRANCE AND THE WEST
1951-1953

CHAPTER XIII

FRANCE HESITATES

IN September 1950, at the same time as the United States made its first proposals for the rearmament of Germany, the Internal Security Act (the McCarran Act) went into operation. Intended to discriminate against unsuitable immigrants, it forbade the admission to America of any ex-Nazis, even those who had only been in Hitler organizations during their childhood; and those who enforced it saw nothing inconsistent in refusing to admit one ex-Nazi to the United States while expecting the French to integrate thousands of them into a European Army. Nor did the French, in their turn, see anything inconsistent in admitting ex-Nazis to the Foreign Legion (they fought consistently well in Indo-China) while hesitating to join forces with them in the supra-national army of the Pleven Plan.

That there was hesitation, even active opposition, became clear almost as soon as the passage of the French Rearmament Law became part of the accelerated rhythm of Atlantic strategy. General Eisenhower, once again Supreme Commander, assumed direction of Supreme Headquarters Allied Powers in Europe (S.H.A.P.E.) and his return to Paris in January was the occasion of a Communist demonstration against him on the Champs Élysées, the scene of his triumph in 1945. The Western Union at Fontainebleau, which had served as a stop-gap till N.A.T.O. was organized, was now superseded for all major purposes by the new S.H.A.P.E. headquarters to be constructed at Rocquencourt, not far from de Gaulle's old retreat at Marly, and work began, under American direction, on five new air bases in Morocco. On February 15th a conference on the European Army opened at Paris, to the accompaniment of new hostile demonstrations; and the participants, France, West Germany, Italy, Belgium and Luxembourg, decided that eighteen months would be necessary to bring all the groups into a standard form. M. Pleven had a very successful trip to America,* returning with the announcement that French and Vietnamese forces in Indo-China would receive $5 millions in American aid, and his statement that 'Europe must be defended — not liberated' met with general approval. But in their enthusiasm the Western allies went too fast for France. The concessions to West Germany became too numerous: the return of Heligoland, the release of war criminals including Alfred Krupp, the anticipated end to the juridical state of war and the reduction of obligatory coal exports by Germany, had the cumulative effect of alarming the French; and meantime the Russians lost no opportunity of pointing out that mobilization and rearmament undertaken jointly with America were entirely contrary to de Gaulle's treaty of alliance with them in 1944.

That René Pleven could fall from power at the moment when his master-project was about to be implemented was perfectly bewildering to Western opinion, especially since he and his cabinet resigned on February 25 on a matter which had nothing to do with international politics, being a technical point in the voting of a new electoral law. As usual there was very little difference in the composition of the new cabinet, formed by Dr. Queuille on March 10; M. Pleven was back as vice-premier, and the premier himself, one of the most astute politicians of the day, soon found a solution to a problem which had been wasting the Assembly's time for more than two years.

At the 1945 and 1946 elections voting had been by proportional representation, which the Third Force feared would now work to the advantage of the two 'monolithic' parties, the Gaullists and Communists. From 1948 onwards sixteen bills were laid before the Assembly, each offering a new voting formula, before the Queuille cabinet found a solution on the eve of the elections required by law to take place in 1951. The bill they produced was a returning officer's nightmare, for in it the principle of *la combinaison* was pushed to the utmost limit of alliances, split votes and preferential balloting (*apparentements, panachage, vote préférentiel*)

---

* During M. Pleven's visit to America French officials were irritated by an article entitled 'French Communism' in *Life* magazine (January 29, 1951). Accompanied by a picture spread of a 'Red town', it warned: 'Americans . . . must fear that France today lacks nerve and sinew', bemoaned 'the sickness of the French state', the helplessness of the government in face of trained Resistance saboteurs. It was written by a staff member formerly one of de Gaulle's press officers in London, Algiers, Paris.

and the only simplification was that there would be one round of voting by Departments instead of two. This meant that all the 'horse-trading' would have to be done beforehand by the system of alliances; nobody outside the party wanted to be *apparenté* with a Communist, and as the R.P.F. had always announced that they were not a party they might find it hard (so Dr. Queuille reckoned) to ally their lists of candidates with the straight party tickets.

In the event only 87 alliances were formed at the election, but as they affected 368 seats out of 627, nearly all Third Force, this was enough to give the Centre *if it voted solidly* rather more than the majority of 314 required in the new chamber for an absolute majority.

While the premier laid his plans for the victory of the Third Force, the President of the Republic, already applauded on a State visit to London, embarked on a highly successful visit to Washington and Ottawa, where his simplicity and sincerity, no less than his dignified accounts of France's war losses and reconstruction efforts, won many friends for his country. Vincent Auriol was a 'character' perfectly comprehensible to the Americans, who liked his *toulousain* accent and his *méridional* passion for oratory, which not even influenza and the need for an interpreter could quench, and they admired Madame Auriol's graceful wearing of the creations of Dior and Jacques Fath. The Auriols, in their several ways, had enhanced the dignity of their office, for the President, in his own words, had opposed those 'who seek to make of the Presidency of the Republic a passive and silent magistracy, a mere representation', and had tried to be 'a Chief of State at once sensitive and attentive to . . . the will of the people'. Some smears and slurs, of course, the presidential family had had to endure. Monsieur Paul Auriol's wife, Jacqueline, was a daring test pilot, whose unusual career made copy for the satirists; she was destined to make aviation history in France when she broke through the sound barrier.* Paul Auriol acted as his father's secretary, and at the time of their visit to America was in litigation with the Gaullist weekly *Carrefour*, which had accused him of

---

* On December 12, 1952, in the French jet plane *Mistral*, Jacqueline Auriol went *en trombe* at the speed of 855.920 km. per hour. The male record, then held by Colonel Ascani, U.S.A.F., was 1023.038 km. per hour.

taking bribes from Roger Peyré, the Indo-China racketeer. He won his action for slander and obtained damages three months later.[1]

The June 17 elections created exceptional interest outside France. It was felt that the international scene had changed so completely that an Assembly elected in 1946, with Communists in the government, could not adequately represent the will of the people, and the great success of Gaullism in all the non-legislative elections held since 1947 made it appear that the R.P.F. would carry the Assembly and bring General de Gaulle back to power. He had attacked the Communists so incessantly since he founded the Rally that his past transactions with them were forgotten, and there was a good deal of support in Britain and America for his return to power as 'a strong man' who would give France the definite leadership she seemed to need. Moreover, de Gaulle was still supporting the idea of a European Army. As near to the time of the election as January, he declared himself, in a speech at Nîmes, in favour of incorporating Spain as well as West Germany in the organization.[2] On two important counts, therefore, de Gaulle's return seemed to promise well, and there was no doubt of the support his wartime prestige could command in France. There was only one inconvenient question, but it was put by a great many insignificant people: if the general could not govern when he had the whole of France on his side at the Liberation, how does he expect to govern now that the country is divided?

The answer to that, of course, had to come from the R.P.F. propagandists, and their always energetic efforts redoubled as the year moved on to April, when de Gaulle opened the election campaign in the most dramatic manner possible, by addressing 20,000 citizens of Rheims from the *parvis* of the great cathedral where the kings of France had been anointed and crowned. This was followed on May 1 by the announcement of another mail campaign; voters were asked to buy a postcard, price 100 francs, write on it their answer to the question 'What do You Think of State Reform?' and mail it to the general at Colombey-les-Deux-Églises.

To the highly articulate French public, the device made a certain appeal: at all events, writing their own opinions was preferable to listening to the endless speeches of the R.P.F. For this was another handicap to the Rally: their campaign had gone on too long. What had been novelty in 1947 had become repetition in 1951: the demands for a strong Executive, separation of powers, revision of the Constitution, had turned into a barrel-organ tune. The R.P.F. had a number of press outlets, the first of which, a weekly bulletin called *L'Étincelle*, had been followed by *L'Étincelle Ouvrière*; they had *Le Rassemblement*; the pen of André Stibio in *La Voix du Nord;* the weekly *Carrefour;* and the indefatigable Quilici editing a paper with the Stendhalian name of *Le Rouge et le Noir*. The Gaullist editorials became as monotonous as the May Day oratory, when the R.P.F. held its annual Feast of Labour, Youth and Sport.

As the years went by, the general's own speeches grew a little shrill:

> Each man must exercise his mandate, wholly and person-ally — if that is what they mean by personal power, I am in agreement with it. As to what happened in June 1940, in the general collapse, when the voice of the people could not be heard, it is true that I took the power and held it until I could restore it to the people's representatives. Yes! I returned from Egypt and even from Libya, from Italy, from the Rhine and Danube; I entered Paris, Lyons, Marseilles, Rennes, Lille, Toulouse, Strasbourg on the heels of our victorious troops, but did I strangle the Republic?[3]

De Gaulle's 'return-fantasy' was a Napoleonic illusion which he later denied, exclaiming:

> I am not Bonaparte! I am not Boulanger! I am *Général de Gaulle*! It has been so for eight years, and after the experi-ences we have had together, I thought all the world knew it!
> Naturally I do not know when or under what government conditions, normal or — which God forbid — dramatic, party régime will be overthrown. But I know that it will not overcome our determination to wrench the State from it, and it will be renounced by France.[4]

Sometimes he turned from the attack on the party system of government, *le régime des partis*, to social justice and religion:

> Come unto us! You who burn with the Christian flame which spreads the light of love and brotherhood o'er the vale

of human sorrow, the flame which for centuries has kindled
the spiritual and moral inspiration of France —
  Come unto us![5]

Social justice was the keystone of the R.P.F.'s economic policy,
which bore an odd resemblance to several other programmes of
the same kind. De Gaulle's theory of the 'association' of capital
and labour was not particularly original, although it added a new
note to his simple dogma of Leadership and strong government.
The R.P.F. line was that employers and workers should share in the
direction of their enterprises, that wages (called *rétribution de base*
in R.P.F. language; salaries were *intérêts de base* and directors' fees
droits de base) and other 'money returns' should be paid according
to the contribution of the individual, with a balance sheet open
for scrutiny by an assembly of all engaged in the enterprise; and —
most significant of all — that trade unions should give up all action
outside the framework of each trade. This programme had a
flavour of the Vichy *Charte du Travail*, a touch of Mussolini's
Labour Charter and Perón's Rights of Labour, and like them all
it derived from the concepts of social justice of Pope Leo XIII's
encyclical *De Rerum Novarum*. In its mixture of anti-Communism
and corporativism it was not far removed from Father Coughlin's*
National Union of Social Justice.

Through the newspaper *Le Rassemblement Ouvrier* and the creation of Gaullist cells in factories the theory of association had
become well known, if not exactly practicable. Management was
opposed to the idea (although de Gaulle gained some support
among leading industrialists, especially after rearmament began)
and labour did not approve of limiting the scope of the trade
unions. In another important quarter the R.P.F. had not won the
support which might have been expected: although it had come
out on the side of grants to Catholic schools, the Church still gave
its preference to the M.R.P. candidates, and the Vatican was said
to have reserves on the subject of the R.P.F.

The M.R.P., once the 'party of fidelity' to de Gaulle, had forbidden its members to join the *Rassemblement* as soon as it was
founded; and although there had been the inevitable splinter

---

* Father Charles E. Coughlin, 'America's Radio Priest' of the 1930s, anticipated de
Gaulle's mail campaigns by asking for letters approving his views (subscription
enclosed); formed the Radio League of the Little Flower.

movement on the issue of personal loyalty to de Gaulle, it was not a large one, only six M.R.P. Deputies bolting the party to found the Independent Popular Republicans with Edmond Michelet. Twice since 1947 de Gaulle had quietly tried a *rapprochement* with the M.R.P., in 1948 approaching Bidault, who declined, and in 1950 through Michelet, but nothing had come of it;[6] and now his old henchman Maurice Schumann was denouncing 'the precise methods and the imprecise programme' of the R.P.F.

The precise methods included a good deal of brawling with the Communists, or threats of brawling, which put the government to some trouble in enforcing security measures for the public peace. A notable occasion was the ceremony arranged for the summer of 1949 in memory of General Leclerc, at which the Avenue d'Orléans, a main artery leading in to Paris — and the road up which the 2ᵉ D.B. had made its historic entry — was to be renamed the Avenue Leclerc. The Paris streets were filled with milling groups of Communists and Gaullists, one side claiming the dead general for the Resistance, the other for the *Compagnons* of London, and although the government prevented a riot by turning out the C.R.S. shock troops to reinforce the police, the memory of the great Leclerc received less than its due homage, and was partly obscured by the dust of the encounter.

But this, and similar incidents, had slipped into the background by the summer of 1951, and on his pre-election campaign tour of France and North Africa de Gaulle was so well received that he was encouraged to make a definite prediction when he spoke on the outskirts of Paris on May 1.

For some years it had been the practice of the R.P.F. to hold a Feast of Labour, Youth and Sport in the pleasant suburban park at Bagatelle, as a counter-attraction to the Communists' May Day rites in downtown Paris. Every May 1 they recorded a larger attendance, and the thing had developed into a large-scale *kermesse*, with shooting-galleries, fortune-tellers, hot-dogs and other attractions, the general's annual oration being the star turn. In 1951, with the election upon which his future depended only six weeks off, de Gaulle said:

> When the people have spoken, I will make a rendezvous with them to inaugurate our enterprise. Where will it be? On the Champs Élysées![7]

The meaning was clear. De Gaulle, victorious in the election, would repair to the Arc de Triomphe, which he had never visited officially since he ceased to be President of the Provisional Government, and would once again walk down the Champs Élysées, followed by a joyous throng. But this time, instead of following the river to Notre Dame, he would cross the Pont de la Concorde and re-enter the Chamber of the National Assembly. As the election had been fixed for June 17, the full results would be known on the anniversary of the famous Eighteenth: the date, the memories, the mass appeal would all be renewed, and — always provided he had the anticipated 240 R.P.F. Deputies behind him — Charles de Gaulle might even be able to end his promenade at the Palace of the Élysée.

But the R.P.F. won only 118 seats in the election, at which de Gaulle again refused to present himself as a candidate, although strongly urged to do so in his native Nord. They were not even, as in the *raz de marée* of 1947, the party polling the highest number of votes; for although the R.P.F. had the largest number of seats, the Communists had received 5,038,587 votes to the R.P.F. 4,134,885. The two together obtained 48.2 per cent of the total votes cast, which meant that on any question which happened to appeal to them both, ideologically poles asunder though they were, the parties grouped around the Centre would have to use *la combinaison* in all its forms to maintain a power now based on the Right rather than the Left. Endless opportunities for bargaining were thus offered to the 95 Deputies of the *Rassemblement des Gauches Républicains* (which included the Radicals and was presided over by Édouard Daladier) and the 95 Moderates, Peasants and Independents (prominent among whom was Paul Reynaud). The Left wing of the 103 Socialists could, if they wished, link up with the Communists, and the M.R.P., though it had dropped almost exactly half its voters since 1946, was still in an excellent bargaining position with 85 representatives. The *apparentements* had produced an Assembly which bore a stronger resemblance to a parliament of the Third Republic than to the first Chamber elected by the Fourth.

De Gaulle abandoned his descent of the Champs Élysées on June 18 in favour of a visit of homage to the martyred dead of the Mont Valérien, and General de Larminat replaced him at the Arc de Triomphe. A few days later he publicly expressed, in a tone more of sorrow than of anger, his regret that the nation 'in a state of moral depression' had given the R.P.F. only a 'limited victory'.[8] He blamed the electoral law for the results, and let it be known that although his 'formation' was the largest in the Assembly he would allow 'the parties' to govern without its aid. But it was not the electoral law which had limited the general's victory, as the total of votes cast for the Communists (also without *apparentements*) quite clearly showed. The R.P.F. failed because of two basic factors in French political life: splinter groups and scepticism.

At the election of 1951, much more than at those held soon after the Liberation, a proliferation of small groups made its appearance. In the third sector of the Seine, for example, there were eleven seats, captured almost proportionately to the national results by the five principal groups plus one newcomer,* the Union of Independent and National Republicans. But lists were also presented by a collection of small groups which had no hope of winning. The Cartel of the Independent Left; the Independent List of Republican and Socialist Concentration; the French National Party; the National Republican, Economic and Social Union; the Independent wing of the M.R.P.; the Independent and National Republicans for the Defence of the Taxpayer; the Federalist Movement; the Fourth Force Independents; and the Union of Anti-Party Malcontents won no seats in the Assembly, but together they polled 29,430 out of the total of 417,527 votes cast — a respectable proportion which, otherwise distributed, might have altered the representation from Seine 3.

The splinter parties had struck a blow for *les nuances*, the shades of meaning which reduced Anglo-Saxon proponents of the two-party system to incoherence, and they helped to make the 1951 election a victory for nobody. But scepticism also played its part in the 'limitation' of the R.P.F., that scepticism which paradoxically contributes to France's weakness as well as France's strength. The R.P.F. had told its story too often, and whereas they will rally to one great speech, one great action fitted to a momentous hour, the French — unlike the British, who like variations on a familiar theme — are soon impelled by their critical spirit to question the repetition, find fault with the philosophy and pick holes

---

* Elected: 4 Communists (136,884 votes), 3 R.P.F. (112,544), 1 Soc., 1 M.R.P., 1 R.G.R., 1 U.N.I.R.

in the diction; then they begin to smile with the smile of Voltaire, and thus a cause is lost.

Very little of this appeared on the surface of the decorous election of June 1951, conspicuous for the smallness and tranquillity of its public meetings. In Paris the liveliest heckling was heard in Seine 2, where a new group, the *Union Nationale des Indépendants Républicains* (U.N.I.R.) had for its *tête de liste* Maître Jacques Isorni, who had championed the cause of Marshal Pétain since defending him at his trial in 1945. Isorni's election platform was a simple one: freedom for the Marshal; and as the next name on his list was that of Admiral Decoux, who had some controversial things to say about Indo-China during his governor-generalship and since, their meetings provoked the attentions of hecklers armed with blackjacks and tear-gas bombs, and were apt to end in arrests and ambulances.

Maître Isorni was elected to the National Assembly, but before the results were known President Auriol had taken a humane decision which was not announced, for fear of affecting the results, until the campaign was over. The prisoner of the Île d'Yeu was now dying: he no longer rose in the middle of the night to beat vainly on the door of his cell, for at ninety-six years of age he had forgotten that he was a prisoner. By order of the President he was now removed from the fortress to what was called by courtesy the Île d'Yeu annexe of the military hospital of Nantes — actually a little house in the rue Guist'hau at Port Joinville, and there his wife, who had visited him regularly during his six years in prison, took her place beside him as his long life moved towards its close.

Philippe Pétain had lived twelve years too long for his own glory, but six years too long for his opponents. Now that France had aligned herself with the Western powers in opposition to Communist aggression, had voted a huge sum for rearmament against a possible attack by Russia and was contemplating an association with West Germany for the same purpose, it was possible to remind his detractors that Pétain, too, had been an active opponent of Communism. Because his collaboration with Germany had taken place in time of war he was found guilty of treason and sent to prison, but Robert Schuman's co-operation with Konrad Adenauer in time of peace entitled him to be called a good European and Foreign Minister of France.

If it was right to fight Communism, then had Jacques Doriot been right when he raised the *Légion des Volontaires Français* to fight the Russians? They had worn German uniform, but if the European Army took shape the French and the Germans would wear the same uniform. Had Cardinal Baudrillart been right when he gave the L.V.F. his blessing for their anti-Bolshevik crusade, and Admiral Esteva when he told his men to 'fight Bolshevism'? Did the Resistants of Bayeux owe an apology to the townsman whom they paraded through the streets in June 1944 — 'tears mingling with blood flowing from his torn face' — as punishment for having been the president of 'an anti-Soviet league'?[9]

If the Marshal had been guilty of treason against the State when he accepted personal power at Vichy in July 1940, then were four million electors also guilty when they voted for the R.P.F. of General de Gaulle, which stood for the revocation of the Constitution and a chief Executive not responsible to the National Assembly?

These were the important Ifs which tormented France seven years from Liberation, and brought the wheel back full circle to the old *mystique* of the *double jeu*, in which the *Français de Grande Bretagne* had found their secret comfort; Rémy's 'two strings to the French bow'. Pétain and de Gaulle were two faces of the father-image which France sometimes desired and sometimes spurned; that much became increasingly obvious as the general himself entered upon old age. But only the simplest folk, like the peasants of the Île d'Yeu who exclaimed '*Voici de Gaulle!*' when they saw an aircraft circling the island[10] on the day of Pétain's funeral, really believed that the general, prisoner of his past, would ever be reconciled with the Marshal, alive or dead.

Philippe Pétain died on July 23, a few weeks after his transfer from the fortress, and was carried to his island grave without honours, the only decoration being his Médaille Militaire, carried in front of the coffin borne on the shoulders of four islanders.[11] In Paris roses were banked in his honour round the Tomb of the Unknown Soldier, the wreaths stretching away for twenty yards under the Arc de Triomphe; also there was street fighting, with jostling and insults for those who attended a Mass said in his memory. It was evidence, if any were still needed, that what France had experienced was not an undigested Revolution, but an undigested civil war.

CHAPTER XIV

TWO THOUSAND YEARS OLD

THREE hundred miles downstream from the sources of the
Seine, a Gallic tribe called the Parisii had built a primitive
city on a boat-shaped island between a marshland to the
north and a swell of hilly country to the south on which the
Romans, many generations later, established a colony called
Lutetia. It was not really possible to fix the year in pre-Christian
history when the Parisii first lit their fires on the Île de la Cité,
but in 1951 the modern Parisians felt themselves justified in
announcing that their town was ready to celebrate her bimillenary
birthday.

Since the flow of tourists resumed in 1948, France had had no
reason to complain of the numbers who each year admired the
splendid capital and the beautiful land. In 1950 France was once
again the leading tourist country of the continent, with 3 million
visitors replacing the 1.9 millions of 1929, the peak year, and with
receipts in sterling, Swiss francs and Belgian francs higher in 1950
than in 1949. Only in U.S. dollar-receipts had there been a per-
ceptible decline; this was partly due to the Korean War, and the
prevalent dread that the Russians might take it into their heads
to start a war in Europe and liquidate all the American guests in
the Ritz Hotel; but much of it was due, the French realized with
incredulity, to the new popularity of Rome. The Italians, taking
on like chameleons the colour of their conquerors, had swiftly
realized that the Colosseum and the Forum Romanum were not
in themselves enough to rivet the attention of American travellers
in the middle of the twentieth century, but as good luck would
have it American film companies began at that time to use their
frozen assets by making films in Italy, and Rome became a colony
of Hollywood. The sight of film stars was an extra attraction for
American visitors, already cheered to find that the Romans were
progressive enough to install neon lighting, illuminated advertising
and quick-lunch counters; they liked the crowds roaming the warm
noisy streets at midnight, the café singers screeching *Ciri Biri Bim*

in the Piazza dell' Esedra, not far from the Finance Ministry, and the way in which the Via Veneto, where their countrymen gathered at the Excelsior or Doney's Bar, had come to resemble Main Street, U.S.A.

To such tourists Paris seemed forbidding, involuted, cold. The *grands boulevards* pleased them well enough, but the long front of the Louvre and the tall houses of the *quais* struck them as so much advertising space gone to waste, and there were no filling-stations in the Place de la Concorde. When they came in through the Gates of Paris they had to traverse miles of dark streets where tenement windows were shuttered and *portes-cochères* closed in the early evening, iron curtains rolled down over store windows as if riot and siege were expected before dawn. No laughter was heard from those who went by at the pace the Parisians had adopted during the Occupation (a kind of rapid hop, arms close to the body for warmth, chin non-committally buried in turned-up collar); and if any singer had started *La Vie En Rose* under the windows of the Finance Ministry in the rue de Rivoli he would have ended in the adjacent police station of the *I*er *arrondissement*.

Although cleaning squads were kept hard at work, the visitors were greeted here and there by huge Communist slogans in whitewash or chalk saying 'AMIS [for Americans] GO HOME! YANK GOME! GO HOME!' It was no wonder that the free-spending tourists shortened their stay and took their dollars to countries with the wit to offer a surface welcome and show a surface gratitude for the impressive aid of E.R.P.

Some new attraction had to be offered, and it was recalled that a Paris Exhibition was a well-tried device in troubled times. The first, in 1855, had been a frank imitation of London's Great Exhibition of 1851; the second, in 1867, was intended to distract attention from 'Badinguet's' Mexican adventure and the rise of Prussia (the Americans sent a rocking-chair and the Prussians a new gun by Krupps of Essen);[1] the third, to bring foreigners back to Paris after the losses of the 1870 war. The exposition of 1889 added the Eiffel Tower to the Paris skyline. The great show of 1900 (the Americans sent false teeth, the Germans ironclads and torpedo boats) restored national pride after Fashoda. *Expo. 1937* had been so nearly a failure, thanks to the bad planning and recurrent strikes which kept it from completion, that it was wisely decided to make the Bimillenary Birthday a general celebration with no special construction work or set pieces of any kind.

So during *le grand Bi* there was a series of *Nuits* in honour of the different French industries (Lyons silk in the Galerie d'Apollon at the Louvre, jute at the Palais Cardinal), a dress parade at Christian Dior entitled 'De Lutèce à nos Jours', the 2439th production of *Tartuffe* at the Maison de Molière, and window-dressing in a number of the principal streets in honour of some gilded period of the capital's fame. *Le Vray Mistère de la Passion* was performed in front of the Cathedral of Notre Dame, and on July 9, to the sound of fifteen bands and countless exploding fireworks, the civic heads of all the great cities, including Mayor Yasnov of Moscow, assembled to offer their homage to the queen of the world.

On her Bimillenary Birthday the appearance of Paris had undergone some marked changes from the season of Liberation. The empty streets were filled with public and private vehicles, and with crowds wearing civilian clothes instead of khaki; the empty shops were full of merchandise of every description. But there was no change in the majestic outlines of palaces and churches; the topaz-coloured Seine still wound past the island where 'philosophy holds the eternal citadel of light and immortality'; and to those returning after years of absence Paris seemed indeed to be

> always as then she was —
> loveliest, brightest, best,
> blessing and blest.

There were, however, signs that the great beauty was ageing, from the torn-up pavements in the city centre where obsolete electrical installations were being replaced, to the scaffolding which obscured the towers of Notre Dame. St. Germain des Prés was in a chronic state of repair and Versailles was beginning to crumble away, so that soon M. Sacha Guitry, old charges of collaboration forgotten, would be asked to give radio and screen performances in aid of a fund to preserve the historic château. The only new philosophy was that of the blue-jeaned existentialists, American students, profiting by a G.I. Bill of Rights' grant or a Fulbright Fellowship to bask in the light from Sartre's eyeglasses at the Café de Flore; and the liberal arts taught on the Mont Ste.

Geneviève were out of fashion in the atomic age. Behind the churches and schools whose names were part of history there stretched a ring of horrifying slums. In the tumbledown tenements within a short walk of the National Assembly, the kennels behind St. Germain l'Auxerrois and St. Germain des Prés, and the mean streets off the north road which bore the names of dead *Communards* and Bolsheviks, five hundred thousand persons were living in conditions of overcrowding and primitive sanitation which the government reports called *inadmissible*. To the artist's eye there was enchantment in those narrow streets, where houses out of drawing tilted and toppled sideways or forward, and the flaking walls shaded from silver grey and stone grey into beige and cream, but to the tenants the remarkably low rents did not always compensate for the broken stairs, the earth-floored basements, the 10-watt staircase light which went out so many minutes after the switch had been pressed.

The Parisians themselves, however, were dyed-in-the-wool conservatives when faced with the replanning of their city. However much Jean Dupont might wish to have a bright apartment for his family, with *confort moderne*, and a vacuum-cleaner for his wife, he was not prepared to vote for any tampering with the shape of a city which had scarcely altered since the Second Empire.* Le Corbusier, post-war consultant to the Supreme Council of City Planning, had already exhibited plans for a modern Paris at the Salon des Arts Décoratifs of 1925; these included demolition of the city on the north and east and the erection of skyscraper buildings joined by parkways, to spare Paris workers their daily journey across the green belt to ugly suburban dwellings. Le Corbusier's ideas met with a storm of disapproval, and the *avant garde* Cité Radieuse which he had built for the bombed-out citizens of Marseilles was considered by Parisians to be just the thing for the Marseillais. There was some agitation to have the green belt itself built over: it was immune by the *non aedificandi* law of 1919,[2] being part of the old glacis of Monsieur Thiers's 1841 *fortifications*, but experts considered that it could accommodate 18,000 dwellings of the three millions required after the war. This might be better

* A poll taken in 1953 by Le Congrès National des Familles de France showed that 47.5 per cent of French housewives had a vacuum cleaner, 14 per cent a water heater, 1.5 per cent a sewing machine. Money had to be spent on food and clothing instead of equipment.

than nothing for the workers, for the new apartment buildings in the rue Michel-Ange and the avenue Paul-Doumer were co-operatives, meant for bourgeois tenants, but there was no chance at all for Le Corbusier's skyscrapers. A law passed in the reign of Louis XIV limited the height of Paris buildings to seven storeys, and the 'Save the Skyline of the St. Germain Quarter' association had burst forth in petitions when the new Medical Faculty buildings began climbing higher and higher on the rue des Ss. Pères.

Georges Duhamel, Secretary of the French Academy, was one of the opponents of the new medical buildings — 'a chaotic citadel of concrete'[3] — and in the Faculty itself there was considerable agitation among the research workers for the right to stay in the old-fashioned laboratories near the Boulevard St. Germain, where experiments were not shaken by passing traffic. But although Duhamel maintained that *le building américain est le triomphe du provisoire*, the Rector of the University, Jean Sarrailh, was in search of more accommodation, provisional or permanent, for all the faculties. The Sorbonne lecture-halls were overcrowded to the danger point, and there was a project on foot to take over and equip the Halle aux Vins as class-rooms — the vintners moving down to the depot of their tuns and barrels on the Quai de Bercy. Already the University was renting space in the Palais de la Mutualité for its law classes, and was constantly exercised by the housing and health of its sixty thousand students, who were going short of food and textbooks as well as of comfortable living conditions.

If the school age were to be raised to 18, as some educational reformers desired, the shortage of class-rooms would be more acute than ever, for although 1950 had seen a marked improvement in school building (3312 new class-rooms compared with 126 in 1946) town schools everywhere were crowded out and working on two-shift timetables. The newly elected Assembly made no difficulty about voting 13,000 million francs for new school buildings, which war damage and the rising birthrate made essential, but the question of money grants to pupils brought the subterranean quarrel of Church and State to the surface again, and while the future of the European Army remained unsettled M. Pleven's new cabinet (constituted August 10, 1951) spent its first month in arguing with the Assembly that the Republic would not be mortally imperilled by the award of secondary scholarships to meritorious pupils without discrimination, provided the awards were made to the individual and not to the establishment where he was a pupil. Eventually a law was passed giving every head of a family whose children were receiving primary education a grant of 1000 francs per child per school term; but in the case of Catholics this fund was to be administered by laymen — the Parents' Association of each school — and not by the hierarchy.[4] Thus the Republic was saved once again, but even the grant of this pittance was only voted by an Assembly of Rightist tendencies on condition that it was regarded as a temporary experiment, applicable only to existing schools.

For six years the parliaments of Liberated France had conducted envenomed debates on school grants without seriously considering the vital problem of educational reform, although the need for more elementary teachers and better pay for all was presented during the schools debates of September 1951. The *machinery* of education had been under discussion by groups ranging from the original Consultative to the Council of National Education since the heyday of debating and planning in Algiers; of the *purpose* of education, little or nothing had been said.

The first Commission on Education, set up in de Gaulle's time, was successively presided over by two Communist professors, Paul Langevin and Henri Wallon. Their recommendations, submitted in 1947, included raising the school leaving age from 14 to 15 (ultimately to 18), the introduction of an orientation programme and the promotion of social development through group work. One innovation in the spirit of this report (though actually inspired by the work of Maria Montessori) was the 'new Sixths and Fifths' in secondary schools, additional to the classical and modern sides. These classes, of 25 pupils only, had formal studies in the morning and practical classes in art, manual training and 'social environment' in the afternoon; most revolutionary of all, *les classes nouvelles* not only received regular vocational guidance but were exempt from the crushing burden of homework which makes the French child's evenings a burden to his parents as well as to himself. As it turned out, these classes were to be abolished in 1952, with the somewhat optimistic hope that the spirit they had engendered would permeate the whole school system.

Ever since the creation of the Université de France* by Napoleon, French education had been set in a rigidly formal mould. It was a mould which turned out the best students in the world, adding a thorough drilling in all branches of book-learning and a highly competitive system of places and rewards to the French child's natural gifts of a quick apprehension and a mother-tongue more flexible and more lapidary than any other upon earth. It was also a mould from which backward or unadaptable children collapsed like badly-set jellies, but it did turn out young men and women who in their last year in secondary schools were equal to first-year students at British Universities, second-year students at American, in their knowledge of philosophy, mathematics, literature and languages. Whether it also produced complete young human beings was open to doubt.

The school children of 1940, whose youth had been ruined either physically or morally by the Occupation, had now been replaced in the class-rooms of France by a generation whose awareness of current events had begun at the Liberation. To teach them the responsibilities of good Europeans as well as national patriotism was an urgent task for which only enlightened teachers of history and geography could find time in the crowded school day. To teach public-spiritedness, community duties and the obligation to love their neighbour as themselves had never been a part of the State curriculum.

Anti-clericalism had always been rampant among members of the Public Instruction system, and in country districts the enmity of the *curé* and the schoolmaster was traditional. In more sophisticated localities the radicalism of the teachers was translated into a glittering scepticism modelled, in the pre-war teaching generation, on the elegant negations of Émile-Auguste Chartier, *dit* Alain. The learned professor, who in the *lycées* of Rouen and Paris taught the teachers of the future to adapt to their own times the query of Montaigne — *Que sais-je?* — the irony of Pascal, the rationalism of Renan, and above all 'the thesis of Doctor Johnson that "most schemes of political improvement are very laughable things",' was responsible in no small degree for the disillusionment and *je m'enfichisme* of the times.

* Meaning the entire system from *écoles primaires* through *lycées* or *collèges* to the universities.

Nor was the undoubted brilliance of some of Alain's pupils invariably reflected upon their own. The system of *répétiteurs*, by which the supervision of senior pupils in their preparation or leisure periods was confided to a body of ushers, far less highly certificated than the *agrégés* who came and went from the rostrum with little thought for the psychology of their students, did nothing to heighten the moral values of children with little opportunity for team games and group activities. The adult Frenchman's interest in sports was either spectator (watching football or bicycle races) or individualistic (tennis, ski-ing, mountaineering on one social level, *le camping* on another); he had not been trained through all his school years to play in groups of nine, eleven, or fifteen, for his side and not for himself. For those raised in the closed corporation of an anti-clerical family avid of its own interests and possessions, unable to join the Scout or Guide movements because these were directed by the Church, there was no group spirit in the schools to mitigate the ferocious individualism of *chacun pour soi*, which among adults found expression in brilliant creative effort, and also in political manœuvres, black-market traffic and tax evasions.

The adorers of Paris, who came from far and near to *fêter* her two thousand years, were too thankful to find her freed of the German yoke and still resplendent to penetrate very far into the post-war personality of her inhabitants. In one respect this was unfortunate: the new and difficult relationship between France and America demanded that the two peoples should know each other better and criticize each other less, but given the reluctance of the French to invite comparative strangers into their homes, even when business was being transacted between them, neither side got much further than casual encounters. The Americans visited restaurants and paid to attend charity balls: they seldom penetrated to the coteries of the Faubourg; they saw bitter-looking workmen exchanging what sounded like snarls at the street-corner bars and learned nothing of the affectionate and united family lives which such men led in their cold-water flats. Years of patience, which neither people was likely to give to the task, would be necessary for the French and the Americans to arrive at mutual comprehension, for no two white peoples were less well equipped to understand one another. The French were Cartesian thinkers, the Americans pragmatic and empirical doers; the French agnostics or Catholics, the Americans fervent in community worship and member participation in all Church activities; they were the old and the new; the *bidet* opposed to the bath-tub; the *crise de foie* to the hangover; irony against good nature; formal manners versus casual; pessimism versus optimism; Notre Dame confronted by Rockefeller Centre; a slow revolving round past griefs outpaced by the determined pursuit of happiness.

CHAPTER XV

THE WAR IN INDO-CHINA

WHEN the Rearmament Law was passed in January 1951, the French had already spent $2188 millions on the war in Indo-China, and the heavy cost in men and money seemed to them to be a powerful reason why they should hesitate to commit themselves to joining a European Army as distinct from the Army of the N.A.T.O. Powers. The situation in the peninsula had grown steadily worse through 1950, for although through the winter of 1949-50 (the time when the 'affair of the generals' first leaked out) it had been possible to talk confidently of mopping-up operations in the Delta as if the main fighting there were over, there had been no real success since the advent to power in China of Mao Tse-tung. The Viet Minh now held an area from the eastern seaboard to the Laotian border, using it as a base for night attacks on convoys which left the French Union troops at daybreak hunting for an enemy who had vanished into the jungle and the shadows. There were sporadic outbreaks of terrorism in Saigon, where hand-grenades were flung and European dwellings set alight, so that both there and in Hanoi there began to be talk of evacuating French dependants. But the French and Vietnamese forces were strong enough to take the offensive in the spring of 1950, and at the end of March to attack simultaneously in the north and south while defending their supply lines round Hué, the key town of central Viet Nam. Again and again the Viet Minh counter-attacked, using the elements of surprise and mobility to advantage, but by May they seemed to be definitely checked, and General Alessandri announced that a territory inhabited by three million Vietnamese had been won back from the followers of Ho Chi Minh.

The rainy season, ending hostilities for a time, allowed the Viet Minh to prepare with Chinese aid for what their radio announced as a great offensive in the autumn. Reports came in of military supplies moving south from China, roads under repair on the Viet Nam side of the frontier, new airfields under construction in the Chinese border provinces, where training camps for Viet Minh troops had also been set up. Military aid from the United States now seemed very necessary, but there had been a hitch in the matter; General Marcel Carpentier had stated that any such aid to Indo-China (as distinct from economic aid) must go through French hands and not direct to the Vietnamese. The Americans, on their side, were still anxious to see a greater measure of independence given to the Associated States, and approved of the proposal to hold a conference at Pau in the Basses-Pyrénées during the summer of 1950, when the handing over of further French organizations to the States would be discussed.

Unfortunately for the opponents of colonialism, the internal politics of Viet Nam had not evolved with that enlightened harmony which is expected to follow the lifting of the oppressor's yoke. If Vietnamese politicians had learned one thing from France it was the technique of the *crise ministérielle*, and Viet Nam's first government lasted only a few months. Bao Dai, the ex-emperor turned chief of state, granted the members of his cabinet 'powers of personal requisition' to further the conduct of the administrative services, with the further power to inflict punishment upon all who disobeyed.[1] Then on April 27 he dissolved the ministry of Nguyen Phan Long and summoned the governor of south Viet Nam, Tran Van Huu, to form another. Thereupon the leading men in central Viet Nam accused the new premier of favouring his old province in the distribution of favours, and also of being pro-French. His predecessor had been accused of being pro-American. From one quarrel to another, it was not an inspiring beginning of self-government.

Some little time before the agreement of March 1949 which gave independence to Viet Nam within the French Union, Émile Bollaert had been succeeded as High Commissioner by Léon Pignon, secretary of the Brazzaville Conference of 1944 which set the French Union on the path of assimilation from which the government was now finding it expedient to retreat. M. Pignon was well acquainted with Indo-China, for in the troubled days following the end of the war with Japan he had been parachuted into Tonkin province to serve as a political counsellor. Now his position in Viet Nam, to which the first American Minister, Mr.

Donald R. Heath, had just been appointed, was likely to be under discussion at the Inter-State Conference at Pau, for the delegations from Laos and Cambodia as well as that from Viet Nam had set out for France determined, if they could, to secure independence, and if possible complete autonomy, for themselves. An American economic mission, led by Robert Blum, had been studying the needs of the Associated States on the spot, and announced in Saigon on June 6 — two weeks before the High Commissioner, Bao Dai and Tran Van Huu left for France — that the United States would provide $23,500,000 in economic aid for the ensuing twelve months. This sum, of which $6,000,000 was earmarked for medical care to be given by an American team, would be payable directly to the Associated States.

The Indo-Chinese delegations at Pau felt their position immeasurably strengthened by this promise, and it was almost with reluctance that they settled down to such technicalities as the status of the port of Saigon and the rights of navigation on the Mekong river. The news of the Korean War, which began simultaneously with their deliberations, was another handicap to steady consideration of their programme, but under the chairmanship of Albert Sarraut, future President of the Council of the French Union, the French kept them firmly to it. They were determined to effect the transfer of the communications and customs systems to the States, and also to settle inter-State immigration and commerce regulations, but they were also determined that the Associated States should remain inside the French Union, with a new ministry of the French Government to look after their interests, and *la présence française* still represented by a High Commissioner. M. Sarraut used a striking phrase to make this position clear to the delegates; France, he said, was draining her life-blood away in Indo-China and would renounce none of her lawful rights there — 'nor go to eat in the kitchen while the [Associated] States sat down at the dining-room table'.[2]

The acceptance of economic aid from America by the Associated States and their need for military aid from France in the conduct of the war against the Viet Minh had placed the French in an uncomfortable predicament. If they continued to insist on keeping the States inside the Union, they antagonized the large section of American opinion which was opposed to 'colonialism' in any form, and which often wilfully misunderstood the nature of the ties now existing between France and Indo-China. If they did as this section wished by withdrawing their troops, indemnifying their colonists and investors, and leaving Indo-China for ever, they would stand accused of cowardice by all those who understood that the wars in Korea and Indo-China were two interrelated parts of the mass Communist attack on South-East Asia, and if they left Indo-China they ran the risk of having to leave North Africa in short order. By fighting the Viet Minh, they were also fighting the Istiqlal, the Neo-Destour and the Algerian Communists, but at the same time the need to keep two divisions in North Africa to handle the potentially explosive situation there meant putting a strain on the needed volunteer replacements for Indo-China.

The time had come to enlarge and equip the Vietnamese Army, the creation of which was one of the penalties of independence which the wealthy merchants and entrepreneurs of Saigon had not quite foreseen, but while only twelve Vietnamese battalions were in existence the promised Viet Minh offensive punctually began on October 1. The Communists, reinforced by Mao Tse-tung's troops, attacked in Upper Tonkin south of the Chinese border, and on October 3, having captured the border posts, attacked Cao-Bang, a key point on the Sino-Vietnamese frontier. The French Union troops, given inadequate air support, were preparing to evacuate the post and retreat southward down a highway harassed by Viet Minh guerrillas when the little garrison at Thatke was ordered to go to their rescue. A junction was effected between the two forces, but on October 8 the column was attacked by the Viet Minh near Dong-Khe and all but annihilated. With over 3000 French Union troops killed out of a total force of 3500, the slaughter of the Cao-Bang garrison was one of the worst defeats of the four-years war, and when the news reached France the Deputies, standing in homage to the dead, adopted an Order of the Day: declaring that the National Assembly

> Pays homage to the heroic sacrifice of officers, N.C.O.s, other ranks and partisans who fell during the military operations;
> Carries to the armies of the French Union, now fighting in

Indo-China, the gratitude of the nation and assures them of
the nation's complete solidarity;

Has confidence that the government will take all the necessary dispositions to give the maximum support to the com-
batants in Indo-China and to assure the defence of the
Associated States.

This was on October 20, four days before René Pleven laid
his plan for a European Army before the Assembly and just as
the Communists were pressing home their attack on the Minister
of National Defence for his handling of the Revers-Mast scandal;
the alleged sale of the Revers report and the disaster at Cao-Bang
were immediately linked together in the public mind. The confidence in the government expressed in the Order of the Day was
only passed, on a vote, by 349 to 218; drastic measures were
necessary, and General Juin was dispatched to Indo-China for a
quick tour of inspection. A state of siege was proclaimed and
general mobilization ordered for all Frenchmen residing in Viet
Nam* and aged between twenty-one and twenty-five, while
within two months of the Cao-Bang disaster 7000 dependants were
evacuated from Hanoi by sea and air. On December 19, anniversary of the outbreak of war, the troopship *Pasteur* arrived with
4500 reinforcements for the troops of the French Union.

Although the Inter-State Conference was still in session at Pau,
Bao Dai and Tran Van Huu had returned to Viet Nam, and were
ready to confer with the High Commissioner and Jean Letourneau,
Minister for the Associated States, who had accompanied General
Juin to Indo-China. Tran Van Huu was still in a mood to claim
more independence for his country: he had been giving press
interviews saying in substance that the 1949 agreement should be
scrapped in favour of a new Franco-Vietnamese treaty, drawn up
on a basis of total equality between the two countries; the ex-
emperor, for his part, was chiefly concerned with the raising of a
Vietnamese Army provisionally fixed at 115,000 men — being the
same number as the French had had in the field since the summer
of 1946. By the end of the year a number of important dispositions
had been made. The Americans had agreed to provide military

---

* In 1951 there were 30,708 French residents in Viet Nam, 4052 in Cambodia, 900
in Laos. Total, 35,660; Total 1946, 16,254.

credits of not less than 350 and not more than 500 million dollars
for the French Union and Vietnamese forces, on the understanding
that the United States would not demand, in return, the right to
establish bases or control the resources of the country, nor
would they encourage the Vietnamese to follow the South Korean
example of appealing for help to the U.N. as long as the French
continued in their way of granting independence by degrees. The
Vietnamese Army, which in its beginning stages had been under
the French High Command, would pass under the command of
Bao Dai from December 12; General Marcel Carpentier was
recalled to France along with Léon Pignon, and their respective
functions of commanding general and High Commissioner would
be filled by one man, General Jean de Lattre de Tassigny.

The arrival of General de Lattre acted like a tonic to the home
government, the troops in the field and the weary, confused
peoples and governments of the Indo-Chinese peninsula. Fully
equal to his double task, de Lattre now had the proconsulship he
had missed in Germany in 1945, and although he had passed the
army age limit (sixty years) he had been retained on the active
list, an honour accorded only to French generals who have been
commanders-in-chief in the field. From his command of the land
armies of Western Union, now assimilated with N.A.T.O., de
Lattre now assumed the command of forces fighting on an unfamiliar terrain, with a mandate to defend the Delta, recover
Upper Tonkin from the Viet Minh and reinforce the naval and
air support needed by the Expeditionary Corps and the Vietnamese.

Jean de Lattre's supple and emotional mind was well fitted to
deal with the subtleties of the ex-emperor, who like other Asiatic
and African personalities of his time was caught between his own
Oriental inheritance and the Occidental affinities formed by his
education in France. Bao Dai was still enough of a despot to
interpret executive power in his own way; once again he provoked
a *crise ministérielle* by dismissing his cabinet, although — quite in
the French manner — he immediately charged the outgoing
premier, Tran Van Huu, to form another. From January 22 to
February 18, 1951, Viet Nam was without a government, and
when the *crise* was over Tran Van Huu was not only still prime
minister but held the ministries of Foreign Affairs, National

Defence and the Interior as well. A week later Cambodia caught the infection and opened a government crisis of its own; Laos, which had a National Assembly of only thirty-nine members, held out until September before indulging in a ministerial crisis, two months long.

The High Commissioner of France looked with a certain indulgence on these upheavals, incidental to the establishment of democratic government in feudal territories, but he was insistent that Viet Nam in her new independence should be set *devant ses responsabilités*, a phrase often used by the more irresponsible elements in the Palais Bourbon. In October 1951 the last of the administrative services directed by the French — the Treasury — would be turned over to the Viet Nam, and de Lattre felt that the young Vietnamese should understand that they were being asked to fight a war not in defence of *la présence française* but in defence of their own free nation. Among the wealthy Vietnamese of Saigon, Hanoi and Hué there was the same spirit of *attentisme* as had existed in Occupied France, a waiting to see whether France or Ho Chi Minh would win the war, as if the only Vietnamese who need be involved were the peasants whose rice paddies had become battle-fields. De Lattre spoke his mind firmly to their sons when he attended graduation exercises at the high school of Saigon.[3]

> Be men! [he said] If you are Communists, go and join the Viet Minh. They have soldiers who are fighting well for an evil cause. But if you are patriots, fight for your country. This war is your own war.

At last the Viet Nam cabinet published the order for general mobilization which on July 18 — four and a half years after the outbreak of hostilities — put their countrymen finally on a war footing. A contingent of 60,000 men was called up, followed by another of 15,000 in October. One thousand young men possessed of school certificates were drafted into officer cadet schools. A census, the first ever taken in Indo-China, was organized to ascertain the number of men of military age.

The government initiative owed much to the dynamism of de Lattre, who was giving his troops their first successes since the Chinese Communists appeared on the frontier. Like most generals in the field he had to contend with amateur strategists at home, notably with Édouard Daladier (who had had some experience during the 'phony war' of 1939-40) and who believed that central Viet Nam was the key sector, Hué the town to be defended. De Lattre's opinion was 'who holds Tonkin holds Indo-China' and he kept to his mandate to defend Hanoi and fortify Haiphong. Against the attacks of the Viet Minh — now numerically stronger and fanatical in their intensity — he opposed a fortified line of over 1000 bunkers holding dug-in defenders, supported by mobile columns for emergency action, and from this defence line he won a number of decisive actions in the 'rice battle' of the spring.

In one of the phases of that battle Lieutenant Bernard de Lattre de Tassigny, the general's only child and a boy soldier of the Resistance, was killed in action at the age of twenty-three, and the bereaved father briefly left his post to escort the body of his son to their little village of Mouilleron-en-Pareds (Vendée) which had also been the birthplace of Georges Clemenceau. Just before Lieutenant de Lattre's death, the general had attended the Singapore Conference, together with the three British commanders-in-chief in the Far East, Vice-Admiral Dewey Stribble, U.S.N., and observers from the Australian and New Zealand general staffs, and had succeeded in persuading them also that Tonkin, more than any other part of Indo-China, was the key to South-East Asia. It was, understandably, with less of his old mannered charm and flair for the spoken word that the bereaved de Lattre continued his international negotiations, but the man who had cheerfully defied Devers and listened to *Poet and Peasant* with Patch still believed in his ability to communicate with the Americans. Their promised aid was coming in very slowly to Indo-China, for the war in Korea was inevitably deflecting a good deal of the necessary matériel. De Lattre therefore prepared to visit Washington in the hope of influencing the large section of American opinion which persisted in seeing the whole situation as the result of colonialism. It was said later in Paris that during one of his visits there at that time he had warned the government to rest on their laurels and make haste to negotiate peace with the Viet Minh as long as they could do so from the strength of his successes in the 'rice battle'. If these were his secret thoughts, they were not allowed to diminish the conviction of his arguments in Washington, strengthened as these undoubtedly were by the just-published opinion of a good friend of France, the American ambassador to Paris, David Bruce.

Mr. Bruce's statement on the French position in Indo-China was the rebuttal of President Franklin Roosevelt's old accusation that France was 'milking' the country for selfish reasons. He said that the French Government could indemnify and repatriate all the French nationals engaged in business or cultivation in the peninsula for a total sum of $250 millions, whereas to fight the Communists was costing them $850 millions a year.[4] Mr. Bruce could have added that whatever profits French enterprise had previously derived from rice, rubber and the other products of Indo-China were steadily shrinking as the war went on, and the awareness of this fact caused a number of French not emotionally involved in the war to wonder why it was necessary to maintain *la présence française* in a territory 8000 miles away. Many Socialists thought in this way, and Pierre Mendès-France, the minister who had urged Draconian measures of austerity after the Liberation, was one of the few Radicals who wanted immediate evacuation. But in de Lattre's Year it was still possible to hope for an eventual victory.

The general's *exposé* in Washington was given with his old verve. He pointed out that while the Vietnamese Army had still to be officered by the French, being 3000 short of the required number of officers, the French had lost 1000 young graduates of the military academy of St. Cyr out of a total loss of 38,000 French Union troops. He called Hanoi:

> what Bastogne was in 1944 and Berlin in 1947. If Hanoi falls, there is no other barrier [against Communism] before Suez . . . The war is not a colonial war, because Indo-China is no longer a colony.
>
> There is nothing left we could grant, nothing more we could transfer; *everything* — save in exceptional cases of delays asked by the Associated States — *everything* has been handed to the governments of the three independent States. We have given our shirt, and now, alas! we must give our lives.

And then, with a touch of the old flamboyance:

> Last October [Ho Chi Minh] thought he had won the game. He inflicted a serious defeat upon us and brought his forces

to the boundary of the Red River Delta. Strong in his five divisions armed with the matériel sent by the China of Mao Tse-tung . . . he shouted from the treetops that he would be master of Hanoi for the New Year. I picked up the challenge and decided to be there myself. It was a question of him or me. Twice since then he has thrown all his forces into the assault. Twice he has failed.[5]

Such was Jean de Lattre's last challenge to the world, the final appearance of 'Général du Théâtre de Marigny'. Two months after returning to his command he was flying west again on sick leave, and at Christmas, when the war was five years old, he entered a Paris clinic for a serious operation. He died there in January at the age of sixty-one.

Once again mourners thronged the Champs Élysées to pay a last tribute to the second of the great soldiers of the Liberation to leave the scene. They were paying homage to a Marshal of France, for the National Assembly had voted the ultimate honour to the man who had led the 1st French Army across the Rhine, and on January 15, when the coffin was conducted from the Invalides to the Arc de Triomphe, President Auriol laid upon it the marshal's baton with the twenty golden stars and the inscription *Terror belli decus pacis*. At the same time, the posthumous honour was conferred on General Leclerc.

The list of the pall-bearers at Notre Dame read like a roll-call of the Liberation. General Eisenhower and Field-Marshal Montgomery represented the Allies; General Juin was there, and Bethouart, and de Montsabert who had liberated Marseilles with de Lattre, and Guillaume, and Vallin, but not Charles de Gaulle. He had gone earlier to the Invalides, and had stood alone beside the coffin, pensive in the wintry afternoon.

Twenty-two years before, de Lattre and his young wife had been almost the only mourners when the body of Georges Clemenceau was carried to Mouilleron-en-Pareds for a secular burial on which the Catholic Vendée closed its pious shutters. 'Such was the farewell of his native village to the saviour of France!' de Lattre had savagely said in later years;[6] but such was not the farewell homage to himself. The whole province seemed to have gathered at Mouilleron with bared heads, even as all the roads across

France had been lined with watchers as the cortège went by. The new gravestone of Bernard de Lattre, so recently killed in action, and the pathetic figure of the Marshal's blind father, ninety-five years old, led to the grave by the still youthful Maréchale, composed such a frieze of grief as had been repeated again and again in France's pantheon. Nothing could have brought home more sharply to the French people the accumulating loss and sorrow of the Indo-Chinese war.

This was the end of de Lattre's Year, and also the end of hopes for a speedy victory or even of a satisfactory ending to the war. The Americans had been sufficiently impressed by the buoyant personality of the general to believe that with increased aid from themselves the thing could be done quickly, but, as the spring campaign of 1952 went on, it became increasingly clear that Indo-China was another Korea: when the weight of the Chinese military machine came in behind the native Communists, the Western forces could not win unless they were willing to start a global war. After a year of fighting the Americans had been willing to agree to a cease-fire and truce negotiations in Korea, and although these did not at once materialize there was an impatience in the United States, a desire to be done with the war in the Far East which indicated that the return of *les boys* would be an important issue in the presidential election of 1952. And yet in Syngman Rhee the Americans had an ally in South Korea who whatever his defects was at least bellicose, whereas it had taken de Lattre himself to wring from Bao Dai, just before the Singapore Conference, a written statement of his determination to wage war on the Communists. The chief of state and his cabinet seemed to be victims of a kind of inertia, a malaise creeping through the cities, and recruiting for the Vietnamese Army again grew slack. Even the spread of the war into Laos, which the Viet Minh invaded on April 12, 1953, did not unduly disturb the *attentistes*, although an airlift of French Union forces to support the tiny Laotian army depleted the defences of Viet Nam. Above all, the departure of Bao Dai himself for Europe, where he moved tranquilly between Switzerland and the Riviera, lowered the morale of even the bravest Vietnamese. An army in the Delta could hardly fight its best for a commander-in-chief at Cannes, who maintained contact with his followers through messages carried by his cousin Prince Buu

Loc, Ambassador at Paris and aspirant to the leadership of an eventual council of regency.

During his term of office General de Lattre had taken severe sanctions against one of the most flagrant abuses current in Indo-China, the traffic in piastres. The monetary unit of Indo-China had been fixed by the second Provisional Government of Charles de Gaulle at the rate of exchange of 17 French francs, being twice its current free market value. This artificially high rate of exchange was confirmed in 1949, when the Associated States became independent, although by then the purchasing power of one piastre was only equal to 5 or 6 francs. It was therefore possible and legal, by obtaining a permit from the Office des Changes in Indo-China, to convert piastres to francs at a considerable profit. The permit, which cost 10 piastres or 170 francs (.50 cents) was issued to all residents in Indo-China regardless of nationality, so that the poorest coolie could earn something by selling his to those who had piastres to transfer; and operation one, which was the *trafic de piastres* in its simplest form, consisted of using the permit to buy a piastre money order convertible into francs in Paris. Operation two consisted of using the francs so obtained to buy U.S. dollars in Paris, smuggling the dollars back to Saigon and selling them for piastres at over 100 per cent profit. With the piastres the vicious circle could begin again, and this was one reason why there were *attentistes* in Indo-China. The big operators, who were not interested in the risk of running dollars into Indo-China, preferred to work at import-export level, using a commercial enterprise in Paris, a branch office in Saigon, a correspondent in New York and another in Hong Kong or Singapore, all handling invoices faked for the benefit of the Office des Changes, but even at that level the circuit worked in the same way: piastres-francs-U.S. dollars-(possibly Hong Kong dollars)-piastres.[7]

In November 1951 President Auriol asked René Pleven, then premier, to arrange a judicial inquiry into the piastre racket, but it was not until *Le Monde* began to publish details of the operation that steps were taken to devalue the currency. On May 10, 1953, the piastre was devalued to 10 francs, and a further devaluation was in view for 1954; but by then the commission of inquiry had had to extend its investigations to cover a book called *Le Trafic de Piastres*, written by a former employee of the Office des

Changes. Jacques Despuech, apparently driven by some curious instinct of self-immolation, was not content with an *exposé* of how the piastre racket worked, for — backing up his allegations by photostats — he named a number of well-known people involved in the black traffic. This led to a side-issue with the Communists, who — no doubt with a view to reviving a circulation which had fallen from 400,000 in 1946 to 145,000 in 1953[8] — published excerpts from the book in *L'Humanité*; and although the editor omitted to publish credits or by-line, he found himself in court, side by side with the indignant M. Despuech and his publisher, when the actions for slander began coming in. Despuech himself was lightly handled by the press, which agreed that the former Resistance agent and ex-sergeant of Marines was an honest man who had felt that his duty lay in exposing scandals which hampered the conduct of a war in which his comrades had fallen and he himself had fought, and the damages which the court found against him were not severe — 50,000 francs ($142; £50) — for a slander on Émile Bollaert, the former High Commissioner, who had no difficulty in clearing himself of Despuech's charges. But there were more actions than one; Paul Auriol was at law again with an accusation of false witness against Henri Dupuy; a business man named Olivier Monasterio started proceedings against Despuech; the witnesses in all these suits read like a roster of Indo-Chinese administrative history as General Revers, Admiral Decoux, Premier Tran Van Huu and ex-Ambassador Xuan successively appeared before the commission of inquiry. Finally, the action for slander brought by André Diethelm[9] against Despuech opened a whole new view on the operations of the R.P.F.

André Diethelm, a *Compagnon* of 1941 and the first Gaullist *Commissaire National à l'Intérieur*, was a former inspector of finances who had devoted himself, in recent years, to the affairs of the R.P.F.

Photostats in *Le Trafic de Piastres* showed that Diethelm, using the names of himself, his wife and his brother-in-law, Jean Bourgoin, had transferred 38,878,000 francs from Saigon to Paris through the Office des Changes, for the purpose of effecting building repairs in France. The allegation that this sum was really intended for the party chest of the R.P.F. brought a number of leading Gaullists into the fray — not the general, who was on tour in Africa, and declared through the party secretary that he 'did not know why the R.P.F. should be summoned [to furnish names and addresses of persons qualified to appear before the commission], since the commission seemed to know all the answers already' — and not, for any length of time, M. Diethelm, who died three months later; but the refusal of the ex-treasurer of the R.P.F., M. Bozel, to testify on the grounds of 'professional secrecy'[10] caused the National Assembly to open a debate on the extent of such privilege in investigating committees. These were the customary side-issues when a financial scandal was being aired, but the piastre story itself did a great deal of harm in the country, for taken in conjunction with the Revers-Mast sensation it persuaded a number of patriotic people that while their sons were fighting in Indo-China for soldiers' pay, a few Frenchmen and their Vietnamese contacts were living in luxury off timely deals in the overvalued currency. The nation as a whole was sick of the war; it had already cost twice as much as the credits obtained through E.R.P.* and had taken the lives of 16,000 French volunteers, 1530 of them officers. Of France's entire officer corps, 26 per cent were serving in the peninsula, making, with 37 per cent of the army's non-commissioned officers, 38,000 of the 180,000† men in the forces of the French Union, who were, and always had been, the thews and sinews of anti-Communist resistance in Indo-China.

---

* Total cost of the Indo-Chinese War to France, to end of 1953, 5478 million dollars. Total aid from E.R.P. to end of 1953, 3849 million dollars. U.S. aid (supplies and equipment) to Indo-China, 1952-53, 682 million dollars.

† The remaining 60,000 effectives in the French Union Forces were Indo-Chinese volunteers.

CHAPTER XVI

THE EUROPEAN DEFENCE COMMUNITY

AFTER the perennial schools question had been dealt with by the newly elected Assembly, the Western Allies hoped that the Deputies would give steady attention to foreign affairs, particularly to the creation of the European Defence Community which was to regulate the European Army. But a full-dress foreign debate scheduled for November 9, 1951, was put off until the 23rd, and again until the 30th while an increase in the price of petrol was thrashed out. From there the Deputies went on to a general debate on the cost of living; in the two years since the franc was last devalued prices had risen by 32 per cent, wages by 15 per cent and taxation to 30 per cent of the national income. René Mayer's austerity finance programme, which included a tax levy intended to yield 2000 million francs, met with such opposition both from the Socialists and the increasingly vocal Peasant Party that the premier squeezed through a vote of confidence by only eighteen votes.

That autumn Winston Churchill had returned to power in Britain at the head of a Conservative government, and General Eisenhower's command at S.H.A.P.E. had been completed by the appointment of Admiral Robert B. Carney, U.S.N., as commander of N.A.T.O.'s southern European sector. Two of the trio who met in the wood near Portsmouth had resumed their former places as Prime Minister of Great Britain and Supreme Commander in Europe, but Charles de Gaulle was not only not in a position to confer with them but in active opposition to an Atlantic Alliance on their terms.

The failure of his Rally to win a commanding majority in the Assembly had marked the end of his anti-Russian phase. He was once again openly anti-American, and he had also reversed his position on the European Army, at least in the form in which it had been seen at the Paris Conference. When the R.P.F. held its *assises nationales* at Nancy at the end of November he intervened in the early discussion to exclaim: 'We need not be American subjects because Americans give us arms!' and his set speech at the closing session was a bitterly sarcastic attack on American approval for the European Army plan.

So our Army must disappear in a hybrid creation, called — to throw us off the scent — European! But since Europe as a responsible and sovereign entity certainly does not exist . . . this force must be handed over to the great American chieftain! [Eisenhower] I ask, in whose name can ardour, confidence, obedience be demanded of French citizens incorporated in a stateless body? . . .
German energy, supported no doubt by our own allies, will soon use the subterfuge of the European army to restore German power and unity . . . It is only in the framework, the bonds of a confederated Europe — which we desire to see — that the various armies of Europe, including the German, may be joined, not confused, in the proper condition.[1]

Thus the general presented the R.P.F. counter-project to the European Defence Community which his followers put before the Assembly in the next few weeks.

This took the form of two bills tabled on December 28, one by Gaston Palewski proposing a referendum open to the whole of Europe, *for or against* a European confederation in spheres of defence, economics and culture, and *for or against* a European Constituent Assembly. The other, in the name of General Pierre Billotte, called for a European Army which should be an association rather than a fusion of the different military systems, and placed under the French commander-in-chief of N.A.T.O.'s central European sector.[2]

These proposals challenged the whole policy by which Robert Schuman had been painfully working towards a new European structure. They denounced the existing European associations from O.E.E.C. to the Council of Ministers as 'fictions, more or less decorative', the Coal and Steel Community as a 'subterfuge', and the idea of a supra-national army as a threat to French leadership in Europe.

Palewski's bill was presented two weeks after the treaty* creat-

---

* Treaty became effective July 25, 1952. Since February 1953 there has been a common market for coal and iron ore for 155 million people in Western Europe. The

ing a European Coal and Steel Community was ratified by the Assembly by 377 votes to 233, a reaffirmation not only of the government's policy but also of the European spirit which had animated men like Schuman, Bidault, Jean Monnet, Pleven and others through all the confusion of the post-war period. The R.P.F. voted almost solidly against ratification. 'What we fear in this projected pool', said Soustelle, '. . . is that we are asked to relinquish a sector of prime importance to a technocracy without a country and subject to no control.'[3]

To this Pleven replied:

> We have at last understood that the unification of Europe cannot be realized except by democratic methods, negotiations, treaties. This is the first such treaty to be concluded, without pressure of any sort, by negotiators convinced that the time for the European Community is ripe. No thinking European can fail to understand that, opposite or beside the Soviet and American economic systems, it is necessary to have in modern Europe an economic system offering equal, if not greater chances of success.[4]

The men who were trying to *faire l'Europe* from small beginnings believed that they had history on their side. More than one Frenchman had tried and failed to remake Europe on a federal basis since the Thirty Years War. The Duc de Sully and his master Henri IV had planned their 'grand design', the Most Christian Association of Europe, to fight against the Turk after uniting fifteen European states under one Council-General. The Abbé de St. Pierre, who unlike Sully included Russia in his scheme, had planned a 'European Society for Perpetual Peace' in which twenty-two states would be represented by a States-General meeting at Utrecht. Less visionary than either of these, the Concert of Europe of 1815 had fallen apart under the pressure of rival nationalisms, though it could at least be said that after its inception Europe enjoyed a long period of peace broken only by Prussia's rehearsals in Denmark and Austria for the victory of 1871. Believing that the federal idea had in all cases led only to

---

Community ranks third among coal, second among steel producers of the world. Pooled resources of the six countries give employment to $\frac{1}{10}$ of their labour force, represent 300 million tons of products, resources valued at 6000 million dollars a year.

rivalries, the men of 1950 had attempted to remake Europe on supra-national lines, creating a parliament in the form of the Assembly of the Council of Europe with its headquarters at Strasbourg and an economic federation in the Coal and Steel Community with its headquarters at Luxembourg, and going on from there to supra-national military defence. They thought the Gaullist idea both out of date and time-wasting; with the threat of Russian aggression never very far away they were not prepared to organize the favourite Gaullist device of a referendum, conducted presumably by means of that other device, the mailing campaign, through all of Europe:

Answer Yes or No to the following Question:

'Do you desire a confederated Europe with supra-national powers?'[5]

On February 19, 1952, by a majority of 327 to 287, the Assembly ratified the *principle* of a European Army. A Gaullist amendment, on the lines of Palewski's bill, was thrown out, and the R.P.F. and the Communists voted together against ratification.

There was a formidable list of reservations and restrictions attached to the ratification, expressive of French uneasiness at the prospect of rearming Germany. Among the most important were:

That the government ask the British and American governments to guarantee, in case of a breach or violation of the treaty by a member nation, the engagements entered into with the European Defence Community by maintaining sufficient American and British forces on the continent for as long as it appears necessary.

That the government renew its efforts to obtain the participation in the European Defence Community of other democratic nations and especially of Great Britain.

That the European Army be subordinated to a supra-national political power with limited but real jurisdiction, responsible to the representatives of the European Assemblies or peoples.[6]

The defeat of the R.P.F. amendment by 474 votes to 119 brought de Gaulle to the Vélodrome d'Hiver four days later, ready to denounce the European Defence Community (by that time under discussion by the N.A.T.O. Council at Lisbon) and to castigate American influence in French affairs. It was now a very sore point with the R.P.F. that American air bases were being constructed in Morocco, where the first two had been installed at Sidi Slimane and Nouasseur near Casablanca, with three others to follow at a total cost of $600 millions by the end of 1955, and Soustelle took up the theme of N.A.T.O.'s forcing France to play a subordinate and dependent rôle on her own soil, while failing to let the French know *why* there had to be a divided command of the N.A.T.O. Army, *why* air bases were necessary at all. In this, Monsieur Soustelle did less than justice to the intelligence of his countrymen, who knew that there were American bases in Morocco and would presently be others in Champagne and Lorraine because the Russians were only three hundred miles from Paris.

At the Vél' d' Hiv' de Gaulle lamented that

matters had been arranged so that through S.H.A.P.E., N.A.T.O., the Permanent Committee, the Committee of those who modestly call themselves the Three Wise Men, etc. etc., France has no more say in her own affairs.

It was the old nationalistic line, and there would always be millions of Frenchmen to respond to it, just as they had responded to the *revanchards* of an earlier generation: the important thing was, as Hitler knew when he attacked the Jews, to find some object for aversion. Thus a Boulanger or a Déroulède had attacked the Germans, but Charles de Gaulle had outclassed the *revanchards* by fighting on two fronts. Only a few months before he had been insisting that

France must arm to the point where we can one day dictate peace to the U.S.S.R. and make the Soviets either renounce their ambitions or disappear.[7]

Now it was the Americans, who wanted to dominate France and make an end of the French Army, who were the object of his attacks. But in spite of him the work of 'making Europe' went forward, and a treaty founding the European Defence Community was signed in Paris on May 27.

On the previous day Monsieur Schuman was in Bonn, where he and Dr. Adenauer (the Briand and Stresemann of their day) signed with Mr. Eden and Mr. Acheson the peace contract which ended the Occupation Statute in Germany, abolished the Allied High Commissions and admitted the Federal Republic as an equal partner in the European Community. The next step would be the West German Army, and Bonn had already been demanding a regular army of 250,000 men, a tactical air force and complete representation in all N.A.T.O. groups. The E.D.C. treaty of May 27 gave the West Germans even more advantageous terms. To the 43 European Army divisions planned for the end of 1954, they were to contribute 12 (against the French 14) and they fixed their peacetime strength at 410,000 men, 500,000 in time of war.

Another problem which the French regarded as part of the E.D.C. idea was the status of the Saar. The tiny territory on the Franco-German border north of Lorraine, only 990 square miles in extent, now enjoyed the most prosperous economy in Europe, and in 1952 was able to contribute 3 million tons of steel and 16 million tons of coal to the Coal and Steel Community. By the Saar Constitution of 1947, which gave the territory political autonomy, an economic union with France had been established, and this meant that the joint coal and steel production of France and the Saar was, particularly as regards steel, within measurable distance of the German output. But, as had happened in the early days of the Hitler régime, there was a tendency in Germany to regard the Saar as an ethnological and economic part of that country, and the Quai d'Orsay was increasingly anxious to have the status of the Saar defined even more precisely than by the Constitution of 1947. In February 1952, therefore, Schuman put forward proposals to Europeanize the territory, confirming the sovereignty of the Saar and abolishing the special rights until then reserved to France's representative. The defence of the Saar by France would be made subject to international agreement, a Court of Arbitration would be presided over by a neutral personality connected with either the Council of Europe or the Coal and Steel Community, and the monetary and customs union already established with France would become a complete contractual partnership.

That these proposals were satisfying to the Saarlanders there could be little doubt, because in the following November, at legislative elections held for the Landtag of sixty members, 87.3

per cent of the votes cast were in support of parties favouring the Europeanization of the Saar. The German reaction was less favourable, and the talks initiated by Robert Schuman with the Federal Government early in 1952 were broken off prior to the Saar elections. It was apparent that further negotiation would be necessary, but the hitch served to stiffen French opposition to the integration of Germany, already showing renewed intransigence on such a familiar point of difference as the Saar, with the European Defence Community.

Although France signed the treaty, there were several points which clashed with the recommendations of the Assembly. When the Pleven Plan was first formed, the idea had been to integrate the forces at the lowest possible echelon, so that national cadres and commanders might be eliminated as much as possible and so frustrate a German national predominance. The French had proposed integration at battalion level (800-1200 men) and had opposed the American proposal of combat teams of 5000-6000 men, but the treaty provided for integration at divisional level, which would keep the national units at the peacetime infantry division strength of 13,000. Britain and America signed, with France, a supplementary agreement promising that they, as Great Powers, would maintain protective forces on the Continent, but the 'guarantees' required by the Assembly were not given in any precise form.* Instead of the recommended 'supra-national political power', a complicated organization consisting of a proportionally elected Council of Ministers, plus the Assembly running the Coal and Steel Community, plus an Executive Bureau might be called 'supra-national', but would not, as the French had wished, be responsible to individual governments. From the National Assembly's viewpoint there were plenty of holes to pick in the E.D.C. treaty, and when it was remembered what the Deputies could do with a debate on the price of petrol it might be expected that the debates on ratifying the treaty — which had to be sent back to the parliaments of each signatory — would be prolonged and inconclusive, as indeed they were.

The opponents of E.D.C. therefore prepared to fight a long

* They were finally given in April 1954, in the form of an Agreement signed between the French and British Governments, and a Declaration by the President of the United States.

delaying action, and Gaullists and Communists (each side trumpeting defiance of the other) made common cause against those who wished 'to discipline a continent and defend a certain concept of mankind'. Their task was made all the easier by upheavals within the government.

History had repeated itself for René Pleven. In 1952 as in 1951, at the very moment when the original Pleven Plan was about to take another step forward, he had been obliged to give up the premiership, this time over a wrangle about the nationalized railways, which were running at a loss. His successor, Edgar Faure, was a brilliant financier whose period in office just covered the ratification of the European Army plan before he was succeeded on March 6 by Antoine Pinay, an Independent, and the first politician from a party to the Right of Centre to take office since the Liberation. Three prime ministers in three months challenged the record of the cabinet changes of 1948, but M. Pinay had the merit of being a novelty — as Minister of Public Works he had been little known; he was not a *résistentialiste* (a Sartrean nickname now in favour with the Right); he was an unassuming small man who ran a tannery as a regular occupation, and he had a definite and comprehensible object: to save and stabilize the franc.*

The advent of Antoine Pinay had a considerable effect on the fortunes of Charles de Gaulle. All his objectives — the defeat of E.D.C., the passing of a new electoral law abolishing the *apparentements*, restoring the two-round voting and giving the R.P.F. a real chance to sweep the country — depended on his keeping his parliamentary strength intact *and using it*. To do so, of course, he would have had to be in the *hémicycle* himself, and there he would not venture; all the other party leaders were in the Chamber with their followers, and nothing could have been more cumbersome than the coming and going of messengers bringing the Oracle's instructions from R.P.F. headquarters in the rue de Solferino (they were often relayed from Colombey) to the R.P.F. Deputies assembled in the Salle Colbert. It was the fact that its strength

---

* The Budget Laws of April 1952 (*l'Expérience Pinay*) declared a fiscal amnesty to bring out hoarded capital but suspended future tax evaders from exercising trade or profession or holding a driver's licence; ordered the making out of bills, complete with the buyer's name and address, to cover all sales. (Selling without billing was a favourite tax evasion among shopkeepers, who also disliked payment by cheque.)

was not being used that splintered the party, for among its 118 Deputies there were a number who had taken to the Palais Bourbon like ducks to water, and resented the endless opposing without constructive opposition forced upon them by de Gaulle's decision that the R.P.F. should wait upon events — preferably catastrophic events — before taking action. They wanted to change the laws before they changed the régime; they knew that their deadweight of resistance made the R.P.F. a valuable asset of the Communist Party. On March 5 their spirits were further shaken by the cold and harsh terms of an address made by de Gaulle to the R.P.F. groups in the Assembly and Senate (as the Conseil de la République had come to be called) in which he said:

> The French people (*la masse française*) has not really suffered yet. As long as they can live on their own fat and on international beggary, they will feel no need to resort to us. But when they again come close to drama, then it is to ourselves that they will have recourse again.[8]

La masse française n'a pas encore vraiment souffert. It was the old Indo-China theme ('not enough blood has been shed here yet') and it undoubtedly influenced the group of Deputies who wrote to the general that Antoine Pinay stood for many of the same principles as they did, and for these they would work rather than support his 'sterile and unpopular' objections to party government. Next day twenty-seven R.P.F. Deputies bolted the party and voted for Pinay's investiture.

They were duly purged from the party, and after being joined by a few more dissidents formed, under the leadership of Edmond Barrachin and General Billotte, a splinter Assembly group under the name of *Action Républicaine et Sociale* (A.R.S.). Once the struggle between the R.P.F. steering committee (all hand-picked by de Gaulle, like the Free French National Committee of 1941) and the would-be people's Deputies had opened, it was easier to go on than to stop. On November 7 the committee expelled several members of the Paris Municipal Council from R.P.F. membership. Paul Coirre, who had succeeded Pierre de Gaulle as council president, and Jean-Louis Vigier, head of the Gaullist *Agence Parisienne d'Information*, were among the purged; other city councillors resigned in sympathy, until eventually the R.P.F. had only 27 members out of the 90 in the Paris Municipal Council against 52 in 1947. At the next municipal election, the Rally lost 2000 seats throughout France.

But at midsummer 1952 the general public was relatively undisturbed by either the instability of the cabinet or the beginning of what *Paris-Match* picturesquely called the slow agony of the R.P.F. There were livelier topics for discussion — topics which had the merit of association with the past; one, in particular, which caused the Church and State quarrel to flare up again.

This was the *cause célèbre* of the Finaly children, two little Jewish boys whose parents had been deported under the Occupation and had died in a German concentration camp. Robert and Gérard had been mere infants when they passed under the kindly care of Mdlle Brun, a devoutly Catholic lady who was in charge of the municipal children's home at Grenoble, and who waited for five years — the last wish of the unfortunate parents had been to have their sons brought up as Jews — before she had them baptized into the Catholic faith. Some years passed before their nearest surviving relative, an Israeli citizen, discovered their whereabouts, but once Mrs. Rosner had found them and had laid her petition before the Grenoble courts in July 1952, she was given the custody of her nephews.

For Mdlle Brun this was not merely a matter of parting from her foster-children, but of two Christian souls at stake. She enlisted the help of the Church; the boys were spirited away, and it was believed that they had found sanctuary across the Spanish border. Six priests and two nuns were arrested as accessories to the kidnapping.

All France took sides in the case of *les enfants Finaly*. That they were Jews by birth added piquancy to the story, for the Jewish element in the country was acutely conscious of its wartime sufferings and also of the anti-Semitism which was creeping back in certain quarters; there was a spirited attempt to turn the two little lads into a kind of composite Dreyfus. But the anti-clericals at heart cared little if Robert and Gérard were Jews, Buddhists or Confucians, for it was the weapon they had provided against the Church which mattered — the Church which had resorted to such medieval illegalities as kidnapping and sequestration — and news pictures of the stout and sobbing Mdlle Brun, begging the sentries at Rambouillet to admit her to the President, aroused no sympathy in radical hearts. Months later the Church and the Rabbinate arrived at a concordat; Robert and Gérard were unearthed near San Sebastian (three more priests were arrested in the process), Mrs. Rosner joyfully dropped all the suits she had filed against those who had come between her and her nephews, and the children were removed from France to a new community in Israel, where they were told they could practise the Catholic religion if they liked.

As if this tale of souls at stake, youths lost to France, interference by the religious orders and the rivalry of foster-mothers had not contained enough human interest to drive the integration-levels of the European Army out of everyone's mind, General Juin provided some new sensations.

The award of the posthumous title of Marshal of France to General de Lattre and General Leclerc earlier in the year had posed a delicate problem in regard to Juin, whose claim to the highest military honour was at least as good as theirs. In May the Assembly decided to confer it upon him, and so for the first time in a number of years France was to have an active Marshal — for Pétain had been a deportee and a prisoner for seven years before his death, and Marshal Franchet d'Esperey had died during the Occupation, at an advanced age. Marshal Juin, when he took the baton from President Auriol's hands under the Arc de Triomphe on July 14, was a virile, burly figure at the age of sixty-six: he got a lot of cheering from the *populo*, which had always liked in him the combination of the lucky general, the *bon viveur* and the policeman's boy from Bône. Just how active he was likely to be he had proved three weeks earlier, when he delivered a commemorative address in honour of the dead of Verdun, that terrible battlefield inseparably and nobly associated with the name of Philippe Pétain.

There is a name upon the lips of all [said Juin] which the subsequent vicissitudes of history cannot dissociate from the days of Verdun: the name of the leader whose mortal remains ought one day to be united with those of the thousands and thousands of soldiers whom he commanded and inspired in that battle, and who are here mingled with the soil they fought so bitterly to defend.[9]

It was known to have been Pétain's great wish to be buried among his soldiers, a wish which the charge of treason upheld against him had caused to be denied. It was emphatically not the government's wish to stir up trouble by ordering an exhumation and a reburial at Verdun, with all the veterans' associations brawling for and against the Marshal; even President Auriol, for all his final act of clemency, had no desire to play Louis Philippe to the ashes of a new Bonaparte. René Pleven, at the time Minister of National Defence, reminded Juin that officers must submit manuscripts of their speeches and writings for publication for his approval, but this made little impression on the new Marshal. In October he was fulminating against the United Nations, to which Morocco had appealed:* France should walk out of the U.N., he said, if that body interfered in Morocco, where the French Protectorate had been recognized by all the Powers at the time when it was signed. It began to be said that the Marshal, who had always liked to share in a rollicking song, now thought very well of himself as an orator and would be heard of further. His championship of Marshal Pétain had given offence to the Left, but this was less remarkable than the fact that he had been able to pay such a tribute (carefully phrased as it was to 'Pétain, the commander of the 2nd Army', not to the former chief of state) only seven years after the Marshal's arrest and abasement. Not long before, Jean Paulhan, a leading and authentic Resistant, President of the *Comité National des Écrivains*, who had left *Les Lettres Françaises* when the Communists moved in and was now literary director at Gallimard, had startled the French with the published statement that from 1940 to 1944 'the legal government of France was that of the Marshal', from which he deduced that to 'condemn the collaborators and let the victims judge the hangmen was to make sport of justice'. This brochure, entitled *Lettre Aux Directeurs de la Résistance*, had to be withdrawn from circulation: the time was not yet ripe for it, but taken in conjunction with Juin's speech it indicated a change in the attitude of sensible men towards Vichy, and of men of sensibility towards the Vichy chief.

* See chapter XVII.

Religious quarrels and Vichy retrospects, while passionately interesting to the French, impressed the Americans as being quite irrelevant to the burning question of the day: the raising of a European Army to fight Communism. But the American pressurizing defeated its own ends, for it alarmed the French; they saw themselves participating willy-nilly in a 'police action' beyond the iron curtain if the Americans decided to liberate some of Russia's satellites — perhaps requiring liberation themselves as a result, and the prospect was not enticing. Why, they inquired, should they be in an unseemly hurry to ratify the E.D.C. treaty? Congress had refused to ratify the peace treaty signed by President Wilson after World War I, and that, however fatal an error, had been the concern of Congress, just as E.D.C. was the concern of the National Assembly. But to the Americans of 1952 the days of Wilson were as dead as the dodo. They were about to elect General Eisenhower as President of the United States, by one of the record majorities of their history, and they felt it typical of the perverse French, with whom *le général Ike* had been so popular, to exhibit a preference for his opponent, Governor Adlai Stevenson.

French anxieties about a Republican administration had been obvious from the beginning of 1951; in 1952 they were a major cause of delay in ratifying the E.D.C. treaty. The 'Great Debate' in Congress, when the principle of sending 'American boys' to fight on foreign soil had been exhaustively examined, had been succeeded by markedly isolationist statements by former President Herbert Hoover, who wished all American ground forces withdrawn from Europe, and future presidential candidate Robert A. Taft, who similarly ruled out the use of American ground troops in Indo-China. Both believed that American defences should be based on the United States, with arms supplies for European allies.

When General Eisenhower was elected President early in November, the event moved de Gaulle to tell the R.P.F. *assises*, held in Paris on November 10-11, that his victory represented 'a tide of action, ambition and exigence' against which French independence and security could only be assured if France 'stood up for herself' without any 'half-baked nonsense about a so-called European Army'. Other observers were less concerned with what

Eisenhower might do on his own initiative than with the concordat he seemed to have made, through a well-publicized meeting with Senator Taft, with the isolationist element in the Republican Party. Would he go over to the idea of a peripheral strategy, or the defence of the American continent by a super-airforce and the atomic bomb, or — while honouring his election pledge to bring *les boys* back from Korea — would he get the Taft element to compromise on bolstering anti-Communism in the Far East at the expense of American commitments in Europe? Either way, would Europe be left to her fate? Or would the new men in the State Department, reversing the Acheson policy of containing the Communist world, persuade the Liberator to a new 'Crusade in Europe'?

France, in the closing days of 1952, stood between the devil of American impetuosity and the deep sea of American isolationism, and was nearly as far from realizing the European Army plan as she had been two years before. She was also without a government, by now a chronic state, for the M.R.P., tiring of Monsieur Pinay, had brought him down on a matter of the family welfare funds, on which, since they were oversubscribed, he had proposed to draw for his budget. He left office on December 23, breathing what were for any French premier the most unusual oaths of never again assuming the leadership of such a pack of ingrates. When General Eisenhower was inaugurated as President in January the United States had had one change of party government since 1944, the first in twenty years; Britain had had two, while France was embarking, with René Mayer at the helm, on her eighteenth cabinet since the Liberation.

CHAPTER XVII

END OF THE *SEPTENNAT*

I N October 1952 President Vincent Auriol made a journey to Provence to inaugurate the new hydro-electric works at Donzère-Mondragon. Three years previously he had opened the power station at Génissiat, in the gorges of the upper Rhône, which with the André Blondel power-house at Donzère completed two parts of the great project to canalize the natural reservoir of Lac Léman, create a navigable waterway to the Mediterranean, and harness the leaping force of the Rhône to provide hydro-electric power for the darkened homes and factories of France.

The Compagnie Nationale du Rhône,* which was about to start on the third part of its project at Montélimar, had prepared its blueprints as far back as 1934, and the Génissiat station, on which work had been interrupted during the war, had been constructed entirely with French funds. In the case of Donzère, the E.R.P. counterpart funds had been drawn upon ($33,880,000 was transferred through the Fonds de Modernisation et d'Équipement up to December 31, 1950) and used for the purchase of American machine tools. Twice the amount of the counterpart sum was subscribed by other sources: a public loan, a grant from the Caisse des Dépôts et Consignations and a capital allocation by the C.N.R. itself. Donzère was thus a striking proof of the confidence of the French investor as well as of the ability of French engineers and workmen, and it would produce 2000 million kilowatt hours of electricity annually for the whole of France. The barrage, the largest in Western Europe, had been constructed with a regard to the human element which amazed American engineers. The little *bourgades* of Provence, dating back to Gallo-Roman times, had all been spared, and the necessary expropriation or purchase of farms and dwellings had been followed by the erection of six *Cités Ouvrières* of chalet-type houses, equipped with modern school

---

* The C.N.R., an example of mixed economy, was partly run by private enterprise, partly nationalized through a connection with Électricité de France.

buildings, field hospitals, stores and recreation centres for the 10,000 workers and dependants on the project.

Donzère — which traced its own origins back to A.D. 674 and had witnessed dramatic episodes in French history from the defeat of the Saracens to Napoleon's return from Elba — thus stood for one of the great technical successes of Liberated France, but it had received little attention in the world press. Anything written about the region, in the months when the André Blondel power station was nearing completion, had to do with Pont-St.-Esprit, a little town near the barrage, where a content of ergot in the bakers' flour had afflicted many of the population (5000) with a painful illness accompanied by compulsive dancing and delusions of demoniac persecution. It was not amusing for the promptly formed *Association pour la Défense des Victimes Intoxiqués par le pain de Pont-St.-Esprit*, but it was the kind of story about France which made the headlines: sensational, with overtones of disparaging pity. The pathetic little old town with its tainted bread and whirling natives presented just the right contrast to the cities of West Germany, now rising from the rubble of the war to new levels of progress and productivity.

At Donzère on October 25, in the presence of the *corps diplomatique*, President Auriol spoke dramatically of the Allied tendency to praise and pamper Germany at the expense of France.

> I shall not attempt to conceal [he said] that although we feel no hatred for those who have made us suffer, and could forget their cruel acts if they themselves would but remember, we are profoundly wounded by comparisons now made between their discipline and will-to-power, and the alleged softness and heedlessness of France.
>
> We are wounded, because it seems as if the defeated enemy is to enjoy all the care and attention on the pretext that he has renewed his strength — as if the aggressor deserved more encouragement than his victim![1]

It was a well-deserved reproof to Britain and America. Having overridden France's steady objections to the centralization of German government and the rebuilding of German war potential, they now disregarded the fact that — as President Auriol pointed out — the efficient Germans had not only failed to repay France more than 1/1000th part of their war reparations, or make good more than 1/1000th part of the damage they had wrought, but had profited by the personal spending of the Occupation troops at a time when France, instead, was incurring new burdens of defence expenditure. At Donzère Auriol drew the conclusion that under such circumstances 'France had the right to take refuge in her own sufferings' — a gloomy prospect for the second *septennat* of the Fourth Republic, but one anticipated by English-language publications, which steadily reported that France had gone within herself in an access of sensibility, her genius in eclipse and her political processes deliberately immobilized.

As President Auriol's term of office drew to a close, however, it was possible to assess the position of Liberated France in a fairer way. In seven years the country had literally risen from its ashes and for the second time since 1914 had repaired almost completely the physical destruction of a great war. It had been estimated when the Monnet Plan was first set on foot that if the whole proceeds of the French economy could be put into the work of reconstruction, the total income of three and a half years would be required to rebuild ruins which stretched from the English Channel to the Côte d'Azur. This of course had not been possible but, even while what came in by way of aid from America was spent twice over in Indo-China, the indestructible French had somehow made good their losses. Not only had all roads and bridges been rebuilt but two great new auto-routes running from north to south, with terminals at Marseilles and Lille, were about to be added to the auto-route running from Paris to the west. The Paris continental airport, shattered when Leclerc's men and the F.F.I. won the battle of Le Bourget in August 1944, had been rebuilt on the same impressive scale as the international terminal at Orly, where the services of Air Transport Command had operated in icy sheds during the Liberation winter. At Le Havre, where transatlantic passengers had scrambled over planks and rubble in 1947, a magnificent maritime terminal had been erected by 1950.

The towns destroyed by the Germans in World War I — notably Lens, Bapaume and Cambrai — had not been completely rebuilt until 1928. Yet with heroic energy the task was resumed after the second German aggression, and the little towns were rebuilt in styles suited to their climate and culture from Sotteville-les-Rouen's modern rectangles to the curved Provençal arcades of Sanary (Var). New villages sprang up, as at Siracourt in the Pas-de-Calais, at Saint-Dié in the Vosges; ancient Saint-Dizier (Haute Marne) became Saint Dizier-le-Neuf; Orléans developed a plan of urbanism of an elegance suited to its royal history. At Saint-Lô, one of the first towns destroyed in the Liberation fighting (demolition of the ruins alone occupied two years), 96 per cent of the town site had been rebuilt by 1953; at Royan, one of the last — it was blitzed just before the Germans surrendered the Atlantic pockets in April 1945 — 2650 out of 3800 ruined homes had been replaced.

It is true that the experts of the Monnet Plan, now more accurately called the modernization programme — for Jean Monnet himself had departed to direct the Coal and Steel Community at Luxembourg and had been succeeded by Étienne Hirsch — were disappointed with the rate of housing production (80,000 houses built in 1952-53) and with the farmers, who had fallen short by 42 per cent of the production target set for them, and even with industrialists who, though only 5 per cent behind in production, seemed to have settled down into the old 'sclerotic' economy, with no impulse of expansion, as soon as the 1929 peak had been slightly passed. But on the other hand gold-hoarding had declined, and the franc was so much stronger that the black-market rate had dropped to 366 to the dollar, very near the official rate of 350. The dollar gap was no wider and the trade balance with foreign countries was much improved. There were far fewer registered unemployed in France than in Britain, Belgium, Italy or West Germany, and France was the only major country in the West to have applied the principle laid down by the Geneva Convention of 1952, giving employed women equal pay for equal work.

All through the land there were new developments. Where the desolate Camargue swamps stretched south from Arles, the gipsies going towards their annual meeting at Les Saintes Maries de la Mer now crossed a transfigured area where 50,000 acres had been reclaimed for rice growing. Petro-chemicals in the south and plastics in the north were new additions to French scientific products, while rapid progress in artificial textiles accounted for

5 per cent of the world output. Seventeen new liners were launched in 1952-53. Construction was begun on a gas feeder, 435 miles long, to carry to Paris and towns along the line a daily volume of 260 million gallons of gas released in the coke ovens of the Lorraine and Saar basins. Two atomic piles, the second completed at Saclay in 1952, formed the basis of a Five-Year Plan (1952-57) to transform atomically generated heat into electric power.[2]

The list of positive achievements was impressive, but in the eyes of the world it was dwarfed by the ever-lengthening tale of French political instability. René Mayer lasted as premier from January 7 to May 21, 1953, when his defeat on a well-worn issue, the right of a cabinet to govern by emergency decree-laws, opened the longest of all the *crises ministérielles* since the Liberation. This crisis produced some interesting candidates for office, among them Paul Reynaud, who came fairly near to regaining the premiership which he had resigned in June 1940 in favour of Marshal Pétain. The political indestructibility of MM. Daladier and Reynaud had indeed made false prophets out of the *émigré* pamphleteers; furthermore, both were now completely *rangés*. M. Daladier had remarried at the age of sixty-five; while M. Reynaud, the physical culturist, was at seventy-four enjoying a happy and fruitful second marriage.

The constant reappearance of the two pre-war party leaders, with others like themselves, in the political carrousel was entirely consistent with the Third Republican system in which most of their working lives had been spent. But one of the *pressentis* in the crisis which dragged from May into June 1953 had the advantage of being a man who had kept out of the struggle for office since his resignation, on April 5, 1945, from the post of Minister of National Economy in de Gaulle's cabinet. Pierre Mendès-France was still only forty-six years old; consistently re-elected as Radical-Socialist Deputy for the Eure, which had sent him to the old Chambre des Députés at the early age of twenty-five, he had been employed since 1945 in high executive posts in the International Bank for Reconstruction in Washington, the International Monetary Fund and the Commission des Comptes. Now, seeking investiture as premier from the Assemblée Nationale, he warned the Deputies — as sternly and as vainly as he had advocated an austerity programme at the Liberation — that the sail the nation was carrying must be shortened: specifically, that the war in Indo-China, impossible to win, must be brought to an end before worse things befell in the danger spots of North Africa. But the day of power had not yet dawned for Mendès-France. He missed investiture by thirteen votes, and on June 26 the *crise* ended with the election of the conservative Joseph Laniel, *ci-devant* Lisieux of the National Resistance Council, as the nineteenth premier of Liberated France.

It was not a popular choice, for there was jealousy of the large fortunes accruing to M. Laniel from the family textile concern in Normandy, and from his marriage into a family of wealthy Marseilles contractors; while the premier himself was a plethoric, fumbling, ambitious man who by a maladroit application of his first programme of economies plunged France almost immediately into a series of lacerating strikes, which incidentally paralysed the tourist traffic of August 1953.

At that time, as the weeks without public services followed the weeks without a government, Paris once again lay silent and empty, supine and relaxed along the banks of the Seine like some antique and ailing deity awaiting the transfusion of a new supply of strength. As so often before, and so deceptively, the inhabitants gave the impression of being more interested in superficialities than in urgent problems. There were increasing interest in and discussion of television, for the retail of TV sets had been greatly stimulated by the televised Coronation of Queen Elizabeth II, and the annual Tour de France bicycle race was followed with even more than the usual passionate enthusiasm. The hero of France, at midsummer 1953, was neither soldier nor statesman: he was Louis Bobet, the first Frenchman for years to win the 3000-mile race and break the series of Italian and Swiss victories recorded when the Coppis, Bartalis, Kublers and Koblets came speeding up the last lap at the Parc des Princes. Bobet won the Yellow Sweater, auspiciously enough, in the Tour du Cinquantenaire, the fiftieth anniversary of the event which for boys and men in France takes the place of the World Series in America or the Test Matches in Britain, and his success caused far more popular emotion than the news that three thousand North Africans had started a riot on Bastille Day after a Communist parade through Paris, where *les sidis* presented much the same problem as the Puerto Rican population of New York. Yet North Africa, so close to France geographically and economically, was — as Mendès-France had warned the Assembly one month before — the area of all others where a repetition of the Indo-China disaster might be expected to take place.

The geographical land mass called the Maghreb, enclosed by the Atlantic, the Mediterranean, the post-war kingdom of Libya and the Sahara desert, included the three Algerian Departments and the two Protectorates of Tunisia and Morocco, the latter having passed into the French sphere of influence by treaty, in 1881-83 and 1912 respectively. In all three countries a number of similar conditions existed: the representation of *la présence française* by French colonists in groups of varying sizes (800,000 in Algeria, 240,000 in Tunisia, 100,000 in Morocco); an economic situation jeopardized, like French prestige, by World War II; an openness to Communist propaganda; and above all the strong nationalistic influence, emanating from Cairo, of the Maghreb Committee and the Arab League. All had the same monetary unit, the metropolitan franc, and all were included in the modernization and re-equipment schemes of the Monnet Plan, which called for the public and private investment of 244,000 million francs in North Africa between 1946 and 1950.[3]

These schemes had opened new zones of industrial development in the northern Sahara, along the Morocco-Algeria border, while coalfields were already being worked at Djerada and Colomb Bechar. Lead, zinc, copper, manganese and cobalt were being prospected in an area of great strategic importance, the turntable for all French Africa. These developments were spectacular enough, in one way, to overshadow all that French resources and energy had already accomplished in territories which within the space of fifty years had been brought up from the level of the fourteenth century; in another, they failed to counterbalance the steadily rising demands for total independence, too often expressed by acts of violence and terrorism against the French colonists. There was a Communist Party in Algeria which could always count on support from such members of the nationalist groups as were dissatisfied with the compromise terms of the Organic Statute of Algeria. Voted in 1947 by a large majority (325-86) of the National Assembly, the Statute provided for a separate Algerian Assembly of 120 members elected by universal suffrage, enabled to vote the budget and 'direct the interests of Algeria in agreement with the Governor-General'. It was the presence of the latter, a Frenchman assisted by a government council of six, which irritated the nationalists, among the most vocal of whom were the *Union Démocratique du Manifeste Algérien*, led by Ferhat Abbas, and demanding an autonomous Algerian Republic within the French Union. Another group, the *Triomphé des Libertés Démocratiques*, adopted the slogan of 'Suitcase or Coffin!' meaning that the French could either leave Algeria of their own accord or stay to be massacred.

When the French protectorate was established in 1881-83, the Regency of Tunis, a vestigial relic of the Turkish Empire in Africa, had been under the absolute rule of the Bey. The administration was on a feudal level, with the civil and religious life of the one and a half million inhabitants centred on the Great Mosque. The French gave the Tunisians civil liberties, abolished racial and religious discriminations and introduced freedom of the press, all of which improvements were generously employed by the Tunisian nationalists, after World War II, to attack *la présence française* in their country. The nationalists were grouped principally in the two Destour movements: the Vieux Destour, strongest among the students of the Great Mosque, and the Néo Destour led by Habib Bourguiba, who returned to Tunis in 1949 after four years of close contact with the Arab League and the World Islamic Movement in Cairo. With a large following in the trade unions, he was the natural spokesman for Tunisian aspirations.

The havoc caused by the military operations of 1942-43, when the ports and 39 per cent of the bridges were destroyed, and the unrest caused by the presence of foreign troops in the country, was used by the nationalists to foment ill-feeling against France. All that France had done for the Protectorate, the modernization of methods in a pastoral country, the introduction of industries, the infrastructure of five modern seaports, eleven airports, eight dams, and 9000 miles of road laid across what had been a trackless land, was ignored or belittled by those who clamoured for independence. The 1000 schools and 7000 teachers (there had been 150 in 1883) and the free medical services provided by 1000 doctors working in 236 hospitals and dispensaries[4] were not benefits which made any appeal to the fanatics of the Destour. Aware that the French Socialist party sympathized with the movement for independence, Habib Bourguiba visited France with the Bey's approval in May 1949. The outcome of his visit was the series of reforms proposed by a new French Resident, M. Perillier, giving Tunisians more share in the government and administration of the country. Unfortunately the French colonists, numbering some 240,000, strongly disapproved of the proposals, and formal opposition was made by the General Union of French Civil Servants in Tunisia. Strikes broke out among the 50,000 Tunisians employed in the French-directed industries; the French Government fumbled with the problem through 1950 and, by the time an agreement was reached on the composition of the administrative councils of the country, Habib Bourguiba's followers were screaming for either the termination of the protectorate or 'Blood and War!'

In Morocco the same spirit was abroad. The physical aspect of the country, like that of Tunisia, had changed very much since the French assumed the Protectorate in 1912, for at the turn of the century the Shereefian Empire was a barbaric land with a coastline but no seaports, where the few communication lines were horse or mule trails. Then, when a man left the semi-civilization of Fez or Marrakesh, Casablanca or Rabat, he stepped straight into Bled-el-Khouf, the country of fear, or Bled-el-Sif, the country of the sword. The Alouite dynasty, which had ruled the land since the seventeenth century, was represented by a weak sultan who in 1900 offered the British a Protectorate over Morocco if they would restore order in the land.

It was the period just after Fashoda, when Lord Lansdowne for Britain and the Foreign Minister, Delcassé, for France, were laying the foundations of a better understanding between the two countries, whose rival aspirations in Africa had brought them to the verge of war in 1898. Rather than take up the sultan's offer, the British preferred to trade influence in Morocco with the French in return for unchallenged influence in Egypt, a clause in the Entente Cordiale which caused heartburnings in Germany. Baron Speck von Sternburg, German Ambassador at Washington, tried to persuade President Theodore Roosevelt to object to the French infiltration of Morocco, but the President thought he might be 'sharply attacked in political circles and public opinion' for doing so, because 'Americans believe that the interior of Morocco is inhabited by quite lawless tribes over whom the Sultan has no authority, and thinking people would gladly see Morocco civilized by a foreign power, just as Egypt was'.[5] Out of office, the Rough Rider stuck to his guns, and in 1910, two years before the French Protectorate was declared, he told the German chancellor, Bethmann-Hollweg, that 'in Africa all white men ought to feel they were standing together as against the blacks'.[6]

The Democratic President Roosevelt held views on the white man's burden which were the reverse of his Republican predecessor's. Franklin Roosevelt met the Sultan of Morocco at Casablanca on January 22, 1943, and as a side-issue to his mission of bringing Generals Giraud and de Gaulle together he apparently assured Mohammed ben Youssef that the status of dependent territories would change radically after the war, when United States capital would enable Morocco to develop on a nationalist basis.[7] These assurances, coupled with the strong impression made on Moroccans by the French defeat in 1940, outweighed all that the French had done in their forty years' Protectorate, when to the Makhzen, the small cabinet of viziers which then existed to carry out the sultan's will, was added the French *Grandes Directions* which constructed 28,000 miles of roads and highways, 1100 miles of railway, 8 modern ports and a school system of 288,000 students and 9000 teachers. The French paid half the equipment expenses of the Protectorate and gave free medical care through a staff of 3000 doctors and nurses.[8]

In 1947, when Alphonse-Pierre Juin became Resident-General, Morocco was the most prosperous of all the territories directly or indirectly under the influence of France. With no war damage to speak of, and increased employment on the American installations at Casablanca and elsewhere, the Protectorate had a rising population, an 'open door' commercial system and a stimulating new programme of electrical and mineral development. The Monnet Plan had here developed into a quadrennial plan (1949-52) to be financed by $314 millions from French public funds. On the debit side, the textile and building trades were lagging; new garments were urgently needed, while the shanty towns of corrugated iron which had sprung up outside the towns and factories were deplored by the name of *les Bidonvilles*. There was the beginning of an attempt to replace them by honeycomb-like urban dwellings, each provided according to Moslem custom with an eastward window looking towards Mecca and an enclosed interior court.

During General Juin's term as Resident, France built seven major civil and military airports in Morocco, while rich mineral deposits of strategic materials (antimony, asbestos, beryl, cobalt, lead, manganese and zinc) were prospected and worked. Large corporations, financed in one-third proportions by Morocco, France and private investors, developed petrol, coal and thermoelectric power. There was enough work of all sorts going on to ensure prosperity, but *la présence française* was denounced by two opponents: the Moslem Nationalists and the Communist Istiqlal. The Istiqlal was led by young men who had been educated in Paris and had picked up Marxist ideas there as Ho Chi Minh had done, and who were suffering from the deep spiritual malaise of men who had jumped three or four centuries of civilization in as many years of schooling. They had gone home to the Bled-el-Sif from French class-rooms, back to a feudal society where the village caïd was overlord, and where they were expected to obey their elders and take to wife girls who were incapable of sharing their mental experiences.* They were ready for the persuasions of the North African Liberation Committee, a front for the Maghreb Committee at Cairo, recently strengthened by the arrival of the old Moroccan rebel Abd-el-Krim,† who had escaped from his French exile on La Réunion to the hospitality of King Farouk's palace of Inchass.

It was fortunate, for the time being, that General Juin, who knew his North Africa from birth and had been schooled in its ways by the great proconsul Lyautey, should become Resident in Morocco. He had always been a lucky general, lucky in the way that Cardinal Mazarin meant, when he got into the habit of asking about any rising soldier in the armies of Turenne or Condé: '*Est-il heureux?*' To the cardinal, who had seen the Marquis of

---

* Moslem prejudice slowed down the extension of education to female children. Cf. Moslem girls in school, 1953, 32,915; Moslem boys in school, 1953, 207,883.

† Abd-el-Krim, rebel against the sultan, surrendered to Marshal Pétain in 1926, was exiled, and in 1947, while ostensibly travelling to France from La Réunion, disembarked at Port Said and escaped to Cairo.

Montrose and Rupert of the Rhine defeated, luck was an important military attribute denied to some of the best soldiers of his age: to General Juin, it was the touchstone he had carried since he first gained his place at St. Cyr. He had won his campaign in Italy at the very place and time where the *furia francese*, famous since the sixteenth century, could be used to the most advantage. Thereafter his career as Chief of Staff of National Defence and Resident in Morocco was to keep him out of the thankless war in Indo-China, while he had the supreme satisfaction of serving where his background and training made him most useful to France. The schoolboy of Bône, the aide of Lyautey, knew how to enjoy a *diffa* with some friendly caïd, how to talk to El Glaoui, the eighty-year-old Pasha of Marrakesh, an important ally of the French power in Morocco who could summon up one million Berber tribesmen from their fastnesses in the Atlas Mountains, and also how to handle the Istiqlal. During his term of office as Resident-General, which lasted until August 1951, Juin made it abundantly clear that the intention of France was to hand over the reins of government progressively to the Moroccans — but not to withdraw *la présence française* from such a vitally important strategic and economic area.

Within two years from his departure the situation in Morocco had become so tense that on August 21, 1953, one month after the North African demonstrations in Paris, the French Government took the extreme step of deposing the Sultan Sidi Mohammed Ben Youssef. The son of the ruler who had signed the Treaty of Fez which established the Protectorate in 1912 had been perverted by the Communist doctrines of the Istiqlal; it was with the enthusiastic support of El Glaoui that he was escorted out of the country and eventually exiled to Madagascar with a portion of his harem, his offspring and pet animals. His elderly cousin Mohammed Ben Moulay Arafa was hailed as sultan in his stead.

In America there was an outcry at this sudden resort to the methods of the seventeenth century, but it was quickly stifled, for the State Department realized that strong government by France was the best protection for the American air bases in Morocco. When the two Protectorates came before the United Nations in October with a demand — supported by the whole Arab-Asian bloc — for full sovereignty and independence, the United States voted against it. The Rooseveltian policy of opposition to what the President loosely called 'colonial expansion' had brought its grim reward in Indo-China, and in regard to Morocco the State Department deemed it prudent to announce that the situation 'called for a middle of the road policy . . . in which it was not to America's interest to "choose sides" for the sake of choosing sides'.

The docile new sultan's rule began with the announcement of further concessions by France to the Moroccan desire for autonomy: democratization of the representative assemblies and the end of absolute monarchy. These were among the achievements claimed by the Laniel cabinet, now fully embarked upon a policy of minor reforms and major evasions which had more in common with the *immobilisme* of Guizot's government in the eighteen-forties than with the aspirations of the early Liberation days; but the North African concessions of September-October 1953 bore an uncomfortable resemblance to the temporizing in Indo-China which had failed to halt the onward march of Communism. There were demonstrations against the new sultan; acts of terrorism across the border in Tunisia to avenge the exile of Habib Bourguiba, and even in the Departments of Algeria there were threats of a violence engendered to some extent by the nationalist movement in Egypt. By all tokens it would require, as Mendès-France had warned, some original and truly liberal action in North Africa to save the two Protectorates and Algeria for France, and to prevent the extension of Communist power to the southern shore of the Mediterranean.

★

As President Auriol's term of office drew to a close through the sombre weeks of late autumn there was increasing impatience with the 'immobility' of the Laniel cabinet, as difficulties accumulated in North Africa and defeat came nearer in Indo-China, where a revision of strategy had called for the last ditch defence of a key fortress named Dien Bien Phu. To Charles de Gaulle it appeared to be an appropriate moment for a general review of the world situation and a few sharp criticisms of some of his former friends.

The year had brought a strange development in the relationship between the general and the French People's Rally. The lack of party discipline, apparent when the first splinter group bolted the party during the Pinay government, had been shown again in January, when the rump of the R.P.F. in the Assembly had again disobeyed de Gaulle in voting for the investiture of René Mayer. The May Day rally at Bagatelle was cancelled, and on May 8 the general made the sudden announcement that the R.P.F. would present no more candidates at elections, and that the R.P.F. Deputies already elected to the Assembly were thenceforth free to vote in any way they pleased. The Rally itself was not to be disbanded. It would continue its mission and would yet find its opportunity in 'a future consultation or upsurge of opinion'. It was the tale of 1946 retold: de Gaulle, impatient of any check to his progress, was weary of the attempt to discipline his Deputies and preferred to lead an amorphous group more responsive to his emotional and nationalistic appeals. Meantime the rump of the R.P.F. in the Assembly, eighty-five strong,* continued to vote along the old lines, which in the case of the European Defence Community treaty meant making common cause with the Communists. They took the name of the *Union des Républicains pour l'Action Sociale* (U.R.A.S.), but like the Free French of 1940 and later they were usually referred to as *les gaullistes*.

In November, when de Gaulle gave his survey of the French position, he did so by means of a press conference, for even the *assises nationales* of the R.P.F., usually held in that month, had been postponed until the following year. The press conference had been for some time his preferred means of self-expression, and these occasions, taking place at the Palais d'Orsay hotel or the Continental, had become events in the social calendar, to be attended by as many men and women of fashion as by reporters. Through the years the general's style, while still pontifical, had become more persuasive, and he had developed a talent for giving sharp answers to the written questions submitted to him, but on November 12, 1953, his tone was sombre and bitter rather than witty. He reviewed the war years and the part he had played in them, the reverses he had suffered since and the consequent (he said) reverses for France, in the manner of a man who has seen his old comrades leave him one by one. The faithful among his *Compagnons* were still around him, although André Malraux had

---

* Early in 1954 another splinter group, led by René Capitant, chose the name of the *Union des Groupes d'Action pour l'Indépendance Nationale*.

recently turned his undoubted genius to more fruitful ends than R.P.F. publicity, and was preparing to publish his great work on aesthetics, *Les Voix de Silence*, but the passage of nearly ten years had brought many changes. Pleven, Philip, Maurice Schumann, Billotte had left him to follow their own careers. Brossollette had been killed in the Liberation fighting, Pierre Bourdan had been drowned in a boating accident. Rémy, the beloved disciple, the *cher Compagnon*, had been estranged from him on the amnesty issue and Passy had been disgraced. Thierry d'Argenlieu was once more Père Louis de la Trinité, sequestered in his monastery of Avon, and Elisabeth de Miribel was about to leave the Carmelite convent which she had entered in 1949.

Charles de Gaulle himself was now sixty-three years old, or one year older than the age at which Philippe Pétain had received the marshal's baton from President Poincaré on the Esplanade at Metz, with his victory over Abd-el-Krim and his failure at Vichy still many years ahead of him. But that the general was ageing faster than the Marshal had done was plain to those who observed the thickening body — for a fall, reopening an old wound, had made him disinclined for exercise — and the dulled glance which had followed an operation for cataract earlier in the year. As the dewlap grew heavier and the arrogant nose grew more pronounced, it became apparent that de Gaulle was, as he himself had said, not Bonaparte and not Boulanger. He was a Bourbon of the Bourbons, having learned nothing and forgotten nothing.

The long rancour he had nursed against Britain and America was expressed again and again at the November press conference, particularly in his attacks on the E.D.C. treaty. He had a sneer for America: if the Americans admired fusion so much, he said, why did they not themselves federate with Canada, Mexico, Brazil and the Argentine? He had another for the British, insinuating that 'Lord Louis Mountbatten, Commander-in-Chief in the Mediterranean, and Lord Alexander of Tunis' would find 'interesting possibilities' in France's loss of her overseas territories; and another, more bitter still, for his first and greatest patron, Winston Churchill.

The Prime Minister had recently referred to Europe as 'the unfortunate continent'. This prompted de Gaulle to declare that Britain did not wish to be involved in continental troubles.

Since France [he said], Italy, Belgium, the Netherlands, Luxembourg, appear willing to destroy themselves in the frightful carnage which would follow another war, Britain declares herself disinterested and *abandons them to their fate.**[9]

If Britain had abandoned France to her fate, and the other occupied countries of Europe with her, by surrendering to Germany during the year between June 1940 and June 1941, when the motherland and Commonwealth had no foreign allies, there would have been no liberation of Europe, and Charles de Gaulle would never have returned to France in triumph in the private aircraft of an American general.[10] And if Britain had abandoned de Gaulle to *his* fate, thirteen years earlier, then the great schism in France between the followers of the Marshal who chose to stay and the general who chose exile might never have been opened, or, being opened, have been quickly closed. It was the opportunities given by Britain for the development of the Gaullist legend which helped to turn the ambitious Leader of All Free Frenchmen from a soldier into a politician; and it was the politician who, more than any other single person, was responsible for the divisions and polemics which distracted Liberated France from the work of renovation. Not that these opportunities had been given gratis. The French taxpayer, who had not been consulted at the time, would go on paying interest for many years to come on the capital outlay made by Britain on the Free French movement. The balance of the British Government's loan at September 1, 1946, was £99,188,750, which the Provisional Government then undertook to pay in twelve annual instalments, with interest at 5 per cent per annum, beginning on September 1, 1950.†

The 'de Gaulle mortgage' would thus be payable until 1962, or twenty-two years after the start of the Free French movement in London. This had not been foreseen at the time, for, as Prince Bismarck had once said, five years was as long as any statesman could be expected to see into the future. On that premise it was not impossible that France, where so many politicians get a second chance, might one day provide the drama, shock, disaster, which

* Author's italics.
† The French Government's *Inventaire de la Situation Financière* (1946) gives the complete balance sheet.

de Gaulle had always seen as paving the way for his return to power. If that upheaval ever came, it would find the general fixed in his personal delusion of grandeur. His identification of himself with his country was crystallized on the day* when he exclaimed:

> I was France, the State, the Government. I was the independence and the sovereignty of France. That is why in the end everybody obeyed me.

If the picture presented by France at the end of 1953 had been entirely one of war and incipient rebellion abroad, stagnation and megalomania at home, that portion of the world which had always looked to France for inspiration might well have been discouraged. But the bad and the good, the Angel of Punishment and the Angel of Liberty of Hugo's epic vision of his country, were still bound up with one another. In the world of the mind the triumph of Liberated France was absolute, for there she had preserved and nourished the vitality and power of creation which had been manifest through all her long, splendid and troubled history.

France was still the leaven in the world's bread, and the ferment worked in many ways. In art and music, theatre and cinema, there was constant experimenting, including plays which had something new to say and a new way of saying it on such traditional themes as the martyrdom of Joan of Arc and the voyage of Christopher Columbus. Masters of satire, the French themselves were the first to criticize, in literary form, the tribulations through which they had just passed. Henri Clouzot's *Manon*, a film having the additional interest of being a modern version of the classic *Manon Lescaut*, took the French-American black market of 1944-45 as one element of its theme. Jean-Louis Curtis won the Prix Goncourt in 1947 for *Les Forêts de la Nuit*, a novel which dealt far from gently with aspects of the Resistance; in 1953 Jean Dutourd won the Prix Interallié for *Au Bon Beurre*, a bitter take-off of life under Vichy. Robert Merle, the Goncourt prize-winner of 1948, described a French soldier's reaction to the epic of Dunkirk in *Weekend à Zuydecoote*.

The French capacity for self-analysis, very highly developed, was not fully understood by their Western Allies, who usually adopted one of two attitudes: an attack on 'French weakness' or a senti-

* Press Conference, April 7, 1954.

mental and unbalanced defence of all things French. In fact, the French needed no defenders, for what was so often overlooked — notably by those who saw no further than the washrooms of the Palais Bourbon — was that the people of France enjoyed being French. They had their moments of humiliation and despair (*j'ai honte d'être français*) and of transcendent pride (*il n'est clarté que de Paris*) but there was nothing apathetic or standardized about either mood. Both were part of belonging to *la grande Nation*, whose grandeur lay most of all in the constant self-renewal, self-examination and ferment by which France produced ideas where others built machines. Moreover, the French were faithful to their country. Even in the darkest days of hardship after the Liberation, polls revealed an overwhelming majority of opinion in favour of staying in France, or remaining French by nationality — Swiss was the second choice, if choice there had to be.[11] In January 1947, with half of Europe begging for admission to the United States, the French immigration quota was one of the only two not filled. The French were satisfied with themselves as they were, and had no desire to be regimented like the Russians, fanaticized like the Germans, or made over into a poor imitation of the inhabitants of the United States.

It was not only in the world of letters that the ferment was at work, although the extraordinary number of new intellectual reviews (four appearing in Paris in 1953 alone) bore witness to an unquenchable appetite for the written word. The *Nouvelle Revue Française*, purged of its old collaborationist stigma, reappeared as the *Nouvelle N.R.F.*, with its old galaxy of talent: Jean Paulhan, Malraux, Schlumberger, Montherlant. A brilliant young correspondent of *Le Monde*, Jean-Jacques Servan-Schreiber, founded a new weekly called *L'Express* which published some uncomfortable documentaries on the Indo-Chinese War, and was said to be a vehicle for the opinions of Pierre Mendès-France. The Catholic review *Esprit* enhanced its intellectual reputation. It seemed as if even the increasing sales of TV sets, rising to 5000 a month, would not quickly wean Frenchmen from their passion for written polemics.

In school-rooms there were more and more young scholars, for the population of France had increased by nearly three millions since 1946. These were the children who thrilled to the exploits of Maurice Herzog, when he planted the *tricolore* on the peak of Annapurna, and of Captain Cousteau and Commandant Huout, whose daring explorations of the ocean bed opened a new door on the silent world of the seas. Such men were living evidence, for those who had eyes to see, that the spirit which had given a Cartier, a Champlain, a Cavelier de la Salle to the New World was not dead in the Frenchmen of the Old.

That adults as well as children were capable of being touched by a genuine appeal to generosity and self-sacrifice was proved by the quick response to an appeal launched in the bitter winter weather of 1953-54 by the Abbé Pierre. Born Henri-Antoine Grouès, the Abbé Pierre at the age of forty-one was deeply concerned with life outside the monastery where he had once taken the vows as a Capuchin monk. He had been in the Resistance, in the famous Vercors *maquis*, and had afterwards founded the Community of Emmaus, led by a group of two priests, five seminarians and twelve laymen. Theirs was a mission to the poor and homeless, and just as devout war prisoners in Germany had taken as their protectress *Notre Dame des Barbelés*, represented by little terra-cotta statuettes of the Virgin and Child swathed in the wire of the concentration camps, so the little company of Emmaus raised a shrine in its refuge at Lagny, near Paris, to Our Lady of the Homeless, *Notre Dame des Sans Logis*. With this inspiration the Abbé Pierre told his tale of the homeless to their countrymen, who were neither so hardened nor so selfish, so absorbed in the latest religious quarrel — between the Gallican Church and the Vatican, which had ordered the disbanding of the worker-priests — as to refuse to respond to a simple and touching appeal.

The election of a President of the Republic, due to take place in December, was an implicit promise of the novelty which was an indispensable ingredient in French politics, although the leadership which France desired must of necessity come from a strong premier in the Palais Bourbon rather than from the Élysée. Vincent Auriol had declined to consider a second term of office. He had come through his *septennat* with great credit, for the constant friction in the government had sharpened his gifts as a negotiator, and his handling of crisis after crisis had given the limited Executive an actual power much greater than its written terms. At sixty-nine he declared himself too old and weary to go on; he

s*

proposed now to turn to writing and to an agreeable division of his time between Muret and a new *pied à terre* in Paris, on the left bank of the Seine. Younger men were ambitious to succeed him. Joseph Laniel, Maurice Naegelen — a Resistance leader who had served as Governor of Algeria — and Georges Bidault, whose ardent Catholicism made anti-clericals tremble for the safety of the Republic, were among the eight potential Presidents who faced up to the new barrage of television cameras when the full parliament met on December 16 in the Congress Hall at Versailles. There were too many of them, it was pointed out, for any one to obtain a clear majority like Auriol's in the very first round; but as the third ballot followed the second and the voting went on through the ninth, tenth, eleventh, the public dismay and consternation grew. The *Garde Républicaine* practised the *Aux Champs* assiduously, the TV cameras destroyed old reputations and made some new ones, and still *l'immobilisme* held the palace of the Sun King fast. Finally, and almost deprecatingly, a conservative senator from Le Havre came quietly forward, and on December 23, in the thirteenth round of balloting, René Coty became President-elect of the French Republic.

In his person the wheel of Liberation had surely turned full circle, for M. Coty was one of the 569 Deputies who had voted for plenary powers to Marshal Pétain in the Casino at Vichy, and one of the few who had since been rehabilitated by the *Jury d'Honneur*. Like all those so distinguished, he had been expected to give proof of Resistance activities subsequent to 1940, but, as he pleasantly told reporters after his election, 'all that seemed very far away now' and he added with a smile, 'I didn't blow up many trains'. It was possible that in this genial and shrewd old man — for he was older than President Auriol, nearly seventy-two, and a Third Republican politician literally since his schooldays — who professed the classic French interests in Lafontaine, Debussy, rose gardens and good cooking, France had found a President willing to let bygones be bygones, and to pass the sponge over the Purge which in the long run had been as much an instrument of division as the Occupation.

The Republic, emerging from a profound traumatic experience, was still in need of rebuilding and recuperation as well as of realistic leadership, and the pause while a new President was elected was a purely artificial dam in the irresistible current of French history. France had been liberated, and her fervent wish was that she need never be liberated again, but that period was now part of the past of a country perennially able to say with Mary Queen of Scots: In my End is my Beginning.

Few Frenchmen were likely to be abroad on Christmas Eve, when René Coty made his state entry into the capital, in that valley of the Côte d'Or called 'the solitude where the Seine is the sole element of life'. Ice-clad in its little grotto, the statue of Sequana flumen *leaned unvisited over the hard ground where the half-frozen rills bubbled up and started on their way to cross the plateau where other living waters rise. But three hundred miles nearer the sea the Seine flowed on in majesty between the crowded dwellings of the proud and the humble, the thinkers and the craftsmen, the soldiers and the women who were in process of renewing the unique contribution of their country to civilization, and of making France, no less than her greatest river, a source of life, a living stream.*

BIBLIOGRAPHY

PRIMARY SOURCES

Parliamentary Debates. Documents. Reports
House of Commons: *Parliamentary Debates*, vols. 368-404.
Assemblée Nationale: *Journal Officiel*: Débats. 1946-53.

L'Année Politique (8 volumes), 1945-52. Paris, Éditions le Grand Siècle, 1946-53.

Dugdale, E. T. S. (translator): *German Diplomatic Documents, 1871-1914.* London, Methuen, 1930.
Fondations Nationales des Sciences Politiques. *Études sur la Banlieue de Paris.* Paris, Armand Colin, 1953.
O.E.E.C. *Economic Progress and Problems of Western Europe.* O.E.E.C., 1951.
R.I.I.A. *Atlantic Alliance.* London, Royal Institute of International Affairs, 1952.
Union Gaulliste. *Manifeste, Programme et Statuts.* Paris, Union Gaulliste, 1946.
Government Publications:
   British White Papers (H.M. Stationery Office): Cmd. 6220: Exchange of Letters between the Prime Minister and General de Gaulle, London, August 7, 1940.
   Cmd. 6662: Relations between H.M. Government and the Vichy Government in the autumn of 1940.
   République Française: Documents Diplomatiques et Accords Internationaux rélatifs a l'établissement du Protectorat Français au Maroc, 1912.
   General Report of the First Plan of Modernization and Equipment, 1947.
   Inventaire de la Situation Financière, 1946.
   Le Général de Gaulle et le Problème Constitutionnel, 1946.
   Economic Progress in the French Union, 1946-53.
   La Zone d'Occupation Française en Autriche, 1945.
   Deux Ans et Demi de présence française en Autriche, 1948.

Memoirs and War Diaries
AURIOL, VINCENT: *Hier . . . Demain.* Paris, Charlot, 1945.
BORDEN, MARY: *Journey into Fear.* New York, Harper & Bros., 1946.
BRADLEY, GENERAL OMAR N.: *A Soldier's Story.* New York, Henry Holt & Co., 1951.

BIBLIOGRAPHY

CATROUX, GÉNÉRAL: *Dans la Bataille de la Méditerranée; Egypte-Levant, Afrique du Nord.* Paris, René Juilliard, 1949.

CHURCHILL, WINSTON S.: *The Second World War* (6 volumes). Boston, Houghton Mifflin Co., 1948-53.

CLARK, GENERAL MARK: *Calculated Risk.* London, Harrap, 1951.

CLAY, GENERAL LUCIUS: *Decision in Germany.* New York, Doubleday & Co., 1950.

DECOUX, ADMIRAL: *A la Barre de l'Indochine.* Paris, Plon, 1949.

DUFF COOPER, ALFRED: *Old Men Forget.* London, Hart Davis, 1953.

EISENHOWER, GENERAL DWIGHT D.: *Crusade in Europe.* New York, Doubleday & Co., 1948.

HULL, CORDELL: *Memoirs* (2 volumes). London, Hodder & Stoughton, 1948.

LEAHY, ADMIRAL: *I Was There.* New York, Whittlesey, 1950.

LEBRUN, ALBERT: *Témoignage.* Paris, Plon, 1945.

PASSY (André DeWavrin, pseud.): *Souvenirs*, vols. 1, 2 and 3. Monte Carlo, Raoul Solar, 1947 *et seq.*

PÉTAIN, MARSHAL PHILIPPE: *Quatre Années au Pouvoir.* Paris, La Couronne Littéraire, 1949.

RÉMY (Gilbert Renault, pseud.): *Mémoires d'un Agent Secret de la France Libre.* Paris, Aux Trois Couleurs, 1945.

SHERWOOD, ROBERT: *Roosevelt and Hopkins: an Intimate History.* New York, Harper, 1948.

SOUSTELLE, JACQUES: *Envers et Contre Tout* (2 volumes). Paris, Robert Laffont, 1947.

Military History

EISENHOWER, GENERAL DWIGHT D.: *Complete Report by the Supreme Commander on the War in Europe from the Day of Invasion to the Day of Victory.* New York, Arcos Publishing Co., 1946.

GAVIN, GENERAL JAMES M.: *Airborne Warfare.* Washington, Combat Forces Press, 1946.

DE LATTRE DE TASSIGNY, GÉNÉRAL JEAN: *Histoire de la Première Armée Française.* Paris, Plon, 1949.

LINKLATER, ERIC: *The Highland Division.* London, H.M. Stationery Office, 1942.

MONTGOMERY, FIELD-MARSHAL VISCOUNT: *Normandy to the Baltic.* London, Hutchinson, 1947.

MOUNTBATTEN, VICE-ADMIRAL EARL: *Report to the Combined Chiefs of Staff by the Supreme Allied Commander South-East Asia.* London, H.M. Stationery Office, 1951.

WILMOT, CHESTER: *The Struggle for Europe.* London, Collins, 1952.

BIBLIOGRAPHY

Journals and Reportage

ANON: *Le Général de Gaulle* (pictures and text). Paris, Hachette, 1945.

AURY, BERNARD: *La Délivrance de Paris* (pictures and text). Paris, B. Arthaud, 1945.

BOURDAN, PIERRE: *Carnet de Retour avec la Division Leclerc.* Paris, Editions Pierre Tremois, 1945.

BRUCKBERGER: *One Sky to Share.* New York, Kenedy, 1952.

BUTCHER, HARRY C.: *My Three Years with Eisenhower.* New York, Simon & Schuster, 1946.

CURIE, EVE: *Journey Among Warriors.* New York, Doubleday Doran, 1943.

DELAGE, FRANCK: *Oradour Ville Martyre.* Paris, Editions Mellottée, 1945.

FABRE-LUCE, ALFRED: *Journal 1951.* Paris, Amiot-Dumont, 1952.

GALTIER-BOISSIÈRE, JEAN: *Mon Journal sous l'Occupation.* Paris, La Jeune Parque, 1944.

GALTIER-BOISSIÈRE, JEAN: *Mon Journal depuis la Libération.* Paris, La Jeune Parque, 1945.

LIEBLING, A. J.: *The Road Back to Paris.* New York, Doubleday Doran, 1944.

LIEBLING, A. J.: *The Republic of Silence.* New York, Harcourt Bruce & Co., 1947.

KERNAN, THOMAS: *France on Berlin Time.* Philadelphia, J. B. Lippincott, 1941.

DE MALGLAIVE, PIERRE: *Un Français vous Parle.* Liverpool, C. Birchald & Son, 1944.

OBERLÉ, JEAN: *Jean Oberlé Vous Parle.* Paris, La Jeune Parque, 1945.

PENDAR, KENNETH: *Adventure in Diplomacy.* New York, Dodd Mead & Co., 1945.

ROOSEVELT, ELLIOTT: *As He Saw It.* New York, Duelle, Sloan and Pearce, 1947.

SANDAHL, PIERRE: *De Gaulle Sans Képi.* Paris, La Jeune Parque, 1948.

THOMAS, EDITH: *La Libération de Paris.* Paris, Editions Mellottée, 1945.

SECONDARY SOURCES

Biographical and Historical Studies

BARRÈS, PHILIPPE: *Charles de Gaulle*, New York, Doubleday Doran, 1941.

BOEGNER, MARC: *Le Protestantisme Français.* Paris, Plon, 1945.

BONNEFOUS, ÉDOUARD: *L'idée Européenne et sa Réalisation.* Paris, Editions du Grand Siècle, 1950.

BROGAN, D. W.: *The Development of Modern France (1870-1939).* London, Hamish Hamilton, 1940.

BIBLIOGRAPHY

BROGAN, D. W.: *French Personalities and Problems*. New York, Alfred A. Knopf, 1947.

CHAPMAN, BRIAN: *Introduction to French Local Government*. London, Allen & Unwin, 1953.

DANIEL, YVON: *Aspects de la Pratique Réligieuse*. Paris, Éditions Ouvrières, 1952.

DARIEL, JEAN: *Chez les Prêtres-Ouvriers*. Paris, F. Chambriand, 1950.

DANSETTE, ADRIEN: *Leclerc*. Paris, Flammarion, 1952.

EARLE, E. M. (editor): *Modern France*. Princeton, Princeton University Press, 1951.

EINAUDI, MARIO AND GOGUEL, FRANÇOIS: *Christian Democracy in Italy and France*. Indiana, University of Notre Dame Press, 1952.

FAUVET, JACQUES: *Les Forces Politiques en France*. Paris, Le Monde, 1951.

GOGUEL, FRANÇOIS: *France under the Fourth Republic*. Ithaca, Cornell University Press, 1952.

GROSSER, ALFRED: *L'Allemagne de l'Occident, 1945-52*. Paris, Gallimard, 1953.

GUEDALLA, PHILIP: *The Second Empire*. London, Hodder & Stoughton, 1922.

GUEDALLA, PHILIP: *The Two Marshals*. London, Hodder & Stoughton, 1943.

DE JOUVENEL, BERTRAND: *L'Amérique en Europe*. Paris, Plon, 1948.

LIDDERDALE, D. W. S.: *The Parliament of France*. London, The Hansard Society, 1951.

MAILLAUD, PIERRE (Pierre Bourdan, pseud.): *France*. London, Oxford University Press, 1943.

MAY: *Rapports de la France à la Civilisation*. Paris, Éditions Albin Michel, 1951.

MORSE STEPHENS: *Revolutionary Europe*. London, Rivingtons, 1928.

PICKLES, DOROTHY: *French Politics: The First Years of the Fourth Republic*. London, Royal Institute of International Affairs, 1953.

RÉMY (Gilbert Renault, pseud.): *De Gaulle, cet Inconnu*. Monte Carlo, Raoul Solar, 1947.

SCHWARTZ: *French Administrative Law and the Common-Law World*. New York, New York University Press, 1954.

SIEGFRIED, ANDRÉ: *The Character of Peoples*. London, Jonathan Cape, 1952.

TAYLOR, O. R.: *The Fourth Republic of France*. London, Royal Institute of International Affairs, 1951.

THOMSON, DAVID: *Two Frenchmen* (Pierre Laval and Charles de Gaulle). London, Cresset Press, 1951.

THOMSON, DAVID: *Democracy in France*. New York, Oxford University Press, 1952.

BIBLIOGRAPHY

WRIGHT, GORDON: *The Reshaping of French Democracy*. New York, Reynal & Hitchcock, 1948.

Polemics

ARAGON, LOUIS: *Servitude et Grandeur des Français*. Paris, La Bibliothèque Française, 1945.

ARAGON, LOUIS: *Le Crève-Cœur* (poems). London, Horizon-France Libre, 1942.

CRAPOUILLOT (editors): *Pétain-de Gaulle: le pour et le contre*. Paris, Le Crapouillot, no date.

DEBU-BRIDEL, JACQUES: *Histoire du Marché Noir*. Paris, La Jeune Parque, 1947.

DEBU-BRIDEL, JACQUES: *Les Partis contre de Gaulle*. Paris, Somogy, 1948.

DESPUECH, JACQUES: *Le Trafic de Piastres*. Paris, Deux Rives, 1953.

FARGE, YVES: *Le Marché Noir* (speech delivered October 18, 1946). Paris, Éditions du Mail, no date.

DE GAULLE, GÉNÉRAL: *Le Fil de l'Épée*. Paris, Éditions Berger-Levrault, 1932.

DE GAULLE, GÉNÉRAL: *Vers l'Armée de Métier*. Paris, Éditions Berger-Levrault, 1934.

DE GAULLE, GÉNÉRAL: *Trois Études*. Paris, Éditions Berger-Levrault, 1945.

DE GAULLE, GÉNÉRAL: *Discours aux Français, 18 juin 1940-2 janvier 1944*. Algiers, Office Français d'Édition, no date.

GIRAUD: *L'Appel de l'Île d'Yeu*. Paris, André Bonne, 1951.

MAZÉ, JEAN: *Le Système*. Paris, Ségur, 1950.

ROUFFIC, MARCEL: *Le Protectorat a-t-il fait Faillite?* Casablanca, Éditions de la S.I.P.E.T., 1951.

THOREZ, MAURICE: *Une Politique de Grandeur Française*. Paris, Les Éditions Sociales, 1950.

Newspapers and Periodicals

Files of: *The Times*, 1940-44; *Le Figaro*, 1944-53; *Le Monde*, 1945-53; *New York Times*, 1950-54.

Issues of: *France*; *La France Libre*; *Les Français de Grande Bretagne*; *Le Figaro Littéraire*; *Carrefour*; *Le Rassemblement*; *Combat*; *Le Canard Enchaîné*; *Études*; *Paris-Match*; *France-Illustration*; *Sondages*; *New York Herald Tribune* (Paris); *L'Orient* (Beirut); *The Economist*; *Foreign Affairs*; *Time*; *Life*.

REFERENCES

Previous writers on post-war France have commented on the difficulty of establishing accurate statistics for certain phases of Occupation and post-Liberation history. This is due to the confusion of the period, and to the claims (number of recruits, achievements, losses, etc.) made by many of the rival factions. It is possible, for instance, to produce several different sets of references for punishments meted out under the Purge; yet those are accurate by comparison with Occupation records, which being of necessity clandestine were often reproduced from memory alone.

For the statistical background of the present book I have relied to a large extent on the tables and figures published annually in *L'Année Politique* (1945-52) a comprehensive and objective chronological review compiled under the direction of a distinguished editorial committee including MM. André Siegfried and Édouard Bonnefous. Official facts and figures for the year 1953, as well as some for earlier years, have been taken from the publications grouped under the name of *La Documentation Française*, and from those issued by the French Embassy's Press and Information Section in New York.

PROLOGUE

[1] Duff Cooper, *Old Men Forget*, p. 328.
[2] Butcher, *My Three Years With Eisenhower*, p. 562.
[3] Eisenhower, *Complete Report by the Supreme Commander*, p. 12.
[4] De Lattre de Tassigny, *Histoire de la 1ere Armée Française*, p. 10.
[5] Linklater, *The Highland Division*, p. 30.
[6] Oberlé, *Jean Oberlé Vous Parle*, p. 29.
[7] Cmd. 6220, *Exchange of Letters between the Prime Minister and General de Gaulle, August 1940*, p. 8.
[8] Churchill, *The Second World War*, vol. II, p. 649.
[9] Form Letter from the headquarters of *Les Français de Grande Bretagne* dated May 8, 1942.
[10] Catroux, *Dans la Bataille de la Méditerranée*, p. 20.
[11] Cmd. 6662, *Relationships between H.M. Government and the Vichy Government in the Autumn of 1940*, pp. 6, 7.
[12] *The Times*, August 5, 1940; cf. Soustelle, *Envers et Contre Tout*, vol. I, 27.
[13] *Le Figaro*, Oct. 4, 1944.
[14] *Le Monde*, Jan. 1, 1946; see also issue of Oct. 13, 1947.
[15] Rémy, *Mémoires d'un Agent Secret de la France Libre*, vol. I, p. 366.
[16] Ibid., p. 367.
[17] Catroux, op. cit., p. 163.
[18] *True Comics*, issue no. 8. Published by The Parents' Magazine Press Inc., 52 Vanderbilt Ave., New York.
[19] Passy, *Souvenirs*, vol. I, p. 157.
[20] Oberlé, op. cit., p. 140.
[21] Passy, op. cit., vol. II, p. 69.
[22] Ibid., pp. 219-30 (text of Brossollette's letter to André Philip).
[23] De Gaulle, *Discours aux Français*, p. 203.
[24] Passy, op. cit., vol. III, p. 44.
[25] Hull, *Memoirs*, vol. II, p. 1222.
[26] *The Times*, June 7, 1944.

CHAPTER I

[1] Oberlé, op. cit., p. 292.
[2] Ibid., p. 295.
[3] Sandahl, *De Gaulle Sans Képi*, p. 167.
[4] Marshall, *The White Rabbit*, p. 30.

REFERENCES

[5] Eisenhower, *Complete Report*, p. 8.
[6] Galtier-Boissière, *Mon Journal sous l'Occupation*, p. 252.
[7] Aury, *La Délivrance de Paris*, p. 17.
[8] Galtier-Boissière, op. cit., p. 256.
[9] Aury, op. cit., p. 26.
[10] Bradley, *A Soldier's Story*, p. 392.
[11] Ibid., p. 392.
[12] Pictures of this event, suppressed at the Liberation, were freely reproduced at the time of Marshal Pétain's death in 1951. Cf. *Paris-Match*, August 4, 1951.
[13] Giraud, *L'Appel de l'Île d'Yeu*, p. 113.
[14] Bruckberger, *One Sky to Share*, p. 14.
[15] Bradley, op. cit., p. 392.
[16] Georges Duhamel in *France-Illustration*, July 28, 1951.
[17] Rémy, *De Gaulle, Cet Inconnu*, p. 84.
[18] Eisenhower, *Crusade in Europe*, p. 297.
[19] Butcher, op. cit., p. 656.
[20] Rémy, *Mémoires*, vol. I, p. 330.
[21] Galtier-Boissière, op. cit., p. 24.
[22] Raymond Mortimer, quoted in Cyril Connolly's preface to Louis Aragon's *Le Crève-Cœur* (London, Horizon-La France Libre, 1942). In this volume appear the lines from 'Complainte pour l'Orgue de la Nouvelle Barbarie' quoted in chapter I, p. 19.
[23] Chevalier, *The Man in the Straw Hat*, p. 229 (New York, Crowell, 1949), cf. Mazé, *Le Système*, p. 25.

CHAPTER II

[1] Passy, *Souvenirs*, vol. III, p. 399.
[2] Ibid., vol. II, p. 120.
[3] *Journal Officiel* (Débats), November 4, 1950, col. 7478.
[4] Ibid., November 11, 1950, col. 7525.
[5] *L'Année Politique*, 1945, p. 113.
[6] Bruckberger, op. cit., p. 51.

CHAPTER III

[1] Duff Cooper, op. cit., p. 337.
[2] Ibid., p. 339.
[3] Churchill, op. cit., vol. II, p. 97.
[4] Pendar, *Adventures in Diplomacy*, p. 119.
[5] Clark, *Calculated Risk*, p. 380.
[6] Dansette, *Leclerc*, p. 9.
[7] Ibid., p. 41.
[8] Ibid., p. 88.
[9] Sandahl, *De Gaulle Sans Képi*, pp. 48-9.
[10] Dansette, op. cit., p. 173.
[11] De Lattre, op. cit., p. 40.
[12] Ibid., p. 194.
[13] Ibid., p. 197.
[14] Raymond Cartier in *Paris-Match*, February 2, 1952.
[15] *Journal Officiel* (Débats), October 29, 1944.
[16] Churchill, op. cit., vol. II, p. 150.
[17] Ibid., vol. VI, pp. 43-5.
[18] Sandahl, op. cit., pp. 133-134.
[19] Passy, op. cit., vol. I, p. 233.
[20] *L'Année Politique*, 1945, p. 87.
[21] Ibid., pp. 526, 527.
[22] Churchill, op. cit., vol. VI, p. 257.
[23] *L'Année Politique*, 1945, p. 532, gives text.

REFERENCES

CHAPTER IV

[1] Sherwood, *Roosevelt and Hopkins*, p. 847.
[2] Duff Cooper, op. cit., p. 348.
[3] Information given by the President of the Syrian Republic to the author, in an audience at Damascus, October 1945.
[4] Duff Cooper, op. cit., p. 354.
[5] Borden, *Journey Down a Blind Alley*, pp. 361-2.
[6] Giraud, *L'Appel de l'Île d'Yeu*, p. 131.
[7] Georges Duhamel in *France-Illustration*, July 28, 1951.
[8] *Journal Officiel* (Débats), November 4, 1950, col. 7455.
[9] *Le Figaro*, February 20, 1946.
[10] *L'Année Politique*, 1945, pp. 156, 157.
[11] Duff Cooper, op. cit., p. 358.

CHAPTER V

[1] *Sondages*, October 16, 1946.
[2] Census figures published by the Division de la Statistique Générale: *Premiers résultats du recensement général, le 10 mars 1946*. Paris, 1947.
[3] Soustelle, *Envers et Contre Tout*, vol. I, p. 286.
[4] Oberlé, op. cit., p. 79.
[5] Wright, *The Reshaping of French Democracy*, p. 51.
[6] Decoux, op. cit., p. 477.
[7] Duff Cooper, op. cit., p. 362.
[8] Union Gaulliste, *Manifesto*, p. 8.

CHAPTER VI

[1] From the article on Louis Jouvet in *Current Biography*, 1949 (New York, The H. W. Wilson Co., 1950).
[2] *L'Année Politique*, 1946, p. 262.
[3] Ibid., p. 261.
[4] Chapman, *Introduction to French Local Government*, p. 26.
[5] La Documentation Française, *Notes Documentaires et Études*, no. 401, p. 1.
[6] *Le Figaro*, May 9, 1946.
[7] *Combat*, August 10, 1946.
[8] *Le Figaro*, August 11, 1946.
[9] *Notes Documentaires et Études*, op. cit., p. 1.
[10] Ibid., p. 5.
[11] *New York Times*, August 28, 1946.

CHAPTER VII

[1] General Report of the First Plan of Modernization and Equipment, p. 11.
[2] Ibid., p. 83.
[3] De Lattre, op. cit., p. 580.
[4] Ibid., p. 596.
[5] Ibid., p. 596.
[6] Ibid., p. 616.
[7] Ibid., p. 621.
[8] Clay, *Decision in Germany*, p. 105.
[9] *Le Figaro*, May 24, 1946.
[10] Clay, op. cit., p. 113.

CHAPTER VIII

[1] Text of President Auriol's Message to Parliament, given in *L'Année Politique*, 1947, p. 321.
[2] Ibid., p. 264.
[3] *New York Times*, August 2, 1945.
[4] Hull, op. cit., vol. II, p. 1597.
[5] Decoux, op. cit., p. 301.

REFERENCES

[6] Ibid., p. 301.
[7] Ibid., p. 464.
[8] Ibid., p. 323.
[9] Memoirs of Jean Sainteny, published in *Le Figaro*, December 12, 1953.
[10] Ibid.
[11] Dansette, op. cit., p. 183.
[12] *L'Année Politique*, 1947, p. 305.
[13] Dansette, op. cit., p. 198.
[14] Sainteny in *Le Figaro*, December 14, 1953.
[15] Ibid.
[16] Hull, op. cit., vol. II, p. 1596.
[17] Ibid., p. 1599.
[18] Ibid., p. 1599.
[19] Eisenhower, *Crusade in Europe*, p. 457.
[20] John Foster Dulles, Speech to the Overseas Press Club of America, March 29, 1954.
[21] *Le Figaro*, October 14, 1952.
[22] Roosevelt, Elliott, *As He Saw It*, p. 24.

CHAPTER IX

[1] De Gaulle, *Le Fil de l'Épée*, p. 70.
[2] Hitler, *Speeches 1922-39*, vol. I, p. 81 (Oxford University Press, 1942).
[3] De Gaulle, *Le Fil de l'Épée*, pp. 154, 97, 66, 77.
[4] *L'Année Politique*, 1947, p. 305.
[5] Ibid., p. 62.
[6] Debu-Bridel, *Les Partis contre de Gaulle*, pp. 195-6.
[7] Ibid., p. 209.
[8] De Gaulle, *Discours aux Français*, p. 217.

CHAPTER X

[1] *L'Année Politique*, 1947, p. 128.
[2] Dansette, op. cit., p. 216.
[3] Ibid., p. 223.
[4] De Jouvenel, Bertrand, *L'Amérique en Europe*, p. 122.
[5] Grosser, *L'Allemagne de l'Occident*, p. 288.
[6] Clay, op. cit., p. 162.
[7] Ibid., p. 361.
[8] *Le Figaro*, December 4-5, 1948.

CHAPTER XI

[1] Chapman, op. cit., p. 26.
[2] Taylor, *The Fourth Republic of France*, p. 173.
[3] Goguel, *France under the Fourth Republic*, pp. 126, 127.
[4] Boegner, *Le Protestantisme Français*, p. 6.
[5] Ibid., p. 12.
[6] Daniel, *Les Prêtres Ouvriers*, from the introduction.
[7] Wakeman, *Ascendancy of France*, p. 251.
[8] Einaudi and Goguel, *Christian Democracy in Italy and France*, p. 192.
[9] Pickles, *French Politics*, p. 114.
[10] Communiqué issued from R.P.F. headquarters and reproduced throughout the Paris press on April 13, 1950.
[11] *Journal Officiel* (Débats), November 4, 1950, col. 7474.

CHAPTER XII

[1] *L'Année Politique*, 1949, p. 365.
[2] Despuech, *Le Trafic de Piastres*, p. 89.
[3] Clark, *Calculated Risk*, p. 39.
[4] *France-Illustration*, May 5, 1951.

REFERENCES

CHAPTER XIII

[1] *Le Figaro*, June 19, 1951.
[2] *L'Année Politique*, 1951, p. 4.
[3] At a press conference, April 24, 1947.
[4] At Nice, August 12, 1948.
[5] At Bagatelle, May 1, 1949.
[6] Einaudi and Goguel, op. cit., p. 166 and cf. pp. 215-16.
[7] *Le Figaro*, May 2, 1951.
[8] Ibid., June 24, 1951.
[9] *The Times*, June 10, 1944.
[10] Fabre-Luce, *Journal 1951*, pp. 295-8.
[11] Ibid., p. 302.

CHAPTER XIV

[1] Guedalla, *The Second Empire*, p. 374.
[2] *Études sur la Banlieue de Paris, passim.*
[3] *France-Illustration*, May 5, 1951.
[4] Goguel, *France under the Fourth Republic*, p. 133.

CHAPTER XV

[1] *L'Année Politique*, 1950, p. 87.
[2] Ibid., p. 213.
[3] Ibid., p. 186.
[4] Senate Foreign Affairs Committee, *Report on the Use of Economic and Military Aid to Europe*, published July 29, 1951.
[5] In an address to the National Press Club, Washington D.C., September 20, 1951.
[6] Oberlé, p. 237.
[7] Despuech, op. cit., pp. 70, 71.
[8] Political Handbook of the World, 1953.
[9] *Le Monde*, October 9, 1953.
[10] *Le Figaro*, October 21, 1953.

CHAPTER XVI

[1] Speech at Nancy, November 25, 1951.
[2] *L'Année Politique*, 1951, p. 347.
[3] Foreign Affairs, July 1952: Jacques Soustelle, *A Gaullist View.*
[4] Documentation of the French Embassy, New York. Document (1952), no. 1, p. 12.
[5] Foreign Affairs, July 1952, *vide supra.*
[6] Documentation of the French Embassy, New York. Document (1952), no. 74, p. 3.
[7] Speech at the Vélodrome d'Hiver, February 23, 1952.
[8] *Le Figaro*, March 13, 1952.
[9] *Le Monde*, June 24, 1952.

CHAPTER XVII

[1] *Le Figaro*, October 27, 1952, gives text.
[2] *La Documentation Française*, France Moves Forward, pp. 6-7, 12-15 *et seq.*
[3] *General Report of the First Plan of Modernization and Equipment*, p. 173.
[4] Documentation of the French Embassy, New York. *Tunisian Affairs*, October 1953.
[5] *German Diplomatic Documents 1871-1914*, p. 230.
[6] Ibid., p. 414.
[7] *New York Times*, July 30, 1953; see also *Current History*, April 1954, p. 229.
[8] Documentation of the French Embassy, New York. *Moroccan Affairs*, October 1953.
[9] Text of de Gaulle's press conference, November 12, 1953, issued by the R.P.F. information service.
[10] Duff Cooper, *Old Men Forget*, p. 336.
[11] *Sondages*, January 16, 1946.

INDEX

INDEX

INDEX

INDEX

Date Due

MAY 14 '62			
MR 12 '63			
DE 4 '64			
APR 2 '68			
APR 16 '68			
APR 30 '68			
JAN 29 '71			
FEB 28 '89			
	PRINTED	IN U. S. A.	